S0-AVR-272

The Securitarian Personality

Hibbing, John R.,
The securitarian
personality : what reall
[2020]
33305248936613
mi   10/19/20

JOHN R.

HIBBING

The Securitarian Personality

What Really Motivates Trump's Base and Why It Matters for the Post-Trump Era

OXFORD
UNIVERSITY PRESS

OXFORD
UNIVERSITY PRESS

Oxford University Press is a department of the University of Oxford. It furthers
the University's objective of excellence in research, scholarship, and education
by publishing worldwide. Oxford is a registered trade mark of Oxford University
Press in the UK and certain other countries.

Published in the United States of America by Oxford University Press
198 Madison Avenue, New York, NY 10016, United States of America.

© Oxford University Press 2020

All rights reserved. No part of this publication may be reproduced, stored in
a retrieval system, or transmitted, in any form or by any means, without the
prior permission in writing of Oxford University Press, or as expressly permitted
by law, by license, or under terms agreed with the appropriate reproduction
rights organization. Inquiries concerning reproduction outside the scope of the
above should be sent to the Rights Department, Oxford University Press, at the
address above.

You must not circulate this work in any other form
and you must impose this same condition on any acquirer.

Library of Congress Cataloging-in-Publication Data
Names: Hibbing, John R., author.
Title: The securitarian personality : what really motivates Trump's base and
why it matters for the post-Trump era / John R. Hibbing.
Description: New York, NY : Oxford University Press, 2020. |
Includes bibliographical references and index.
Identifiers: LCCN 2020007942 (print) | LCCN 2020007943 (ebook) |
ISBN 9780190096489 (hardback) | ISBN 9780190096502 (epub) | ISBN 9780190096519
Subjects: LCSH: Political participation—Social aspects—United States. |
Political culture—United States. | Social conflict—Political aspects—United States. |
Identity politics—United States. | National characteristics, American—Political aspects. |
Trump, Donald, 1946—Public opinion.
Classification: LCC JK1764 .H529 2020 (print) | LCC JK1764 (ebook) |
DDC 306.20973—dc23
LC record available at https://lccn.loc.gov/2020007942
LC ebook record available at https://lccn.loc.gov/2020007943

9 8 7 6 5 4 3 2 1

Printed by LSC Communications, United States of America

To Taryn, Xander, Matilda, and Penelope

CONTENTS

ACKNOWLEDGMENTS

OVER THE COURSE of my career, I have co-authored with dozens of people but five stand out for putting up with me over extended periods: John Alford, Matthew Hibbing, Kevin Smith, Elizabeth Theiss-Morse, and Susan Welch. This book is the first project I have done on my own in quite some time and it made me realize how much I have depended on co-authors. At several points during the preparation of this book, I was in dire need of them. As an indication of how special they are, all five agreed to read manuscript drafts even though I did not have the decency to give them a reasonable amount of time to do so. Despite this, they provided remarkably probing and insightful comments. Yet again, I am in debt to these bright and generous scholars and friends.

It is fortunate for the planet that I do not have as many members of my immediate family as co-authors but my spouse, Anne, and three children, Michael, Matthew, and Anthony, all agreed to read the manuscript, also on short notice. Their willingness was particularly valuable because my hope is that this book will be useful, not just to scholars, but also to informed and interested laypeople, and I can think of no laypeople more informed and interested than these four. Anne went the extra mile by funneling relevant posts and writings my way and by reading the entire manuscript twice. Careful readers will note that Matthew shows up on both lists and he responded admirably to this additional pressure. My thanks and love to all four of them.

I would also like to thank two graduate students who were crucial to this project: Stephen Schneider and Joaquin Suarez. Stephen produced sensible tables and figures from the chicken scratches I sent him and Joaquin sorted through my jumble of notes, musings, and vague recollections to compile intelligible endnotes and references. My editors at Oxford University Press, David McBride and Emily Mackenzie, shared my vision for a crossover book and managed to be helpful and unobtrusive at the same time. Finally, I would like to thank the many ardent Trump supporters who, despite knowing I was not one of them, were willing to talk at length with me. Some of them were my students; a few were members of my extended family; most were focus group and other research participants; but all patiently explained—well, usually patiently—the basis for their veneration of Donald J. Trump.

CHAPTER 1 | Barefoot over Burning Coals

A N AUTUMN DAY in the Midwest. Blue skies tease to the north but a
layer of clouds persists over the Columbia, Missouri, Regional Airport.
People have been arriving since early in the morning. Parking lots and shuttle
buses fill quickly. Lines of cars stretch for miles as the Highway Patrol's carefully arranged traffic patterns are badly overmatched. A light rain starts. At
precisely 3:30, the huge doors to Hangar 350 swing open and the crowd
streams in. When the hangar can hold no more, people are channeled toward adjacent outside areas where they view the inside activities on huge
screens. The rain picks up. Darkness falls. The assemblage is excited but
restive; the 6:30 scheduled starting time comes and goes. At 6:45, a public
address announcement: "Air Force One is on final approach." The crowd goes
wild. Five minutes later, another announcement: "Air Force One is wheels
down." The crowd loses it. The mammoth aircraft taxis directly behind the
stage, perfectly positioned to provide a dramatic backdrop. At 7:00, Donald
J. Trump appears at the top of the stairs that have been rolled to the plane.
He waves, descends, and approaches the lectern, to rapturous applause and
chants of "Trump, Trump, Trump, Trump . . ." He waits for the loudspeakers
to quit blaring the song "Proud to Be an American," basking in the scene
and adulation.

Donald Trump was in Columbia to stump for Josh Hawley, the Republican
challenger in the 2018 midterm who was attempting to unseat incumbent
Democratic US Senator Claire McCaskill. I was there because I thought
someone writing a book on Trump supporters should observe them in vivo.
Surveys and focus groups are valuable but they place participants in artificial

situations; people attend a Trump rally voluntarily and researchers do not manipulate the setting. Studying non-human animals "in the wild" is revealing and the same is true of studying humans.

So it was that I reserved an electronic ticket, donned a flag-emblazoned baseball cap and red, white, and blue T-shirt, and prepared for the drive. Thinking there might be down time before the event itself started, I grabbed an issue of *The Atlantic* and Francis Fukuyama's latest book. Before I could leave, my wife suggested that taking reading material would surely blow my cover.

"But Fukuyama is conservative," I protested.

"Doesn't matter," she responded coolly—and correctly, as it turns out. I didn't see a single soul passing the hours by reading.

What *did* I see? I expected parking lots jam-packed with pick-up trucks and gun racks. This was a Trump rally in rural Missouri after all. In fact, there were only a few pick-ups and I did not see a single gun rack. Most of the vehicles were late-model SUVs and crossovers. As to the people, they appeared to be from all walks of life. There were a surprising number of women and young people; however, I did not see any people of color.

The attendees were neither bitter nor angry but rather pleased and excited, talking animatedly about Trump, politics, and football. The rain discouraged discussion and made eavesdropping challenging but I heard enough. The focus of many conversations was Trump's persona and mannerisms, his refusal to take guff from anybody. People loved the degree to which he was changing the very nature of politics by his willingness to say and tweet whatever was on his mind and by standing up for his own beliefs—and by extension, theirs. They remarked repeatedly on the horrible abuse he was suffering at the hands of the established media and they compared this Missouri rally to other Trump rallies they had attended. Hats emblazoned with "Make America Great Again" were everywhere, as were signs reading "Finish the Wall."

As to Trump himself, except for praise of Hawley and stinging criticism of McCaskill, he delivered his standard 2018 stump speech. Still, hearing those words while surrounded by adoring Trump supporters drove home several themes. He referred to the roaring economy, tax cuts, deregulation, and the appointment of conservative judges, but the clear touchstones of the speech were immigration, crime, and putting America first. A week before the rally Trump had intimated he would issue an executive order to end "birthright citizenship," the practice of granting citizenship to anyone born in the United States. In his speech, Trump explained why this practice had to be stopped, he railed against "chain migration," and he stressed the urgency of eliminating "birth tourism" which we were told was rampant. He reserved special venom for caravans that at the time of the rally were wending their way across southern Mexico. Trump said there were many, many bad people in the caravans—mostly powerful young men apparently. He repeatedly referenced the gang MS-13 and the need to call up US troops to protect against the impending invasion. He had already mobilized 5,000 soldiers and told the crowd he was contemplating tripling that number. Attendees thought this was a splendid idea.

The crowd cheered every Trump musing and booed any reference to the caravans, the desire of some Democrats to rein in ICE (Immigration and Customs Enforcement), and immigration generally. Those in and around Hangar 350 seemed convinced that the dangers posed by outsiders were everywhere. They were ready to embrace anyone who understood these threats and who took steps to guard against them; they were ready to ridicule anyone who did not recognize the peril and failed to appreciate the urgent need for action. Even a tangential mention of Hillary Clinton generated the prolonged, obligatory chant of "lock her up." In language reminiscent of linguist George Lakoff's distinction between the mommy and daddy parties, Trump told the crowd that leaders had to be "tough" but that leaders of "the left" had "weak little faces" and didn't like being yelled at by Mom and Dad.[1]

His speech ping-ponged from one topic to another but always returned to the threats posed by outsiders and the associated need for security. The barbarians were at the gates. Worse, the indifference of previous leaders had already allowed many barbarians in. Because of these breaches, an ever-growing cadre of criminals, freeloaders, non-Americans, and heretics—people who do not look, think, or behave like our country's mainstream—outnumbered real Americans. Full-scale and immediate vigilance was imperative if we were to prevent more damage to the country's core.

People in the crowd certainly approved of deregulation and Brett Kavanaugh but Trump's deep commitment to putting insiders first and outsiders last was what energized them. Trump could have announced that he was repealing tax cuts and this crowd would have stayed with him; he could have announced that his next Supreme Court nominee would be Merrick Garland and this crowd would have stayed with him; he could have embraced Obamacare and this crowd would have stayed with him. And, yes, he probably could have confessed to shooting somebody on Fifth Avenue and this crowd would have stayed with him. However, he could not have announced plans to open the borders, cut the defense budget, increase welfare spending, release criminals, give the United Nations authority over our military, and ban private ownership of guns without losing this crowd.

Attending a Trump rally was eye opening but perhaps even more eye opening was the reaction of my acquaintances and university colleagues to what I had done. Many were incredulous; many wondered what was wrong with me; many could not fathom doing the same thing themselves. At a faculty meeting the day after the rally, when asked by the person sitting next to me if I had traveled recently, I mentioned that I had attended a Trump rally the night before. In no time at all, the entire table of people ended their own conversations and focused on me. They quizzed me on every detail. What were the people like? What did they wear? Where did they come from? What did they say? What was their mood? How could they embrace such a person? How could they be so hateful toward immigrants and minorities? Was I scared? Would I do it again? Did it change my views? I felt like an anthropologist freshly returned from the Amazon.

Explanation, not Evaluation

Being surrounded by 20,000 Trump supporters one day and a roomful of Trump opponents the next put the depth of the differences between the two political camps into sharp relief but being aware of the deep division between the two camps does not require attendance at political rallies and faculty meetings. American society is split. The consequences are serious and the situation will not improve until we understand others. As of now, we not only fail to understand those in the other camp; we actively misunderstand them.

I wrote this book in an attempt to explain Trump's most ardent supporters to those who, like my colleagues, simply cannot fathom how anyone could embrace such a man. Of course, that is only half the equation but I will leave it to others to explain Trump's most intense opponents to his most fervent supporters. To a certain extent, however, it is impossible to describe one camp without describing the other. I hope that by reading this book Trump's intense opponents as well as his intense supporters will learn something about their political foes and about themselves.

Like the great majority of Americans, I am not a Trump supporter, avid or otherwise. However, unlike the great majority of Americans, I am an empirical social scientist and this means my job is not to rail against people I think are wrong but rather to collect and interpret evidence on the nature of the social world, including people who have political preferences very different from my own. Though it may seem presumptuous for a non–Trump supporter to claim to understand the psyches of Trump supporters, I would argue that a non–Trump supporter has the greatest odds of succeeding in such a task. Analytical distance is essential because humans are terrible at understanding themselves. We are built to construct a narrative about the reasons for our actions and this narrative typically is only loosely tethered to reality.[2]

Presumptuous or not, I am going to describe the inner workings of Trump supporters and I am going to do so, as much as possible, without interjecting value judgments. Often, it will seem as though I am going too far in giving Trump supporters the benefit of the doubt and this will infuriate Trump's strongest opponents, many of whom are eager to label Trump supporters racists or fascists and leave it at that. Please bear in mind that my treatment is not designed to be exculpatory—but neither is it designed to be inculpatory. The description I provide of Trump's most enthusiastic followers may very well suggest to you that they are dyed-in-the-wool racists but I am going to refrain from calling them that so that I can dig deeper into the specifics of their beliefs and motivations. As Jonathan Haidt points out, labels such as racist are designed to end debates that need to begin.[3]

Moreover, determining who is a racist is likely impossible because definitions vary so widely that exchanges quickly degenerate into little more than, "yes, you are;" "no, I'm not." My more constructive goal is to explain to Trump's opponents why Trump's ardent supporters have convinced themselves that they are not racists and to explain to Trump's supporters why his ardent opponents are convinced his supporters are indeed racists. Whatever we might think of each other, the cycle of name-calling, fulmination, and reprisals only intensifies polarization, intransigence, incivility, and gridlock. One-sided ideological rants feel good and sell a large number of books but they do not improve the political system and in fact degrade it even further. As Theda Skocpol and Vanessa Williamson note in their analysis of Tea Party supporters, "It is rarely helpful for analysts to denigrate . . . citizens."[4]

In today's hostile political climate, neither side will be pleased with my account. Trump supporters will be convinced I am too critical of them and Trump opponents will be convinced I am not critical enough. Total objectivity is impossible and no doubt readers will be able to spot biases, but to get the most out of this book, you should suspend the urge to be outraged and instead take the opportunity to ponder what really does motivate certain people to become devoted to leaders such as Donald Trump. Historian Jon Meacham believes this to be the central question of our age and I think he is correct. My purpose is not to change anyone's opinion of Donald Trump and his followers; my purpose is to help people understand attitudes that are very different from their own and this will require everyone to be more reflective and less condemnatory than they might prefer to be. I spent a good deal of time immersed in Trump supporters so that readers could gain an under-standing of them without needing to make a similar investment.

I hope that in calmer moments those of you who oppose Donald Trump with every fiber of your being can see value in understanding the deep motivations of people who fervidly support him.[5] Learning as much as pos-sible about the motivations of the other side will make for better democratic citizens and will even increase the odds that opposing views can be meaning-fully addressed and perhaps changed because in order to modify an attitude it is first necessary to determine the function it serves.[6] I hope people read this book because they want to come to grips with a crucial, politically rele-vant slice of the population; but, failing that, I accept the reality that certain people will read it only because they believe it might help them to defeat those they believe hold dangerously misguided views.

The act of describing a political type is frequently taken to be hostile to that type.[7] The idea seems to be that most people are normal—which appar-ently means devoid of type—and so are in no need of explanation. According to this line of thought, those evincing a political type, persistent tendency, predisposition, or orientation are abnormal and probably pathological. In truth, analyzing a potential type does not automatically demean it because distinct political types are ubiquitous. Having a political type hardly makes a person abnormal. Note, however, that this does not mean all political types are normatively equivalent. Certain political orientations are more dangerous than others are. Strong Trump supporters may well turn out to be problem-atic but the larger point is that the decision to analyze them does not pre-judge them so. All people from all portions of the political spectrum have biases and engage in motivated reasoning, which is the tendency to avoid and dismiss information contrary to existing views but to seek out and believe confirming information.[8]

On the other side, the argument that explaining a politically relevant type—even an odious one—automatically legitimizes it is equally mistaken. The fear seems to be that people are more likely to excuse behaviors and attitudes if they understand the reasons for them. Such thinking, however, is a variant of the naturalistic fallacy—the erroneous idea that if something happens naturally and explicably it needs to be accepted and accorded value. In fact, much of what happens in nature is morally repugnant, and being able to account for a behavior says nothing about its value and legitimacy. Providing a reason for unacceptable behavior does not make that behavior acceptable.

In sum, just as explaining the underlying nature of Trump supporters does not mean they are inherently evil, neither does it mean they should be given a free pass. Description does not mean equivalence. All political orientations have flaws and all political types merit sustained attention. I happen to focus on strident Trump supporters. Those eager to understand the motivations of other political types should write books on them.

Many observers will object to the very concept of political type. They will point out that human variation is typically continuous and that political orientations are unlikely to be an exception, rendering it misleading to force people into discrete political types. This observation has an important element of truth; political views do array across a spectrum—and quite likely many spectrums. That does not mean, however, that the concept of political type is inappropriate. Individuals fall at all points on the political continuum but they are not regularly spaced. People with virtually identical beliefs cluster at various places along the spectrum and we can accurately describe these people as belonging to a political type.

Those who viscerally dislike Trump's core supporters may have a vision of them that is different from the one I provide here just as those who viscerally support Donald Trump may have a vision of themselves different from the one I provide here. However, that does not mean I am wrong. The evidence I marshal is not conclusive but it is suggestive. If scholars conclude that the ideas I offer have merit, they will need to collect more data and conduct analyses that are more sophisticated. That is the way science works. At the end of this process, people will be able to react to Trump supporters on the basis of what those supporters actually believe rather than what conventional wisdom assumes they believe.

I am far from the first to try to capture the ethos of Trump supporters. In fact, the field has become quite crowded of late. I have learned a great deal from previous efforts. Still, in my opinion none of them homes in on the essence of strong Trump support. For example, as we will see in the next chapter, numerous observers allege that ardent Trump supporters are angry, afraid, anxious, authoritarian, bitter, closed-minded, conformist, dogmatic, order-craving, pessimistic, reactionary, unimaginative, aggressive traditionalists. My data suggest that few of these descriptors actually apply. Intense Trump supporters are not who they are thought to be.[9]

One reason previous interpretations are often inaccurate is that many of them rely on studies that were designed for a different purpose. Some researchers sought to understand those who jumped on the Trump bandwagon early in the 2016 Republican primaries;[10] some sought to place the 2016 elections in historical context;[11] some tried to explain specific aspects of the 2016 general election;[12] and some attempted to put the 2016 election in cross-national perspective.[13] Though it was a fascinating and consequential election, my interest is in the long-term psychological composition of ardent Trump supporters rather than the specifics of the coalition that elected him to the presidency on November 8, 2016.

Several previous studies rely on intensive interviews of Trump supporters[14] or groups likely related to Trump supporters.[15] These interviews are enlightening but often were conducted only in selected parts of the country and so are not generalizable. Further, many of the works thought (almost always by people other than the original researchers) to be helpful in describing intense Trump supporters were actually intended to describe broader groups, such as conservatives or authoritarians.[16] As we will soon see, generic descriptions of conservatives and, especially, of authoritarians are not helpful in capturing the psychology of avid Trump supporters. These individuals require their own description and analysis.

To provide such an analysis, I conducted four focus groups with self-identified strong Trump supporters and, as I have already described, engaged in participant observation at Trump rallies and elsewhere. The focus groups and participant observations were extremely useful as background in the development of my theory of the motivations of impassioned Trump supporters though I have resisted the urge to cherry-pick selected quotations for inclusion in the text. Instead, the systematic evidence I present comes from a specially commissioned national survey. This survey included many original items and was administered to a demographically representative sample of American adults that was supplemented with an oversample of the group that is of special interest here: Trump's strongest supporters.[17] The survey contained well over 250 items (to avoid respondent fatigue, some items were asked to only half of the sample) and provides a rich description of avid Trump supporters.

The timing of any survey is crucial. Whereas identifying the kind of people who were initially attracted to Trump (that is, his early primary supporters) is important, I wanted to investigate the individuals who were devoted to Trump after they had observed and digested his various successes and failures as president. As a result, I had the survey administered in April of 2019, twenty-seven months into his term. At the time, Trump had just failed to secure congressional funding for a wall along the country's southern border; several Trump associates had been indicted and sentenced; Trump's former lawyer and fixer, Michael Cohen, had just provided sensational public testimony; Trump had declared a state of emergency with the intention of repurposing money originally appropriated for other needs so that he could build portions of the wall; and a remarkable number of departures from the higher echelons of his administration had occurred (Homeland Security

Secretary Kirstjen Nielsen was fired days before the survey went to the field). The economy was growing slowly but steadily, the stock market was strong, and unemployment was as low as it had been in decades. The survey came a couple of weeks after the release of Attorney General William Barr's summary of the findings of the Mueller investigation but before the release of the more damning version of Mueller's report and well before intelligence community whistle blowers provided accounts of apparently inappropriate communication between officials in the administration, including Trump, and the Ukrainian government—accounts that later served as the impetus for the initiation of impeachment proceedings in the House of Representatives. At the time, Trump's job approval was sitting at 40%, a rapidly growing number of Democrats had announced their candidacy for the 2020 Democratic nomination for president, and the novel coronavirus (COVID-19) would not be a part of people's vocabulary for many months. I wanted to obtain a psychological portrait of the individuals who continued to stand with Trump rather than those who may have drifted away after providing early support.

Ardent Supporters, Not Mere Voters

On November 8, 2016, sixty-three million people voted for Donald J. Trump. Many of them were unenthusiastic about him and may even have harbored real concerns, but they calculated that he was likely to reduce their tax burden and nominate socially conservative judges, or thought he was the kind of anti-politician who could facilitate systemic change, or were curious to see how someone with Trump's distinctive personality and reality-TV background would fare in the highest office of the land, or found Trump's general election opponent, Hillary Clinton, to be wholly unpalatable, or were embittered Bernie Sanders supporters who could not bring themselves to vote for the person who defeated their champion in the hard-fought Democratic primaries, or were habitual Republican voters for whom the thought of voting Democratic was simply a non-starter, or were attracted to Trump's purported success in the business world, or wanted someone as different as possible from the previous president, Barack Obama. People voted for Donald Trump for all sorts of reasons.

I am not interested in those who merely voted for Trump in 2016 or in 2020; I am interested in those who adored him in 2019; those who after seeing him in political action for years were wholly smitten. I do not want those who voted for Trump out of curiosity, party loyalty, or distaste for either Hillary Clinton or Joe Biden. I want those who, after acquiring a sense of what they were getting, pronounced themselves dyed-in-the-wool Trump supporters. I do not want those who drifted away after an initial flirtation; I want those who, well after he became president, proudly wore "Make America Great Again" hats, eagerly attended Trump rallies, loudly defended him, angrily decried his treatment by the establishment and mainstream media, and thirstily lapped up his bravado, ethos, and demeanor. I want those who had difficulty imagining what Trump would have to do to lose their support—the people who would walk over burning coals for him. This book is about them—the Trump base, the Trump core, the Trump venerators.

Why a book-length treatment of fervent Trump supporters? If the mindset in question existed only in the followers of a single elected official in a single country in a single decade, the justification would be less compelling. A look around the world and throughout history, however, suggests that the people who aggressively support Donald Trump have counterparts everywhere and always. Rather than being anomalies or products of a highly unusual confluence of events, Trump's core supporters share traits found in people across cultures and epochs—and though the numbers vary from place to place, it is not unusual for at least one in five of a country's politically active citizenry to have proclivities similar to those of ardent Trump supporters in the United States. An understanding of strong Trump supporters will provide a window into a remarkably common political type and in turn into the reasons modern political conflict is so polarized and harsh.[18] In fact, if we are to have any hope of constructing a civil, properly functioning political system, we must first deconstruct intense Trump support. To misdiagnose Trump supporters is to misdiagnose politics.

Whether called populists, nativists, authoritarians, nationalists, prefascists, or worse, the supporters of Donald Trump are eerily similar to the supporters of Rodrigo Duterte in the Philippines, Geert Wilders in the Netherlands, Jair Bolsonaro in Brazil, Viktor Orban in Hungary, Marine Le Pen in France, Makoto Sakurai in Japan, Sebastian Kurz in Austria, Doug Ford in Canada, Mauricio Macri in Argentina, Jaroslaw Kaczynski in Poland, Recep Erdoğan in Turkey, Vladimir Putin in Russia, Nigel Farage in the United Kingdom, Narendra Modi in India, Jimmie Åkesson in Sweden, Miloš Zeman in the Czech Republic, and Pauline Hanson in Australia.[19] Earlier and sometimes extreme incarnations of this mindset can be seen in the followers of Francisco Franco in Spain, Juan Perón in Argentina, Fumimaro Konoe in Japan, Robey Leibbrandt in South Africa, Nicolás Rodríguez Carrasco in Mexico, and Oswald Mosley in Britain.[20]

In the United States, modern-day supporters of Donald Trump would have found kindred spirits among the supporters of Patrick Henry, Andrew

Jackson, William Poole (of the Know-Nothing Party), William Dudley Pelley, Charles Lindbergh, and George Wallace. Anti-immigrant and especially anti-German sentiments were already rampant among the founders generally and Ben Franklin particularly. In fact, the American Revolution grew out of a nativist aversion to meddling outsiders such as George III. Trump may not have come to power without the one-off combination of the Electoral College, a reaction to the Obama presidency, and a wounded Democratic candidate, but the ethos of Trump supporters is neither novel nor new. Long after his departure from the political scene, the mindset that made Trump supporters such an enthusiastic, disruptive, intense, influential, and contrarian bunch will remain—in the United States and elsewhere. Who are they?

Securitarians

Of course, millions of distinct individuals in the United States and around the world do not all share identical motivations. It would be foolish to suggest a single explanation for their political preferences and I will not. That said, intense Trump supporters share many traits and features that to this point have been underappreciated. I describe these characteristics of Trump supporters in full detail in Chapter 4 but a brief summary at this early point serves as a useful prelude.

The central feature of Trump's base is their belief that the noblest and most essential task of a human being is to protect person, family, culture, and country from the tangible threats they believe are posed by outsiders. They do not feel the need to be vigilant against all threats and, in fact, can be surprisingly cavalier about threats that do not emanate from outsider human beings (for example, climate change). In the face of these outsider threats, they believe insiders need to stay unified and strong. Who are these outsiders and insiders?

In Trump supporters' worldview, insiders are the historical and numerical core of the country—the dominant race, religion, and language group—plus those who can be trusted to work to strengthen that core, preferably by defending and enriching it, but at the least by not dividing and placing demands on it. Outsiders are those who do not belong to the aforementioned core. Those who live outside the country are automatically outsiders but so are many people who live among us.[21] These outsiders on the inside are likely to chip away at the unity and strength of the country and dominant culture (in the eyes of intense Trump supporters, there really is no difference between country and dominant culture). Outsiders may weaken the core because their skin color is different from that of insiders, because their political beliefs are different from those of insiders, because they do not follow the customs of insiders, because they violate the norms and laws that protect insiders, or because they advocate public policies that weaken insiders vis-à-vis outsiders (for example, welfare spending, foreign aid, and immigration).[22]

I use the terms "insiders" and "outsiders" rather than "in-groups" and "out-groups" because, from the perspective of Trump supporters, outsiders do not fall into discrete groups but rather are collections of individuals with varying mixtures of traits.[23] Think of it as a point system. Individuals lose points if, compared to insiders, they have a different skin color, come from a different place, practice a different religion, follow different customs, and speak a different language. They also lose points if they are in the public charge or violate norms, especially criminal laws. Another way to lose points is to take actions or advocate policies that weaken insider unity and security—perhaps by opposing patriotism or giving rights and benefits to anyone other than insiders. Thus, in the eyes of fervid Trump supporters, blacks such as Ben Carson can recoup points lost because of skin color if their behavior and policy positions are believed to strengthen the status and safety of insiders.[24] On the other hand, individuals possessing or displaying multiple outsider traits cause Trump devotees particular distress, with perceived demerits seeming to accumulate exponentially. Witness US Representative Ilhan Omar (D-MN) who is non-white, non-US-born, non-Christian, and non-male, and who wears non-insider clothing, follows non-insider customs, and vigorously pursues non-insider-promoting public policies. Send her back indeed.

Though multiple factors go into determining who is and who is not an outsider, race and national origin occupy a special role. With regard to race, evolutionary psychologists Rob Kurzban, John Tooby, and Leda Cosmides note that humans have a "lifetime's experience of race as a predictor of social alliance."[25] They show that other cues, including clothing, can signal belonging. Still, the fact remains that we cannot change skin color, making it a primal marker that occupies a privileged place in the long list of indicators of outsider status.

The default of an intense Trump supporter is to view with suspicion anyone other than those known to be insiders. The onus is on such individuals to prove they are loyal, non-threatening, and contributing. Immigrants, lawbreakers, anthem protesters, and welfare cheats have not done this and so Trump supporters prefer to minimize exposure to them and warmly endorse policies that restrict immigration, enhance national defense, facilitate personal defense, reduce welfare spending, confine and discourage criminals, and diminish the power of external entities such as the United Nations and the European Union. Such policies make them feel safe, satisfied, and virtuous. Individuals who oppose these policies are viewed with a sense of bafflement, concern, unease, and alarm to the point that they are not considered insiders even though their demographic characteristics suggest they would otherwise be insiders. Enthusiastic Trump supporters wonder why anyone would want to emphasize divisive and uncomfortable aspects of our nation's past, even if historically accurate. Trump supporters see the world not through an "us vs. them" lens but rather an "us vs. not-us" lens.

Trump supporters believe they are not racists because race is only part of their (typically unwitting) assessment of insider status and because under the right circumstances—that is, if racial minorities demonstrate they are trustworthy, contributing members of society and that they are themselves ready to take steps to preserve insiders in the face of outsider threats—they can be fully accepted. Trump supporters need to recognize, however, that to Trump opponents, requiring racial minorities to prove themselves in a way that whites are not required to do is blatant racism.

Trump supporters are discomfited by the ability of someone else to get the drop on them but feel a sense of deep satisfaction and even pleasure when they fulfill their duty to be vigilant.[26] Though at times Trump supporters are moved by fear and anxiety, on the whole they are not pessimists with a low sense of social well-being. For Trump supporters, security is not a tiresome, regrettable burden necessitated by unremitting fear; rather, it is an uplifting mission. Doing one's duty is rewarding in and of itself and creating a secure environment for insiders is a duty. The more dangerous the world is thought to be, the greater the psychological rewards that accrue from preserving security. For Trump supporters, outsider threats are as psychologically beneficial as they are unavoidable.

Trump supporters view threats to their person and to their society as existential and see no reason to do anything that might compromise insider strength and security. As a result, they take precautions such as steering away from a leader unless they are certain that leader is as vigilant and vulnerability averse as they are in which case they may well become wholly devoted to that leader. They are convinced that the Boy Scout motto of "Be prepared" pretty much says it all. They work tirelessly to avoid situations that would leave them under the thumb of outsiders and norm violators. They prefer to speak loudly AND carry a big stick. Deterrence of outsider threats and preservation of insider security are their central objectives.[27]

Avid Trump supporters believe successful strategies for achieving their security goals will be furthered by a unified group of like-thinking, like acting, and, if possible, like-appearing individuals who will fend off attacks in the first place and assist in active defense should deterrence fail. As such, they value patriotic displays, bonding exercises, unifying values, and those who risk their lives for the welfare of the in-group—military personnel and first responders. Like other nativists and nationalists, Trump supporters see no reason to be soft on immigration, defense, freeloaders, and law-and-order because softness only increases vulnerability.[28] A good day for Trump supporters is one in which the dominant culture is not compromised and those they love are not the victims of outsiders. They do not like feeling pressured by others, particularly those who are unknown to them. They believe bluster and swagger are useful deterrents.

Extreme types often serve to clarify those with less extreme tendencies. In the case at hand, the extreme version of those with Trump-supporting predispositions is not a fascist as many assume,[29] but rather a survivalist. At the extreme, those with these predispositions lose faith in the ability of society to treat threats with the required seriousness, making it necessary for them to take matters into their own hands by plotting contingencies and stockpiling gold, weapons, water, and perishables in order to be prepared for a time when each person or at least each family needs to go it alone. Survivalists and members of militias often do not vote but when they do, they likely prefer candidates such as Donald Trump.[30]

Fascist leaders such as Adolf Hitler believe the insiders they symbolize are superior. They want to take over the world and kill or subjugate outsiders. Leaders such as Donald Trump believe their insiders are different from outsiders (superiority is beside the point for most of them). They want to isolate themselves from the world and keep outsiders at a distance. If the symbols of Hitler are death camps and Panzer tanks, the symbols of Trump are segregated communities and border walls. World conquest is hardly what Trump and his followers are about; it would require them to have far too many dealings with outsiders.

Alternative Explanations of Intense Trump Support

Positing that a concern for security and a corresponding aversion to vulnerability constitute the motivational core of Trump supporters and their counterparts throughout history accords second-class status to numerous potentially attractive alternative explanations. Financial hardship, anxiety, unhappiness, resentment, social conventionalism, insufficient education, limited mental faculties, fear, aversion to change, a craving for simplicity and closure, and a desire to control reproductive opportunities as well as to submit to authority figures have all been suggested as reasons people hold politically conservative, nationalistic, nativist, populist orientations and therefore as reasons people support Donald Trump. Though relevant to the motivations of some ardent Trump supporter, none of these explanations scores a direct hit; the issues that animate the Trump base revolve around security rather than economics and sex.

For Trump supporters and others like them, homosexuality and abortions are secondary. This does not mean they are incapable of working up a good lather on these issues but rather that, unlike authentic social conservatives, Trump's fervent supporters often support policies limiting such behaviors more for indirect and coalitional rather than foundational reasons—perhaps because the policies happen to be associated with dominant insider religions or norms. In the current political climate, ardent Trump supporters solidly oppose abortion and gay rights but their fundamental political constitution does not demand that they do so . . . and many do not.

Likewise, Trump's core supporters are quite fond of economic policies such as tax cuts, trade restrictions, deregulation, and reductions in welfare spending. On their face, these are not foundational issues for Trump supporters either; however, they can be foundational when they bear on the status and vulnerability of insiders vis-à-vis outsiders.[31] For example, Trump based his attacks on free trade and especially free trade agreements such as the North American Free Trade Agreement (NAFTA) and the Trans-Pacific Partnership (TPP) not on economic theory but rather perceived group competition. One of Trump's most reliable applause lines during the 2016 campaign was that Japan, China, and Europe were "killing" us on trade and that he would quickly put an end to US subservience. Just as is the case for those with vigilant proclivities in all societies, for Trump supporters trade is about national competition, not economics.[32] America First!

Deregulation is typically presented as an economic strategy—one that will free up businesses to be more efficient and profitable so that they can employ more people and improve economic health. From the perspective of Trump supporters, however, another attractive feature of deregulation is that it reduces the ability of government to infiltrate the everyday lives of Americans. If the government can put fluoride in our water and ethanol in our gasoline, if it can tell farmers where they can and cannot plant crops, and if it can dictate which animal species are deserving of special protection, it can restrict our ability to be vigilant. It might even disarm us and then we would be vulnerable to outsider malevolence and unable to defend our families. Trump supporters endorse deregulation less because they worry about the economy and more because they worry about emasculation.[33]

In a similar vein, Trump supporters typically oppose welfare spending not for purely economic reasons but because of the belief that benefits go largely to racial minorities, layabouts, and ne'er-do-wells who have not demonstrated themselves to be certifiable contributors to a secure society. Note that when massive government payments are made to farmers, Trump supporters barely bat an eye because they believe farmers, unlike food stamp recipients, are contributing insiders. Outside of defense spending, Social Security, Medicare, and farm subsidies, Trump supporters suspect most federal government spending is misguided because it does nothing to decrease insider vulnerability and in fact often benefits those who are outsiders. Foreign aid is the clearest example of counterproductive government spending and thus is the most reviled by passionate Trump supporters. In sum, preferences on many so-called economic issues are often derived not from economics but instead from perceptions of group, race, identity, and deservingness.[34]

A final feature of strong Trump supporters that has puzzled many observers is their apparent willingness to support a candidate who intends to enact policies likely to be harmful to their own economic livelihood and indeed even their personal health.[35] How could farmers vote for a candidate who promises, as Trump did, to initiate trade wars that will adversely affect farm commodity prices? The obvious answer is that they place security and in-group concerns above their own economic welfare.[36] Even as the price of soybeans fell in the wake of a string of tariff proposals emanating from the administration, Trump-supporting farmers insisted that they were happy somebody was finally standing up to China; therefore, they were willing to tolerate and even endorse Trump's trade policies.[37] For them, not being under the influence of other countries was a bigger concern than crop prices.

In a similar vein, supporters of Brexit often were acutely aware that severing the United Kingdom's ties with the European Union would lead to financial hardships but they were ready to endure economic losses in order to keep British culture from being overtaken by the arrival of ever more immigrants.[38] The central Brexit slogan, after all, was "Take Back Control." Those with vigilant proclivities are surprisingly willing to trade in their personal economic well-being if doing so will make their country and culture more secure, more unified, more autonomous, and less vulnerable.

Political parlance has words for all kinds of orientations. Those advocating personal freedom and minimal governmental involvement are called libertarians; those who see the people of a country as united, homogeneous, and worthy are called populists; those desiring social freedoms but economic redistribution are called liberals; those favoring social intrusion but economic freedoms are called conservatives; those wanting substantial government involvement in the economy and elsewhere are called socialists; those preferring to subject themselves to strong, unquestioned leaders are called authoritarians; those believing in the sanctity of the community are called communitarians; and those philosophically committed to equality through society are called egalitarians.

Until now, however, there has been no label for those who are vigilant to their core; for those who have a viscerally negative response to finding themselves in a vulnerable posture; for those who elevate security concerns to a way of life; for those who are highly attentive to the threats posed by outsiders, scofflaws, dissidents, non-contributors, and norm violators. Until now, there has been no label for the psychological orientations and concerns resting at the core of Trump supporters. Until now, there has been no label for securitarians.

The Evolutionary Value of Vigilance, but from Whom?

What forces lead millions of people to be securitarians—to harbor vigilant, vulnerability-averse orientations that then predispose them toward nationalist, nativist, law-and-order, defense-first candidates such as Donald Trump? Moreover, why is the division between securitarians and their opposites— whom, with apologies to those who use the term to describe their religion, I label "unitarians"—so common across time and space and why is this division so intense and explosive?[39] Answers to questions such as these are unavoidably speculative—but speculation can be useful as long as it is labeled as such. Consider it labeled.

For most of our existence as homo-sapiens, we lived in semi-nomadic bands of fifty to two hundred people, relying on hunting and gathering to acquire necessary provisions. Rather than being isolated and wholly insular, these bands had a surprising amount of interactions with each other—some hostile and some not.[40] Attachment to a band was more fluid than is typically assumed, with the surplused, ostracized, intrepid, disaffected, captured, curious, and lovelorn regularly shifting allegiances. During the extended period in which we organized social life in this fashion, human-on-human violence was rampant and in fact was the most common single cause of adult deaths so would have been of special concern.[41] As a result, evolutionary pressures would have encouraged particular vigilance against threats posed by other humans.[42]

In such an environment, a reasonable initial suspicion is that evolutionary pressures would have selected for vigilance against outsider threats. After all, cavalier attitudes toward the dangers posed by outsiders would increase the likelihood that those holding such attitudes would be killed, which in turn would curtail reproductive opportunities and the associated inter-generational transmission of genetic material. If this were the entire story, securitarian orientations should have become virtually universal. Why is this not the case? Perhaps because the membership fluidity resulting from tolerance of outsiders brought decided advantages, including new information, ideas, and approaches, not to mention entertainment and genetic cross-fertilization. Anthropologist Kim Hill and colleagues even suggest that the unusual level of human inter-group movement relative to other great apes may have been an important factor in the unparalleled success of our species.[43]

Moreover, a total fixation on the threats posed by outsiders would have blinded individuals to another threat: powerful insiders, most likely an alpha male. Cross a particularly influential member of the band and your life could be ruined. Strategies for securing protection against deadly raids by out-groups will be quite different from those designed to secure protection from the alpha male and the hierarchy that elevated him. In fact, given that powerful leaders are likely useful in conflicts with other groups, it is easy to see that a balancing act is necessary: empower a leader sufficiently to facilitate protection from inter-group violence without creating the possibility of potentially deadly intra-group conflict fueled by an unconstrained, testosterone-addled leader.

Hunter-gatherer bands were notably egalitarian but not because egalitarianism came naturally.[44] They typically countered the threats posed by unchecked internal power with strong norms against so-called big man behavior. Groups immediately ridiculed, shamed, and shunned any member who acted like an arrogant big shot and felt entitled to inordinate respect and deference. An elderly member of a hunter-gatherer band once explained it this way: "When a young man kills much meat he comes to think of himself as a big man and he thinks of the rest of us as his inferiors. We can't accept this. We refuse one who boasts, for one day his pride will make him kill somebody. So we always speak of his meat as worthless."[45] As wonderfully varied as hunter-gatherer bands were, this "anti-big-man behavior" seems to have been universal,[46] leading to the following question: How could a species that spent hundreds of thousands of years meticulously sanctioning any form of big man behavior elect as its leader Donald Trump, the man who said "I alone can fix it," the man who said "I know more about ISIS than the generals," and the man who made a living festooning tall buildings with his name in immodestly sized gold letters?

In searching for an answer, remember these points. First, the fact that these egalitarian norms were necessary in the first place and were so strictly enforced suggests there have long been inclinations to act otherwise. Second, as noted previously, the percentage of the modern population in the thrall of big man leaders such as Donald Trump is in actuality quite small—less than 3 in 10. Many of those who voted for him did so in spite of his big man behavior, not because of it.

Over the millennia, the opposing needs to secure protections from both insiders and outsiders could easily have resulted in widely varying behavioral phenotypes. The ancestors of securitarians were so concerned with the dangers posed by outsiders that they directed all of their energy toward constructing defenses; they were not particularly concerned with threats posed by powerful insiders because they could be useful in leading a united defense against outsiders.[47] Those so inclined eventually begat Donald Trump.

The ancestors of unitarians on the other hand, like the elderly hunter-gatherer quoted above, were most concerned with protection from internal rather than external threats. People with this disposition were more worried about the dangers posed by arrogant, powerful leaders of their own group than the dangers posed by outsiders. In fact, they were quite welcoming to outsiders. Those so disposed eventually begat Bernie Sanders.

The key division in all political systems is the result of these two distinct perceptions of the most dangerous threats. Whether or not to prioritize insider uniformity and security or enhance the well-being of outsiders and degree of outsider diversity is the most basic question for all societies.[48] If I were given the assignment of grasping an individual's political essence with a single question and I knew nothing about politics in that individual's society, the question I would ask is whether that person is most concerned with the threats posed by outsiders or by insiders, whether that person is eager to defend against or to embrace outsiders. Of course, if permitted more questions it would be possible to flesh out the many additional dimensions.[49]

In modern parlance, we place this conflict in left-right terms. For the right generally and certainly for the nativist, nationalist wing specifically, the most concerning threats are those emanating from out-groups and in-group rule breakers. For the left, the most concerning threat is in-group members who hold too much political power and economic influence.[50] Whatever the labels, the cut point is the same.

The evolutionary centrality of this division is why political discussions focusing on groups, safety, identity, culture, belongingness, and unity are especially furious. Capital gains tax rates, residential zoning, tuition costs, alternative energy, infrastructure, center-periphery relations, morning-after pills, and gay adoptions are vitally important and certainly can be controversial but they do not arise from the depths of the primordial dispute between those who are and are not concerned about outsiders; between those who are and are not securitarians. This is the dispute that must be understood if we are to come to grips with the ultimate source of political conflict in the world.

Are You One of Us?

Remember that securitarians are inclined to think of outsiders as those who do not have insiders' dominant skin color, national origins, language, religion, and customs, plus those who fail to appreciate the need to defend insiders against all others. In fact, the people who do not see the peril facing insiders are often seen as the bigger threat. From a securitarian point of view, people who endorse gun control, defense cuts, criminal rights, foreign aid, refugee admittance, parole, and Black Lives Matter are not only making bad policy choices, but they are also rendering it less likely that insiders will be secure within the snug confines of a tight, homogeneous, comforting, impregnable collection of fellow citizens. To a securitarian, all it takes to wipe out the entire insider community is one minor misstep. People who look like insiders but are not on board are especially dangerous.

Given the stakes, securitarians are always on guard against being sold a pig in a poke and they are remarkably adept at spotting politicians who only pretend to be securitarians. Those with vigilant propensities, such as Trump supporters, crave leaders who take up the cause of forthrightly defending group and country. Serious threats require unfiltered action, not consultation, debate, committees, compromise, and sensitivity to dissent. For securitarians, it is a simple world: those who strive to enhance security by putting insiders first are revered; those who do not are reviled. Leaders who use guarded language are not to be trusted because their words may not reflect their innermost feelings. For this reason, securitarians abhor politically correct talk and are suspicious of most all politicians. Securitarians have no time for politicians who fraternize with non-securitarians; on the other hand, securitarians form indelible bonds with politicians who authentically appreciate outsider threats. Many leaders support securitarian policies; few leaders give off authentically securitarian vibrations. Followers with securitarian predispositions have an uncanny knack for telling the two apart.

As an example, consider the case of the late Senator John McCain (R-AZ). In his efforts to appeal to the various Republican constituencies during his turn as the party's presidential nominee in 2008, he had most everything going for him. In the year before his nomination, he supported the agenda of President George W. Bush 95% of the time and voted with the majority of his Republican colleagues in the Senate 90% of the time. Over the entirety of his senatorial career, he supported the positions favored by the American Conservative Union 82.3% of the time. In addition to this conservative, pro-party voting record, he was widely respected in Republican circles for being a defense hawk and standing up to America's enemies, endorsing the Iraq War, the "Surge" in Afghanistan, and sanctions on Russia. A tireless supporter of veterans' causes, he also brought with him a compelling and heroic personal story. As a naval aviator during the Vietnam War, he was on a bombing mission over Hanoi in 1967 when he was shot down, seriously injured, and captured. He spent five and a half years as a prisoner of war and, though tortured repeatedly, still refused the offer of an early release. His wartime experiences left him physically disabled for the rest of his life.

All this should have endeared him to the wing of the Republican Party that would later come to enthusiastically support Donald Trump but this was not to be.[51] Why not? Because in 2000 McCain referred to Jerry Falwell and Pat Robertson as "agents of intolerance"; because throughout most of his legislative career he supported broad-based immigration reform that to securitarians reeked of amnesty; and because he had the temerity to come to the defense of someone who definitely did not get it: Barack Obama. During a campaign rally in Minnesota on October 10, 2008, an attendee stood up and said that he was scared of McCain's Democratic opponent in the election because Obama "cohorts [sic] with domestic terrorists." McCain immediately disagreed, calling Obama a "decent person" and stating that there was no reason to be scared of him, a response that drew boos from the audience. Later at the same event another supporter stated that she did not trust Obama because, among other things, he was "an Arab." McCain cut her off, took the microphone, shook his head, and said, "No ma'am, he's a decent family man and citizen who I happen to have disagreements with on fundamental issues."

These responses created problems for McCain in terms of being accepted by a key wing of the electorate. Securitarians demand politicians who are threatened by the same things they are and securitarians are threatened by the likes of Barack Obama. The fact that McCain did not have a visceral aversion to a potential president who, in their eyes, was perhaps an Arab, probably not born in the United States, and who, as McCain's vice-presidential nominee, Sarah Palin, so memorably claimed, "palled around with terrorists" indicated to the nativist wing of the Republican Party that regardless of his war record, McCain was a nominee unworthy of enthusiastic support. He acted as though he was committed to insider security but this commitment was intellectual rather than emotional.

That same wing of the Republican Party was similarly disappointed with the party's nominee four years on. In 2012, Mitt Romney took all of the right positions on immigration: he stridently opposed amnesty for the undocumented, defended Arizona's controversial "show me your papers" law, famously endorsed a strategy of "self-deportation," and vigorously opposed the DREAM Act. Once again, all this should have pleased those Republicans who would become Trump supporters in 2016 but, despite the fact that he was running against someone they perceived to be the anti-Christ, Romney could not stir enthusiasm. Why not? A denizen of right-wing media, Michael Medved, provided the best explanation for Romney's failure to inspire Trump supporters when he noted that Romney "isn't angry enough." Medved elaborated: "[Romney] looks self-possessed and unflappable, cool and collected, reasonable and restrained. Rage isn't part of his emotional repertoire. . . . [H]e is more perplexed than infuriated." Medved summarized his thoughts by correctly noting that Romney's "real problem isn't a question of ideology; it's a matter of attitude."[52] Romney assumed the desired policy positions but he didn't *feel* them and this rendered him a non-starter in the eyes of soon-to-be Trump supporters. Securitarianism is a demanding mistress.

In fact, for many Trump supporters—before, during, and after Trump—leaders' intentions and emotionality are as important as policy outcomes. Trump's followers never really believed that he would build a big, beautiful wall across the entire US-Mexico border and do so with Mexico's money. Still, his very advocacy of a protective wall—and by the way, there is no better symbol of a securitarian ethos than a border wall—signaled to them that this is a person who shared their orientation; who felt it in his gut and not merely in his pre-frontal cortex; and who would go to the mat for what they believed in. Unitarians should quit expecting Trump's fervid supporters to turn on him because of promises not kept. Making those promises in an emotionally committed fashion was all they needed. Failing to secure Democratic cooperation was lamentable but certainly not enough to cause securitarians to turn on Trump. In fact, Democratic resistance to the wall indicated to Trump's core supporters that he was more necessary than ever. He had them at "I will build a wall."

Securitarians and unitarians also have fundamentally different visions of evidence and argumentation. Securitarians tend to use data and words as tools in service of a greater good (security). After all, they assert, you can claim anything with statistics and you can make whatever argument you want with words.[53] From the point of view of his followers Trump is not a liar, he is a bullshitter. His overstatements and embellishments do not bother them because he is doing what he can do to make America unified and secure. If what he says and tweets is not completely true, it should be. Trump's opponents, on the other hand, have a more elevated view of argumentation and evidence, seeing them as strategies for reaching an objective truth. For them, bullshit is indistinguishable from lies, and banter and puffery are not playful but extremely dangerous.

Conclusion

Delineating the mindset of strong Trump supporters will not cause political conflict to evaporate because intense Trump supporters and intense Trump opponents will go on thinking the other side is dangerously incorrect. Still, grasping the precise differences that drive this dispute could improve the political climate.

Committed Trump supporters would benefit from recognizing that the reason their opponents "don't get it" is that for them there is nothing to get. They do not see a world revolving around the need for vigilance in the face of outsider threats. They are more worried about the unbridled concentration of economic and political power, especially when that power is in the hands of a securitarian who advocates planet-endangering policies. If passionate Trump supporters realized that, when it comes to outsiders, most people are not as averse to vulnerability as they are, they would at least understand the actual reason for political conflict. Trump supporters need to accept that the default of those who disagree with them politically is to be open to people, even people from other parts of the world and even people who in the past may have violated important societal norms. If an illegal immigrant commits a crime, non-Trump supporters will not necessarily take this as cause to tighten restrictions on immigrants, on criminals, or both because they do not organize their lives around deterring outsiders.

At the same time, Trump's most strident opponents need to recognize that for fervid Trump supporters security against outsiders is essential and vigilance is a core part of their beings. Vulnerability to outsiders is distasteful to them at a level that those of us who are not Trump supporters can only struggle to comprehend. Arguments and evidence implying that threats are not real are ineffective to the point of being useless. In the minds of strong Trump supporters, regardless of the crime rate, vigilance will still be necessary. Trump opponents should accept that Trump supporters are attentive to dangers that other people neither see nor acknowledge and that they believe belligerence, honor codes, and tough talk all serve a useful purpose in fending off outsider threats. Some situations simply must be taken as a given and one of these is that a slice of the population is fixated on security from outsider threats and as a result naturally gravitates toward leaders such as Donald J. Trump.

The appropriate response to these differences is not to yell at those on the other side but rather to think carefully about how we can build a constructive society when significant, vocal subsets of the population have such fundamentally different orientations to social life. Name-calling has gotten us nowhere. Belittling, whether of ardent Trump supporters or ardent Trump opponents, only makes the situation worse. Clever arguments, zippy posts, compelling facts, demeaning epithets, or extended Fox News blackouts will not change the stripes of passionate Trump supporters. A far better approach is to work with what we know about the securitarian mindset—however foreign and abhorrent that mindset might be to unitarians.

* * *

This book can be divided into two major parts: the first four chapters and the last four chapters, with the first four being largely speculative and descriptive and the last four being data-based and explanatory. In Chapters 2 and 3, I review existing explanations of Trump supporters and describe the ways in which these explanations come up short; then, in Chapter 4, I provide a detailed description of what I believe to be the defining trait of fervid Trump supporters: securitarianism. Shifting to the survey results, in Chapters 5 and 6, I offer empirical evidence of the psychological and personality characteristics that distinguish intense Trump supporters from those with other beliefs and, in Chapter 7, I explore differences among Trump supporters themselves (they are not all the same). In Chapter 8, I conclude by looking to the likely future role of securitarians in American politics.

CHAPTER 2 | Scared, Resentful, Destitute
Hillbillies?

D ONALD TRUMP GLIDED down that escalator into the national political
scene in mid-June of 2015. Sixteen months later, thanks in large part
to a feverishly supportive base, he had been elected president of the United
States. Those struggling to interpret the mindset of Trump supporters typically sought answers by looking to descriptions of the mindsets of ostensibly
similar individuals such as conservatives and authoritarians. Though understandable, this strategy is flawed. As we will soon see, Trump supporters are
not authoritarians and they are a unique genre of conservatives. They require
an explanation all their own. Recycled data and theories concerning the psychological motivations behind other political philosophies do not hold the
key to understanding intense Trump supporters.

In this chapter and the next, I make the case that the standard, established narrative regarding the makeup of Trump supporters misses the
mark. Describing the nature and weaknesses of conventional wisdom will
set the stage for isolating the actual mindset of those who fervently support
Trump and by extension those who fervently support similar political figures around the world. Many misconceptions are afloat, and before turning
in detail to what Trump supporters are (beginning in Chapter 4), it is important to know what they are not. Elements of the standard narrative fall
into two broad categories: demographic and psychological. I begin with
the demographic.

Does Where You Stand Depend on Where You Sit?

Impoverished, uneducated, elderly, religious, rural, white males. That is the widely circulating demographic profile of Trump supporters.[1] Is it true that an individual's geographic, chronological, and socioeconomic location in society shapes political preferences and ultimately support for a politician such as Donald Trump? The "demography as destiny" vision of politics has been popular since at least the 1940s and has enjoyed a resurgence in the wake of Donald Trump's political successes.[2] How accurate are these accounts?

The standard demographic narrative derives largely from studies of the Trump electoral coalition in November of 2016. Most of the relevant data come from exit polls, which entail a series of quick questions posed to selected voters as they come out of their polling places.[3] Starting in Chapter 5, I will present new data on intense Trump supporters two years into his term, but the preliminary analyses I report in this chapter rely on findings from other researchers often utilizing exit poll data on voters in 2016 rather than data on ardent supporters well after Trump's policies and demeanor in office had become evident.[4]

ECONOMIC STATUS

A common view is that the core of Trump's support in 2016 came from working-class individuals who were financially insecure and frustrated with the rapidly changing, globalized economy.[5] They believed or wanted to believe that Trump would stop factories from moving overseas and secure America-friendly trade arrangements that would restore health to rural and rustbelt parts of the country.[6] Reflecting this belief, Bernie Sanders asserted that Trump's 2016 win occurred because he "appealed to people tired of working longer hours for lower wages."[7] Many of Trump's salient campaign promises had economic elements. He said he would reduce taxes, free businesses from regulations, tear up existing and pending multilateral trade agreements, prevent immigrants from taking Americans' jobs, prioritize bringing employers back from overseas, and stop freeloaders from overburdening the welfare system.

Economic issues are undeniably important but is it the case that Trump supporters are "have nots" locked in mortal combat with the "haves?" Are Trump supporters really the unfortunate victims of immigrant workers and NAFTA? Are they the proletariat to Hillary Clinton's (or Joe Biden's) bourgeoisie? If Trump voters in 2016 are any indication, the answer is no. Compared to those who voted for other candidates in 2016, Trump voters actually were less likely to be unemployed, less likely to be under-employed, and less likely to live in areas of the country with high exposure to job-poaching immigrants.[8]

Exit polls show that Trump lost every income bracket below $50,000/year and won every income bracket above $50,000/year. In fact, Trump's largest margin was among people making $70,000–$120,000 a year.[9]

Maybe the actual economic statistics are irrelevant and Trump voters *felt* less financially secure. This possibility does not withstand analysis either. According to American National Election Studies (ANES) data, Trump voters did not report feeling less financially secure than others did and they may even have felt more secure.[10] Economically marginalized? Hardly.

Moving beyond Trump voters to the broader, worldwide picture, the notion that financial stress sends people of any culture fleeing to the comforts of nationalistic policies, rhetoric, and politicians is a popular one in journalistic circles.[11] Try as scholars might, however, empirical support for the claim that right-wing nativist parties and candidates flourish in bad economic times simply does not exist.[12] To put an exclamation point on this fact, the US economy was booming when Trump—the quintessential nationalist leader—was elected in November of 2016. As a growing scholarly chorus points out, the recent surge in support for nativist, populist parties and candidates around the world is not the result of declining economies and rampant financial insecurities.[13]

AGE

Those attracted to Trump may not be economically downtrodden but other aspects of the popular demographic narrative are at least partially correct. Consistent with conventional wisdom, the 2016 general election exit polls indicate that Trump did much better with older than with younger voters. Among those forty-five and over, Trump defeated Clinton 52%–44%; among those forty-four and younger, Clinton defeated Trump 53%–39%. This pattern appears to be attributable to factors other than Donald Trump, however. According to the Pew Research Center (Pew), Trump actually did better with young voters (18–29) than did his two immediate predecessors as Republican presidential nominee, John McCain in 2008 and Mitt Romney in 2012. Trump voters in 2016 were indeed older than Clinton voters, but this difference reflects a long-standing Republican pattern rather than a peculiarity of 2016.[14]

URBAN-RURAL

The major exit polls do not record the type of community in which respondents live but Pew does and uses this information to compute the share of each candidate's voting coalition constituted by distinct residential types.[15] The results confirm conventional wisdom that rural voters made up a disproportionate share of the Trump voting coalition just as urban voters made up a disproportionate share of Clinton's voters. The suburbs, where most Americans live, were largely a wash.

Fully 35% of Trump voters were rural while 53% were suburban and just 12% urban. For Clinton the numbers were quite different: only 19% of her voters were rural, 48% suburban, and a whopping 32% urban. Clinton's 20-point margin in urban areas was even larger than Trump's 16-point margin in rural areas. The problems for Clinton in 2016 were that there were more rural/small town voters than central city voters and, even more important, that she was not able to win among suburban voters. A key point regarding place of domicile is that nearly two-thirds of Trump voters in 2016 were *not* rural/small town residents.

RELIGION

At first blush, it would appear that churchgoers formed the core of Trump's coalition. Exit polls show that among those who attend church at least once a week, Trump defeated Clinton easily; among those who attend church at least monthly, Trump barely won; among those who attend only "a few times a year" Trump barely lost; and among those who never attend, Trump lost badly. These numbers, however, reflect 2016 voters rather than intense supporters and even at that, the denomination with which frequent attenders are most likely to affiliate may distort the results. A survey by the Public Religion Research Initiative (PRPI) in April of 2018 found that the only religious group that continued to support Trump a little over a year into his presidency was white evangelicals. Jewish people, Catholics, and black evangelicals were unsupportive of Trump and "mainline" Protestants split about evenly.[16] Trump's persistent supporters are not so much religious as white evangelicals.

Still, frequently lost in discussions of Trump supporters is the high percentage who are *not* religious. According to exit polls, 40% of Trump voters admit to going to church only a couple of times a year or less. Another 7% of Trump voters would not answer the question and so are unlikely to be frequent attenders. Then, of course, there is the well-known fact that survey respondents tend to inflate self-reported behaviors such as attending church. In short, it appears that upward of 50% of Trump voters attend church very rarely or not at all. Among strong supporters, this number could be even higher. Contrary to conventional wisdom, many Trump supporters, like Trump himself, are not religious.

In fact, the split between religious and non-religious Trump backers could be quite important. A study by the Democracy Fund Voter Study Group[17] finds that compared to non-religious Trump voters, religious Trump voters are significantly more likely to have favorable attitudes toward racial and religious minorities, to be supportive of immigration, and to be concerned about poverty.[18] Trump backers may fall into two distinct camps: a non-religious camp for whom immigration and outsider threats are central and a religious camp for whom Trump's anti-immigrant, nationalistic rhetoric is a partial turnoff but one that is more than offset by his hostility toward gay and abortion rights and his appointment of socially conservative justices.

GENDER

A clear gender gap was evident in the 2016 elections, not surprising considering that it was the first election in which a female was the presidential nominee of one of the two major parties. According to exit polls, males voted 52–41 for Donald Trump while females voted 54–41 for Hillary Clinton.[19] These numbers seem to suggest that many couples canceled out their votes, though in actuality this is not the case since marital status complicated the relationship between gender and vote in 2016. Single women voted overwhelmingly for Clinton, 63–32; married women, on the other hand, split nearly evenly, voting just 49–47 for Clinton. Though the difference was smaller, married men were also significantly more likely than unmarried men to vote for Donald Trump; thus, intra-couple disagreement in 2016 may not have been as common as the overall numbers for male-female differences imply.[20]

EDUCATION

With regard to education, Trump lost 52–42 among those with a college education but won 51–44 among those without a college degree. Pew's alternative to exit polls showed an even greater educational split, with Clinton winning among college educated 57–36 and losing among non-college-educated 43–52. Educational attainment clearly mattered in 2016 but this may simply be a reflection of the partisan contours of American politics in recent decades. Non-college-educated whites began leaving the Democratic Party many presidencies ago. The Civil Rights Act, shrinking labor unions, Ronald Reagan, and Barack Obama all set the stage for Donald Trump's success with non-college-educated voters. In other words, the education gap in 2016 was less about Trump than about long-standing partisan differences.

To underscore this point, in the 2016 primaries, Trump supporters on average had just three months less education than supporters of the other Republican candidates—a startlingly modest difference.[21] Trump voters also were better educated than the public overall, though to be fair this is due in part to the tendency of non-voters to have less education than voters.[22] Any way you cut it and despite the obvious statistical tendency for Trump voters to be less educated than Clinton voters, tens of millions of college-educated people voted for Donald Trump in 2016.

RACE

Trump supporters are white. This is the conventional wisdom and it is true. In the 2016 general elections, fewer than one in ten African Americans voted for Trump. Voters who identified as Latinx, Asian-American, or "other" were more likely than African Americans to vote for Trump but they still lined up two to one against him (Pew's numbers are similar). To look at it the other way, however, many observers might find it surprising that nearly three of every ten Latinx voters marked their ballots for Trump in spite of his comments on Mexican judges, Central American immigrants, Puerto Ricans, and Democratic members of Congress who are racial minorities.[23]

SUMMING UP

Pulling together two demographic categories, Trump's success is often attributed to white, non-college-educated voters. Trump's popularity within that demographic is undeniable, yet it may be a mistake to give this fact too much emphasis. Non-whites were about as likely to vote for Trump, which is to say not very likely, whether they did or did not have a college degree, but for whites, a college degree made a remarkable difference. Whites without a college degree voted 66–29 for Trump; whites with a college degree split almost evenly, 48% voting for Trump and 45% for Clinton (note that even among the college-educated, more whites voted for Trump than Clinton).

Pew follows a different strategy to put the role of the white, non-college-educated demographic into perspective by comparing the share of all 2016 Trump voters who were whites without college diplomas. When this is done, they find that Trump's share was very nearly identical to the share for other recent Republican candidates. White, non-college-educated voters constituted 61% of George W. Bush voters in 2004, 61% of John McCain voters in 2008, and 59% of Mitt Romney voters in 2012. The popular narrative implies that this number exploded for Trump in 2016 when in fact it went up only modestly, to 63%. Adding gender to the mix, 33% of Trump voters in 2016 were white *males* without a college degree. This is a substantial share but it means that two-thirds of Trump voters were either female, non-white, college educated, or some combination of those three.

A final point regarding demographics and Trump support: Correlations between demographic traits and a fondness for political figures such as Donald Trump do not necessarily mean demography caused that fondness. The environment created by people's place of residence, religious community, and educational peers certainly affects their political attitudes but the individuals involved have substantial control over these environmental factors. Some are attracted to the stimulation and diversity of a college campus; others prefer to do without it. Some long for the hustle and bustle of urban life; others seek the quiet and predictability of the small town.[24] Perhaps individuals who choose to forgo college and live their lives in a rural/small town environment are attracted to candidates such as Donald Trump. Perhaps lifestyle preferences, educational decisions, and psychological predilections are what is really behind the correlation between some demographics and political preferences. Indeed, sociologists David Norman Smith and Eric Hanley present evidence that the apparent influence of demographics largely washes out once they control for ideology. They conclude that Trump's appeal "was more immediately and decisively associated with attitudes than with demographics."[25] What might these "attitudes" be?

Trump Supporters' Psychological Proclivities

A reasonable first step in answering this question is to recognize that Trump voters in 2016 were overwhelmingly Republican and conservative. For all the talk about the novelty of Trump and his candidacy, his voting coalition was not at all novel: 88% of Republicans voted for Trump, as did 81% of conservatives. Pew, with a different method of categorizing conservatives, had the number even higher at 95%. Trump received remarkably few votes from Democrats (8%) and from self-professed liberals (10%). Thus, to a great extent, describing Trump voters requires no special skills beyond being able to describe a Republican or a conservative. Zealous Trump supporters are another story but until we get to the data on them, it will be useful to ponder the attitudes that correlate with being a Republican and especially with being a conservative. What are the personality traits, psychological tendencies, and attitudes that characterize conservatives and how prevalent are these traits among the subset of conservatives who passionately embrace Donald Trump?

In 2003, psychologist John Jost and colleagues conducted an extensive review of studies connecting psychological traits to political conservatism.[26] A list of these traits is shown in Table 2.1.

TABLE 2.1: Traits that Have Been Empirically Associated with Conservatives

1. Dogmatism
2. Intolerance of ambiguity
3. Low integrative complexity
4. Decreased sensation seeking
5. Decreased value placed on imaginativeness
6. Decreased value placed on living an exciting life
7. Decreased openness to new experiences
8. Preference for simplicity in art, literature, and music
9. Reluctance to accept new technology
10. Suspicion of innovation at workplace
11. Preference for order
12. Preference for structure
13. Preference for closure
14. Diminished self-esteem
15. Ego defensiveness
16. Neuroticism
17. Belief that the world is a dangerous place
18. Sensitivity to threats
19. Enhanced fear of death
20. Enhanced mortality salience

The Jost list is extensive but does not include all of the concepts scholars have attached to conservatives. Disgust sensitivity,[27] resentfulness,[28] bitterness,[29] anger,[30] fear,[31] conformity,[32] preference for purity,[33] and decreased concern with inequality also correlate with conservatism.[34]

Conservatives may not take kindly to some of the traits on this list but before concluding it is merely the product of biased, left-leaning academics, remember several points. First, the authors of the relevant studies came to their conclusions because conservative research participants reported they had those traits. To provide a few examples, conservatives are more likely than liberals to agree that "the things I believe in are so completely true, I could never doubt them" (an item in the dogmatism scale). They are more likely than liberals to agree that they "dislike questions that could be answered in many different ways" (an item in the "need for closure" scale). They are *less* likely than liberals to agree that they "enjoy the exhilaration of being in unpredictable situations" (an item in the "value placed on leading an exciting life" scale). In addition, they are more likely than liberals to agree that "sleeping in a hotel bed where a man had died of a heart attack the night before" would bother them (an item in the disgust sensitivity battery). Critics can quibble over question wording and labels but they cannot claim that researchers merely decided on their own to describe conservatives in a demeaning fashion.

Second, recognize that the relationships reported in these studies, though significant and persistent, are relatively weak, meaning the traits listed do not describe many conservatives. Finally, note that not every finding paints conservatives in an unflattering light. After all, being sensitive to threats and preferring order in life are hardly character flaws. Moreover, empirical research has found that, compared to liberals, conservatives are conscientious[35] and polite,[36] traits most people view favorably.

My goal is not to argue that these traits either do or do not describe conservatives but rather to use this list to derive hypotheses regarding the tendencies of fervent Trump supporters. Are Trump supporters similar to conservatives generally? Do the descriptors of conservatives in the list above describe Trump supporters specifically? The list is too long to allow treatment of every single trait but we can make a good start. Consideration will be largely speculative at this stage since, unlike the case with demographics, reliable data on the psychological and personality descriptions of Trump voters, let alone ardent Trump supporters, are not always available.

ARE TRUMP SUPPORTERS CONSCIENTIOUS?

Psychologists are generally agreed that the five core human personality traits are conscientiousness, extraversion, agreeableness, emotional stability (the opposite of neuroticism), and openness to new experiences. Ideologues always like to imagine that their counterparts possess distasteful traits but the truth of the matter is that studies consistently show that liberals and conservatives do not differ much on extraversion and emotional stability. These same studies also show that liberals and conservatives are quite similar with regard to agreeableness.[37]

Personality differences between liberals and conservatives exist but tend to be confined to conscientiousness and openness to new experiences.[38] Compared to liberals, conservatives report themselves to be less open to new experiences (e.g., they are more likely to profess a preference for "work that is routine") and, as mentioned above, compared to conservatives, liberals report themselves to be less conscientious (e.g., they admit that they "can be somewhat careless"). Are Trump supporters similar to their fellow conservatives in that they are conscientious but not particularly open to new experiences?

This is a rare case in which evidence is already available on the psychology of Trump's more motivated supporters. A study by political scientists David Fortunato, Matthew V. Hibbing, and Jeffery J. Mondak found that when it comes to personality traits, early Trump supporters are similar to but also a little different from conservatives.[39] People who supported Trump early in the primary season were similar to conservatives as a whole in that they scored high in self-reported conscientiousness. On the other hand, Trump supporters were also high in extraversion. Given that, compared to liberals, conservatives generally are not particularly extraverted, this discovery is inconsistent with the standard pattern for conservatives even as it is consistent with the general vibe given off by enthusiastic Trump supporters—many of whom hardly seem to be shrinking violets.

Even more, these same authors found that, compared to those who supported other Republicans in the 2016 primaries (e.g., Ted Cruz or Marco Rubio), Trump supporters were low in agreeableness, openness, and neuroticism. The finding on agreeableness is likely to be met with knowing nods by those who are not fans of Donald Trump and his followers. Before they become too defensive, however, strong Trump supporters should remember that these conclusions derive from self-assessments. As such, the authors are not decreeing that Trump supporters are relatively disagreeable but rather reporting that Trump supporters are more likely than Trump opponents to see themselves as, to take one example, "sometimes rude to others." Merely based on my personal exposure to Trump supporters, the finding that they are low on neuroticism also rings true in that Trump supporters do not seem particularly unstable and neurotic.

Are Trump supporters low on openness to new experiences? Numerous studies find that conservatives in general report being less open and a lack of openness seems related to several of the studies included in the Jost meta-analysis. These analyses found that conservatives were more likely to be dogmatic, to be indifferent to new sensations and experiences, to place minimal value on imaginativeness and excitement, to be suspicious of innovation, and to prefer order, structure, and closure. Further, it would not be a stretch to connect many of these traits to a sensitivity to threats and even an enhanced concern with mortality. Playing life relatively close to the vest and not taking unnecessary chances is a sensible strategy for those attuned to threats and their own mortality even if doing otherwise is likely to be more stimulating and exciting. The thinking could be, "If the standard way of dealing with life has not led to my death, why would I want to deviate from the standard way?" Sensitivity to threats and an awareness of mortality are perfectly consistent with a more conservative approach to life and to politics. If Trump supporters are as threat sensitive and security conscious as suspected, it would make sense that, like conservatives generally, Trump supporters would express relatively high support for the tried and true. They prefer patterns and predictability to novelty and nuance.

Still, if Trump supporters are indeed securitarians, they may not be consistently averse to change. The previous way of doing things may have kept people alive but that does not necessarily mean it is sufficiently oriented to vigilance and protection to suit the tastes of securitarians such as intense Trump supporters. Due to their preference for vigilance, many Trump supporters may want their leaders to be less cavalier toward the need for group strength, security, and protection. In this light, Trump supporters may be likely to display a desire to shake things up if doing so enhances their freedom from vulnerability and protects their country's physical and cultural security. Blind devotion to existing norms may be the last thing Trump supporters want if taking chances is necessary to heighten security. Conservatives generally crave structure, order, tradition, and closure. My suspicion, however, is that fervid Trump supporters respect only those traditions, conventions, and established structures that foster personal freedoms and provide security to insiders.

THAT MAKES ME SICK

Would it bother you to eat a bowl of your favorite soup that had been stirred with a used but cleaned fly swatter? Would you eat monkey meat? Would it bother you to see a man with a glass eye take it out of the socket? Researchers commonly employ questions such as these to ascertain the degree to which individuals are "disgust sensitive." Sometimes, however, people may not present accurate portraits of themselves. Perhaps they want to project a certain image—evidence suggests males strive to appear hearty and unfazed; females discerning and sensitive[40]—or perhaps they simply are not very good at self-reflection. Fortunately, scholars have devised ways of measuring disgust sensitivity that do not involve asking people to self-report. We can do this in the lab by presenting participants with disgusting stimuli, such as a picture of vomit or feces, and then measuring each participant's physiological response to that image. Whether gauged by self-report or physiology, disgust-sensitive individuals appear to be more likely to take conservative stances on certain issues, especially those pertaining to gay marriage and other sexual matters.[41]

Given that preferences for purity are likely to accompany relatively high levels of disgust sensitivity, this finding fits well with a related set of findings indicating that conservatives are more likely to value purity when they make moral judgments.[42] After all, one of the items used to assess purity is "people should not do things that are disgusting even if no one is harmed."[43]

As disgust sensitivity and a desire for purity correlate with aspects of conservatism, the obvious question is whether they also correlate with the type of conservative constituting the central topic of this book: impassioned Trump supporters. Trump's own remarks and behaviors seem to indicate he is disgust sensitive. Recall his comment that journalist Megyn Kelly was "bleeding from wherever" and his description of Hillary Clinton's trip to the bathroom during a break in their debate as so "disgusting" that he could not talk about it. In addition, Trump is a self-described clean freak who, even before the coronavirus, hated the tradition of shaking hands.

What about Trump's followers? A recent study found that Trump voters (not necessarily Trump supporters) were more likely to register high levels of disgust sensitivity especially when it comes to sex.[44] Another study found a relationship between body odor disgust sensitivity and voting for Trump in the 2016 primaries.[45] Neither of these studies homes in on Trump's most ardent supporters but they do raise the possibility of a relationship. Skepticism toward immigration and toward other races (a common characteristic of strong Trump supporters) often has a purity component to it—think separate drinking fountains and other Jim Crow laws. In May of 2019, Fox News host and frequent Trump defender Tucker Carlson illustrated this viewpoint when he said that immigrants bring disease and "make the U.S. dirtier."[46] Trump devotees could interpret outsiders infiltrating insiders as a violation of purity standards and in this sense, disgust and a desire for purity may well drive their support for Trump and his wall. Trump's penchant for referring to the novel coronavirus as the "Chinese virus" both illustrates and played into this orientation.

WHAT DO YOU VALUE?

Psychologist Shalom Schwartz offers a circular map of basic human values.[47] On one side of the circle is self-direction and stimulation, along with their subcategories of creativity, freedom, and a desire for an exciting life. On the opposite side are conformity, tradition, and security, along with their subcategories of obedience, humility, and devotedness. Subsequent to delineating the array of basic values, Schwartz and his colleagues analyzed the degree to which those values correlate with political orientations.[48] They found that self-direction and stimulation correlate with liberal political orientations whereas conformity, tradition, and security correlate with conservative political orientations. The question of interest here, though, is whether the values associated with conservatives generally are associated with intense Trump supporters specifically.

There is reason for doubt. I have already questioned whether the conservative values of conformity and tradition are characteristic of Trump supporters. Similar questions attend obedience and humility. At the least, humility is a trait seldom ascribed to Donald Trump himself; thus, it may be that his strongest supporters likewise do not value humility. I also wonder whether Trump supporters are particularly high in obedience and low in a desire for freedom. Relative to other conservatives, Trump supporters may well value obedience less and freedom more (remember they are vulnerability averse). Schwartz's basic value of security, on the other hand, could not be more central to my conception of the ethos of fervid Trump supporters. I predict that Trump support derives from the basic human value of security and will test this and other hypotheses in chapters 5 and 6.

I RESENT THAT

Donald Trump's degree is from the Wharton School of Business at the University of Pennsylvania. He inherited millions of dollars from a father who made it possible for him to succeed in real estate. His primary home is a three-level penthouse at the top of a skyscraper on Fifth Avenue in Manhattan. It is modeled after the rococo Palace of Versailles, complete with opulent gold inlays. Even as a pre-teen, Trump's son Barron had an entire floor to himself. Trump tells people the spread covers 33,000 square feet and, even if it is really just one-third of that, it remains an immense, ostentatious, and ornate residence in a neighborhood where studio apartments smaller than one of Trump's closets routinely sell for millions of dollars. He also owns and sometimes resides in a former 128-room mansion in Palm Beach, Florida, originally built by the cereal heir Marjorie Merriweather Post and since converted into a luxury private club called Mar-a-Lago. If he would rather not go all the way to Florida, he owns a weekend getaway in Bedford, New York. It has a bowling alley, three swimming pools, and sixty rooms, fifteen of which are bedrooms. Then there are his numerous hotels and properties, including Turnberry Golf Course in Scotland. Oh, and don't forget his walled compound on the beautiful Caribbean island of St. Martin.

Donald Trump never served in the military and there is little evidence he has spent a single day doing manual labor. His favorite sport is golf and when he plays, he neither walks nor carries his own clubs. Throughout most of his adult life, servants, drivers, and sycophantic aides have accompanied him. By any measure, he leads a pampered, surreal existence.

Despite wealth and opportunities most people can only imagine, a common claim is that Trump's supporters are attracted to him because they are resentful of wealthy, citified, Ivy-League-educated people who are out-of-touch with the problems of workaday, blue-collar, struggling America.[49] To be fair, some of the writers attracted to the resentment argument stress racial resentment and that particular type of resentment appears to be present among many Trump supporters. Still, the resentment argument is often raised in the context of education, occupation, class, and place of domicile[50] and the notion that those who deeply resent coastal, urban, overeducated, white-collar, wealthy, privileged, condescending, arrogant elites find Donald J. Trump an appropriate vessel for that resentment is rich.

This is not to deny that resentment can drive political attitudes because it can, as is evident in Katherine Cramer's compelling account of the supporters of Scott Walker, former governor of Wisconsin.[51] In her personal interactions with the residents of Wisconsin, Cramer encountered thick layers of unmistakable resentment. The mostly elderly and mostly rural residents that she consulted resented state government workers in the capital of Madison, the lazy city-dwellers in Milwaukee, and the effete, overpaid college professors at the state's flagship university. Mostly, they resented anybody who seemed entitled and did not do honest labor and they respected anybody who was real, knew the worth of a dollar, and showered after work rather than before. A similar theme is evident in J. D. Vance's account of his own working-class family's struggles in rural Kentucky and small town Ohio.[52]

Resentment certainly can be an important motivator and the rural resentment that fueled the rise of Scott Walker might animate ardent supporters of Donald Trump as well. Then again, it might not. Given that Trump perfectly embodies the target demographic of their resentment, the obvious question becomes whether the focus of rural, working-class, white, non-college-educated resentment is actually urban, educated elites or is in fact something else. One distinct possibility is that the real target is liberals and their seeming naïveté in the face of outsider threats. If Donald Trump did not champion vigilance against outsiders, if he assumed liberal rather than conservative positions on immigration, defense, welfare, and gun control, he would probably be the target of rural resentment rather than its consequence. Without the appropriate political positions, demographic profiles are nothing. Imagine that university professors and state workers in Wisconsin suddenly became strident political conservatives. In this alternative universe, the rural resentment directed at bureaucrats and the intelligentsia is likely to melt away.[53]

The brouhaha surrounding a series of Donald Trump's tweets in July of 2019 provide another illustration of this point. In those tweets, he suggested four female Democratic members of Congress should go back to where they came from, places that are "totally broken and crime-infested" and whose governments are "a complete and total catastrophe." His comments were reprised just days later at a campaign-style rally in North Carolina and led the crowd to chant in reference to one of the four, "Send her back, send her back!" No one questions that the race and religion of these four members were highly relevant but it is unlikely that Trump and his supporters would have expressed the same desire to "send back" a member of Congress who consistently voted to increase defense spending, strengthen the police, restrict immigration, promote patriotism, protect gun ownership, facilitate capital punishment, reduce foreign aid, and protect Donald Trump from investigations. What made members of "the squad" so dangerous in the eyes of Trump and his ardent supporters is not merely that they are something other than white male Christian fourth-generation Americans; it is that they are something other than securitarians. Strong Trump supporters hold individuals perceived to be outsiders to a higher standard, but the likelihood that they will be accepted increases significantly if they behave like securitarians.

Emotions and Trump Supporters

In recent years, political scientists have become emotional. After long asserting that people's decisions on whether or not to vote were based on cold-blooded cost-benefit analyses and that voters' preferences for particular parties or candidates were the result of calculated economic self-interest, there has been an explosion of quality work showing that several emotions are central to political choices.[54] I discuss them in turn, focusing most concertedly on fear.

FEAR

We frequently hear that conservatives and Trump supporters are fearful. Consider the following headlines: "Trump Supporters Are Easily Manipulated by Fear"; "People Who Are Fearful Tend to Be Politically Conservative";

"Conservatives Scare More Easily than Liberals, Scientists Say"; "How Fear of a Physical Threat Can Foster Social Conservatism"; "Experiment Proves that Conservatives Are Little Baby Snowflakes"; "Fear and Anxiety Drive Conservatives' Political Attitudes," and "Donald Trump and the Politics of Fear."[55] Pippa Norris and Ronald Inglehart see support for conservative, nationalist leaders around the world as springing from "a cult of fear" and they observe that "fear drives the search for collective security for the tribe."[56] Many of the works on fear trace back to Richard Hofstadter's classic essay, "The Paranoid Style in American Politics."[57] The logic is easy to see. Fear is a reasonable explanation for conservatives' desire to empower the police, fortify the military, place America first, keep immigrants at bay, punish criminals, and sacrifice civil liberties in order to catch terrorists. Nonetheless, as we will soon see, the evidence that conservatives are more scared than liberals is ambiguous at best.

What about Trump supporters? Even if conservatives overall do not report being more fearful, Trump's most devoted supporters might. After all, in the lead-up to the 2018 midterms, Trump himself barnstormed the country, ballyhooing the candidacies of favored Republican candidates. His central strategy during these campaign stops was straight-up fearmongering, with lawbreaking immigrants typically being the primary source of ostensible threat.[58] Does Trump's rhetoric on this single particular type of threat—criminally inclined immigrants—mean that his followers tend to be generically fearful? Not necessarily.

I am skeptical that Trump's most intense supporters are on balance more fearful than non-Trump supporters. Instead, the only entities likely to inspire greater fear among Trump supporters are outsiders and their sympathizers. Contrary to popular belief, conservatives and especially intense Trump supporters do not appear to be inordinately afraid of windstorms and lightning, spiders and snakes, plane crashes and nuclear conflagration. They do report being more fearful of immigrants, criminals, and terrorists but, as we will soon see, even this finding may need to be qualified. If these assertions are true, they suggest that people's level of fear is largely disconnected from their desire to pursue protective policies and that, somewhat ironically, fear is not a prerequisite for being a securitarian or for supporting Donald Trump.

Previously collected data provide support for these counterintuitive claims.[59] Scholars at Chapman University have queried several random samples of Americans about fears, concerns, and political orientations.[60] They were gracious enough to share their 2014 data covering people's self-reported reactions to fifty-seven possible threats, ranging from asteroids to growing old, from identity theft to nuclear accidents, and from heights to power outages. These data make it possible to test the hypothesis that conservatives are more generically fearful than liberals and the results are striking. Despite the widespread belief that conservatives are more fearful across the board, only four of the fifty-seven possible threats listed by Chapman was self-reported as being significantly higher for conservatives than for liberals. Fear of the other fifty-three was either unrelated to political ideology (34 of them) or actually significantly greater among liberals than among conservatives (19 of them).

Some of the potential threats that inspired more fear among liberals were predictable. Compared to conservatives, liberals are more threatened by illness and poverty as well as by oil spills and the loss of the rain forest. Other items on the list, however, cannot be explained away so easily. Why, compared to conservatives, are liberals significantly more threatened by earthquakes and clowns?

The four situations inspiring more fear among conservatives than liberals are civil unrest, economic collapse, US decline, and the government having information on private citizens. All four of these relate either to an overly powerful government or to a weakening of the United States. For those who structure their lives around protecting insiders and avoiding vulnerability, these four situations are especially concerning, so greater fear of them fits nicely with my account of securitarians. A sub-element of the Chapman project provides additional support. Shifting away from fear, a short battery of items asked how worried various situations made respondents. Potential worries included government use of drones, government health care, government corruption, and government restrictions on firearms. Each of these generated positive, statistically significant, and usually large correlations with political conservatism. If you want to worry conservatives, just mention government. It has the power to stop them from pursuing the protective strategies—such as taking steps to defend themselves—that are at the very core of their beings.

Intrigued by the patterns in the Chapman data, Kevin Smith, Clarisse Warren, Stephen Schneider, Sami Lauf, and I drafted survey items of our own and had them administered to a representative sample of American adults in late 2017. We asked respondents how threatened they felt by each of forty-six situations or entities, many of them the same as those found in the Chapman data. These forty-six included dying, reptiles, strangers, blood, fire, heights, the dark, communicable diseases, cyber-attacks, drought, nuclear attacks, physical disabilities, plane crashes, earthquakes, social humiliation, cancer, civil unrest, germs, the grid collapsing, animals, and identity theft.

When we correlated felt threat with ideology, the results confirmed and even went beyond the Chapman findings. Conservatives were not significantly more threatened than liberals by any of the forty-six items listed. Moreover, for forty-three of the forty-six, liberals were significantly more threatened than conservatives. Even for the kinds of tangible, societal, security-based threats that might have been expected to be especially concerning to conservatives—cyberattacks, nuclear attacks, economic collapse, terrorist attacks, civil unrest, and the grid collapsing—liberals were significantly more fearful than conservatives. These findings suggest that liberals are more, not less, likely than conservatives to find most aspects of life threatening. Not surprisingly, liberals find gun accidents and environmental catastrophes more threatening than conservatives do, but they also find shark attacks and clowns more threatening. The only apparent exceptions are threats posed by outsiders and their abettors.[61] A judge, a legislator, or, God forbid, a president who fails to understand the need to relentlessly protect gun rights, patriotic values, and the privileged position of insiders is a much bigger threat to conservatives than a scorpion or a thunderstorm. During the worst of the coronavirus pandemic, Trump supporters were hardly more fearful that they would get sick—if anything, they were less—but they were much more likely to emphasize that the outbreak came from foreign sources.

The reason for these results may be that the survey was conducted during the Trump administration, a time when conservatives wanted to believe that everything was rosy and that nothing bad, like a large asteroid smashing into Earth, could possibly happen. Maybe so, though remember that the Chapman data were collected during the Obama administration so it cannot be explained away by that reasoning. Moreover, even if it is true that liberals believe animal attacks are more likely during conservative presidencies and conservatives believe they are more likely during liberal presidencies, this conclusion is a far cry from the standard narrative that regardless of political climate, conservatives are endemically more fearful than liberals and that this enhanced fear explains their actions and policy positions. If fear is produced merely because the opposing party holds political power, conservatives are no different from liberals. To sum up, with the possible exception of threats posed by outsiders and the government, conservatives are no more fearful than liberals and may well be less fearful, a conclusion that could apply with even more force to the subgroup of conservatives known as strong Trump supporters. The hypothesis that I will develop in subsequent chapters is that avid Trump supporters are not more fearful . . . just more sensitive and attentive to outsider threats.[62]

ANXIETY

Though they are often lumped together, feeling fearful is not the same as feeling anxious. Threat and anxiety appear to lead to quite different orientations and policy desires[63] and we should not assume that the two distinct emotions will play out the same across ideologies. Even if conservatives are not more fearful across the board, they still could be more anxious.

Should this supposition about conservatives prove to be true, we would still need to know whether the pattern extended specifically to strong Trump supporters. Some have claimed that Trump voters in 2016 were particularly anxious[64] but the evidence for this claim is not convincing. Trump supporters are likely to be more anxious about illegal immigration, crime, and governmental overreach but are they also more anxious about income inequality, gun violence, and imminent ecological calamity? I know of no systematic evidence that, compared to those with other political orientations, Trump supporters on balance are more anxious.

ANGER

Anger is an entirely different emotion than either fear or anxiety and it, too, has been alleged to be prevalent among conservatives and to have been the motivation for many Trump voters in 2016.[65] Examples of conservative anger are easy to find and Trump's own tweets often seem angry, but is there evidence beyond anecdotes? Going into the 2016 election, many Americans believed the country was on the wrong track but this is not equivalent to being angry. Moreover, liberals worked up some pretty good anger during the administrations of George W. Bush and then Donald Trump. Many of the same media outlets that eagerly cited anger as the reason for Trump's victory in 2016 turned right around and asserted that Democratic victories in the 2018 midterms were due to anger.[66]

Contrary to popular belief, Americans were not unusually angry in 2016. Toward the end of that year, Barack Obama's approval levels were at 56% and consumer confidence was as high as it was in 1984 when Reagan's "morning in America" was brightening everyone's mood.[67] Vague assertions that, for unspecified reasons, decades of decline in working-class conditions waited until 2016 to manifest themselves in an angry electorate have the feel of post hoc theorizing. Discontent and anger can always be found somewhere in the electorate so they are not useful explanations for particular events.

Do Trump supporters have the market cornered on anger or is each side of the ideological spectrum merely likely to be angry at different times?[68] If it should be the case that conservatives are angrier only when a liberal occupies the White House (and liberals only when conservatives are in control), this pattern is a far cry from one in which conservatives on the whole and Trump supporters in particular are consistently angrier than liberals regardless of the current political climate or topic.

BITTERNESS

On April 6, 2008, during a conversation with a large group of wealthy donors in northern California, Barack Obama tried to explain the motivations of people in the rural Midwest. He said, "The jobs have been gone now for 25 years and nothing has replaced them. . . . Each successive administration has said that somehow these communities are going to regenerate and they have not. And it is not surprising then that they get bitter, they cling to guns or religion or antipathy to people who aren't like them or anti-immigrant sentiment or anti-trade sentiment." Though Obama's statement came eight years before Donald Trump's election, it nicely captures what was to come. The references to anti-immigrant and anti-trade sentiments, to xenophobia and guns, accurately identify the apparent policy priorities of Trump and his followers. Was Obama correct, however, about those in the rural Midwest circa 2008 being bitter? Since data on this specific group are difficult to marshal, we can pose a related and more answerable question: Is it the case that conservatives are bitter? As with the other emotions I have addressed, I think bitterness is more likely to ebb and flow with changes in the ideological make-up of the politicians in positions of authority. Be this as it may, systematic evidence that conservatives overall are bitter people is difficult to find. In fact, as we will soon see, conservatives actually score higher than liberals do on various measures of social well-being and positive emotions.

Conclusion

When it comes to understanding the motivations of core Trump supporters, demographic explanations are of limited use. Trump voters are disproportionately rural, religious, non-college-educated, older, male, and white, thus fitting conventional wisdom, but even so, a remarkable number of young or college educated or well to do or female individuals voted for Donald Trump. In addition, to the extent that demographic traits do correlate with attitudes, the relationships may be spurious. Trump voters' decisions to attend an evangelical church, to live in a rural area, and to refrain from attending college reflect deeper psychological predispositions that may also make political figures such as Donald Trump attractive. This being the case, predispositions and not demographics are the crucial factors. Moreover, to the extent that demographic explanations apply to 2016, they seem to fit with long-standing patterns of Republican support rather than Trump support specifically.

Researchers have identified many of the psychological predispositions of conservatives broadly defined: conscientiousness, wariness of new experiences, disgust sensitivity, dogmatism, intolerance of ambiguity, threat sensitivity, conformity, traditionalism, fear, and anger, to name a few. Far too often, those struggling to understand Trump supporters assume that the psychological portrait of conservatives can be applied to ardent Trump supporters. The brief review in this chapter suggests that the psychological profile of Trump supporters, or at least Trump voters in 2016, is different from that of run-of-the-mill conservatives.

I have expressed doubts about the ability of existing demographic and psychological explanations to explain Trump supporters and I have offered a brief outline of an alternative explanation. It will soon be time to flesh out and then test the accuracy of my alternative. Before doing so, however, in the next chapter I explore a final tenet of the popular account concerning Trump supporters. This tenet has the longest heritage, has the most empirical work behind it, and has been the most frequently employed to explain Trump's supporters. It is time to consider whether strident Trump supporters are authoritarians.

CHAPTER 3 | Authoritarians Who Dislike Authority?

D O YOU KNOW any ardent Trump supporters? If so, would you describe them as eager to submit to all authority? The broad consensus these days is that Trump supporters are authoritarians but I have my doubts.[1] Of course, once convinced Trump was their kind of leader, some became deeply and even disturbingly devoted to him but virtually all people with strong beliefs can develop a powerful affinity for a leader who shares those beliefs—to the point of projecting inaccurate but favorable traits onto that leader.[2] Trump supporters' tendencies on this front might be more pronounced—or they might not be.

Most readers will be familiar with the term "authoritarian" in the context of family arrangements. Authoritarian parents are domineering and controlling, demand obedience, and do not tolerate dissent. They are strict, tough, and punitive; not lenient, indulgent, and soft. In a similar vein, authoritarian political leaders are tough, demand obedience, and do not tolerate dissent. Children have little opportunity to choose the style of parenting they will receive but if they did, it is unlikely they would request to be under the thumb of authoritarian parents. This raises an interesting question: When the context shifts out of the family to society in general, why would anybody voluntarily choose to follow an authoritarian political leader? The answer is that some people enjoy certitude, purpose, and direction, so they want a political leader who simplifies their existence by telling them in definitive terms how they should lead their lives. The dictionary definition of an "authoritarian" is someone who "favors strict obedience to authority at the expense of personal freedom." Seen in this light, are supporters of Trump and similar leaders around the world authoritarians? More than those with other orientations, do they enjoy submitting to authority and being told what to do?

It seems unlikely. The Trump supporters I know are more agitated than placid; more defiant than submissive. Far from devaluing personal freedom, they typically are averse to taking instructions and to having their actions constrained in any fashion. The Trump supporters I know resist rather than submit to authority and they challenge rather than follow the conventions of polite society. The Trump supporters I know do not like being dependent on others and as such are, if anything, closer to being anti-authoritarians than authoritarians.

If these unsystematic observations have any merit, why are Trump supporters so often pegged as authoritarians? Probably because the term itself has morphed well beyond its original, literal definition. To understand the claim that Trump's strongest supporters are authoritarians and to evaluate the claim's accuracy, we must first understand the evolution of the term. It is an involved but intriguing story that begins, as all good stories do, with a mid-twentieth-century continental polymath.

Theodor Adorno and the Authoritarian Personality

Theodor Adorno associated with fascinating people. He collaborated with the novelist Thomas Mann on *Doctor Faustus*. He worked for the renowned Austrian social scientist Paul Lazersfeld. He was an acquaintance, fan, then critic, and later neighbor of the composer Arnold Schoenberg, originator of the twelve-tone technique. He was a colleague of intellectual luminaries such as Herbert Marcuse and Bertolt Brecht. He had a long and productive relationship with the filmmaker Fritz Lang. He and Karl Popper staged a much-discussed series of debates on positivism. He knew Charlie Chaplin. He was a correspondent and interviewer of the playwright and novelist Samuel Beckett. In later years, Angela Davis, the American social activist and campus radical, attended his seminars.[3] Yet, despite all his accomplishments and famous acquaintances, Adorno is best remembered for a single social science study that was directly at odds with the central philosophy of the rest of his life; a study entitled *The Authoritarian Personality*.

Adorno was born in Frankfurt in 1903 to a father who was a wine merchant and a mother who was an opera singer. Young Teddy was a child prodigy and classically trained pianist, performing Beethoven's works by the age of twelve.

His talents were not confined to music, however, and in 1921 he graduated from gymnasium first in his class. Adorno then pursued his dual interests of music and philosophy, writing numerous concert reviews and original music as well as a philosophical manuscript that drew heavily on Freud's notion of the unconscious. In 1931, Adorno's scholarship met the requirements for "habilitation," meaning he had qualified to teach without supervision and was eligible to compete for professorships. Though not a formal member, Adorno soon became involved with lectures, publications, and other projects sponsored by the Institute for Social Research, an independent organization composed largely of Jewish scholars and dedicated to pursuing advances in the social sciences. Those at and around the Institute agreed on many matters, primarily the wisdom of Sigmund Freud and the need to save Marxism by revising it. This orthodoxy became known as the Frankfurt School, connoting a style of thought rather than a formal institution of learning.

Adorno's first major work was published on March 23, 1933, the very day Adolf Hitler seized total control of the German state. Before long, Adorno's right to teach had been revoked, his house and office searched, and his efforts to join the Reich Chamber of Literature denied because membership suddenly had become limited to persons "belonging to the German nation by profound ties of character and blood." Since "non-Aryans are unable to feel and appreciate such an obligation"—Adorno's mother was a Roman Catholic but his father Jewish—Adorno's application was summarily denied.[4] He soon left Germany, spending several years in England, mostly at Oxford. In 1938, the newly married Adorno somewhat reluctantly moved to New York where Max Horkheimer had relocated the Institute for Social Research. To make ends meet, Adorno took a job with the Princeton Radio Project under the directorship of Paul Lazersfeld. The goal of the project was to help RCA understand people's reaction to music heard over the radio. Though potentially of interest to the musically inclined Adorno, by this time he had developed serious reservations about modernity, mass society, and by extension, radio. The curmudgeon in him detested the notion of people listening to music while walking around or lying in bed rather than sitting attentively in acoustically appropriate concert halls. On top of this, a key element of Frankfurt School dogma was deep skepticism of objective empirical data on people's life experiences, an approach sometimes referred to as positivism. Attempting to ascertain people's feelings by using cold-blooded, multiple-choice survey items, as Lazersfeld was doing in the Princeton Radio Project, was anathema to Adorno.

With his work in New York less than rewarding, Adorno soon followed Horkheimer to southern California so that they could continue their collaboration, primarily on a searing critique of progress entitled "Dialectic of Enlightenment." About this time, the American Jewish Committee (AJC) was in the process of putting together a series of works on fascism and anti-Semitism. Adorno was intensely interested in these topics for obvious reasons but also because he saw a chance to further his theory that the cultural standardization endemic to modern life strips people of their autonomy, reduces them to childlike lemmings, and renders them susceptible to fascistic, demagogic messages. Under AJC auspices he conducted an analysis of the propaganda employed by a California preacher named Martin Luther Thomas whose diatribes against Jews and communists attracted a substantial following in the late 1930s.

At this point, Adorno's life took an unexpected turn. As the events in Europe became darker and deadlier, the AJC wanted more than case studies of fascist preachers. The committee envisioned a comprehensive study of anti-Semitism that would serve as the flagship for its "Studies in Prejudice" series. Three Berkeley psychologists—Else Frenkel-Brunswik, Daniel J. Levinson, and R. Nevitt Sanford—were already working with the committee on ethnocentrism and personality. Adorno was brought on board relatively late in the long-running project, primarily to add political and sociological flavor to the perspectives of the psychologists. The volume that ultimately resulted from this collaboration was *The Authoritarian Personality*. Adorno is listed as the first author not because his contribution was greatest but because his last name came first in the alphabet. In a somewhat unusual decision, the authors treated the twenty-three chapters distinctly with each having a separate author list. Adorno's name appears on just five of the twenty-three chapters, though in later years he asserted that he was the primary designer of the F-scale which many see as the heart of the entire project. For their part, his co-authors bore no resentment over Adorno's prime billing and reported him to be an engaged, creative, vibrant, valuable, and occasionally ribald teammate.[5]

Adorno's life continued to be eventful. Close to the publication of *The Authoritarian Personality* in 1950, Adorno decided to repatriate though this move proved to be less than unremittingly satisfying. What he saw as the failure of Germans to face up to their embrace of Nazi doctrines miffed him as did the degree to which preference in the postwar era was given to those who had remained in the country throughout the 1930s and '40s. Frankfurt, of course, had been leveled and along with much of Germany was struggling to remove rubble and rebuild. Adorno agonized over the role of citizens and intellectuals in the wake of the Holocaust, at one point famously asserting that "to write poetry after Auschwitz is barbaric."[6] He never made peace with modernity, and "trivialization" became one of his most frequently used words. He hated jazz, he hated dancing, he hated the elevated status accorded celebrities, and he hated the homogenization of society. One of his most astute observations was that the combination of capitalism and modern culture offers "the freedom to choose what is always the same."[7]

When the Institute of Social Research, with its unmistakably Marxist leanings, was re-established in Frankfurt, Adorno continued his role as a central player in the "Frankfurt School," but with the 1960s literally exploding on college campuses, activists frequently deemed ivory-tower Marxist sympathies insufficient. Despite being a vocal opponent of the Vietnam War and an equally vocal proponent of redistribution and socialist reforms, Frankfurt students increasingly perceived Adorno as too tepid and therefore as part of the problem. One of his students scrawled on the blackboard, "If Adorno is left in peace, capitalism will never cease." A group of them left his class in protest when he refused their demands to interrupt his lecture to endorse the ongoing student protests. During a public presentation, three female students bared their breasts and covered him with flowers. At another, protesters unfurled a banner that read "Berlin's Left-Wing Fascists Greet Teddy the Classicist." In the midst of those tumultuous times, he died in 1969, at the age of sixty-six, after going for a peaceful walk in the foothills of the Alps.

Irony attends the fact that Adorno's name is so tightly connected to *The Authoritarian Personality*. A scholar who spent a lifetime embracing Marxism, extolling the power of social conditioning, and arguing against positivist approaches to modern social science is forever attached to a work that relies on closed-ended survey self-reports, is largely devoid of Marxist rhetoric, and emphasizes deep-seated and perhaps innate personality traits. Adorno himself occasionally tried to square this circle but more often seemed eager to distance himself from the work.[8] Just a year after *The Authoritarian Personality*'s publication, Adorno wrote that "fascism is not a psychological issue"[9] which must have been a revelation to his three psychologist co-authors. At the least, we can say that *The Authoritarian Personality* is by no means an Adorno-esque work.

Perhaps he just happened to have finished a major project at the very time the American Jewish Committee needed someone to come on board another. Perhaps his interest in the substance of the project overrode his concerns about method. Perhaps we would not be engaging in these speculations if his name had been Theodor Zadorno and he had been the fourth, not first, listed author. (Else Frenkel-Brunswik, next in line as the second-listed author, led an equally fascinating, though far more tragic, life—she blazed trails as a very early (1930) female Jewish psychology PhD but suffered severe depression subsequent to her husband's suicide in 1955 and, three years later, after self-administering a massive dose of barbital, died at the age of forty-nine.) Whatever Adorno's attitude toward it, *The Authoritarian Personality* was a blockbuster of a study. Sometimes lauded; sometimes damned; always noticed. Other academics have cited it nearly 17,000 times and finding a social scientist without an opinion of it is a challenge.

No doubt much of the attention stems from the fact that the questions posed by the authors of *The Authoritarian Personality* (Adorno, Frenkel-Brunswick, Levinson, and Sanford; hereafter, "AFLS"), though central to societal governance at any time, were singularly poignant in the years immediately after the Holocaust and the reign of fascism in the 1930s/'40s. They attempted to explain why people are so susceptible to the messages and policies of certain leaders even when those messages and policies are patently repellent; why fascism so effortlessly took root in multiple countries; why ethnocentrism, racism, and anti-Semitism connect so readily with fascism; and why particular individuals are so much more amenable than others to ethnocentric messages, policies, and leaders.

AFLS, as well as those who commissioned their work, hoped to answer these questions so that it might be possible to root out what they called "irrational hostility." As they put it, "Our aim is not merely to describe prejudice but to . . . help in its eradication."[10] They intended to do this by painting a detailed portrait of people with a certain "mentality," "spirit," "character," "type," "syndrome," or "personality" (they use all these phrases and more in the book)—people who constituted a distinct "anthropological species"[11] that is prone to ethnocentrism, is prejudiced against minority groups, and is "particularly susceptible to anti-democratic propaganda."[12]

For two reasons, AFLS believed that this particular "type" merited special treatment: First, no other type posed a graver threat to democratic aspirations, human potential, and basic decency; second, no other type was as distinct and coherent. As they put it, "Anti-fascists do not constitute any single pattern" whereas "individuals who show extreme susceptibility to fascist propaganda have a great deal in common."[13] They set out to identify the nature of this personality type and the reasons it develops in some people but not others. To do so, they employed several diverse and creative research strategies.

Methods of The Authoritarian Personality

Imagine you are presented with a picture of two conversing adult white males, one much older than the other. Your instructions are to tell a "complete" story about the picture, including the events that led up to it, the events that followed it, and the nature of the two men's relationship. What story would you tell? Are they father and son? Did they have issues when the son was a youth? Do they get along or is there friction? What happens to them as their lives continue to unfold? If you are overly terse and omit valuable information, the examiners—who are busily recording your tale verbatim—will prod you. Now imagine this process being repeated for nine other pictures, one portraying a physical altercation; another an elderly African American woman and a young African American man. You have just participated in a Thematic Apperception Test (TAT) of the very sort AFLS administered to eighty participants. Two separate coders assessed whether each completed story contained any of a large number of designated features ranging from "achievement" to "self-pity" and from "abasement" to, of course, "sex." The underlying notion was that these spontaneous stories revealed each individual's needs and fixations.

Storytelling not your thing? Maybe you will do better at answering "projective questions," another intensive technique employed in *The Authoritarian Personality*. Projective questions are open-ended and deal with events and experiences likely to have emotional content. They are designed to be provocative and potentially revealing. AFLS employed eight of them and the following three are illustrative: (1) "We all have impulses and desires which are at times hard to control but which we try to keep in check. What desires do you often have difficulty controlling?" (2) If you knew you only had six months to live, but could do just as you pleased during that period, how would you spend your time?" and (3) "What great people, living or dead, do you admire most?" As you may have anticipated, answers were treated not at face value but rather as signs of the "deeper dynamic sources" that animate an individual's very being.[14]

AFLS also used a much more direct approach to compiling a portrait of people—putting them "on the couch" for clinical interviews. During these sessions, participants were asked highly detailed, open-ended questions about an incredible range of topics that fell within the following broad categories: vocation, income, religion, family background, family figures, childhood, sex, social relationships, school, politics, and minorities/race. To give a flavor of the richness of these interviews, when the topic was income it was not enough to ask which numerical range captured the respondent's family earnings. Participants were also asked: "What do you miss most that your present income does not provide?" "What are your plans for attaining the income to which you aspire and what are your chances for achieving that?" "What is the most important thing money can give a person?" When the topic was childhood, questions included the following: "Were you ever spanked as a child?" "Which parent did you feel closer to when you were age six?" "What were your main satisfactions in your relationship with your father?" When the topic was race and minorities, the questions were quite direct and sometimes loaded: "Which racial groups do you like the least?" "Do you think the Jews are a true menace or just a nuisance?" "What personal experiences with minority group members have you had and were those experiences positive or negative?"

Measuring Authoritarianism

Enriching as these various forms of qualitative data might be, the most influential evidence presented in *The Authoritarian Personality* came from a set of structured survey items that were administered to over 2,000 people. Rather than inviting participants to prattle on in an open-ended fashion that then required coders' subjective assessment, these items forced respondents to select one of a limited number of answer options (e.g., strongly agree, agree, neither agree nor disagree, disagree, or strongly disagree). AFLS included closed-ended items on anti-Semitism (the original motivation for the project; called the A-S scale), ethnocentrism (the E scale), political-economic views (the PEC scale), and anti-democratic, pre-fascist tendencies (the F-scale). In the eyes of the four authors, the F-scale was unquestionably first among equals.

AFLS were convinced that "anti-Semitism and ethnocentrism were not merely matters of surface opinion but general tendencies traceable to sources deep within the structure of the person,"[15] a conclusion buttressed by their observation that the target of prejudiced views was not nearly as important as the psychology of the person holding those views. AFLS found few participants who were prejudiced against Jews but not blacks, or vice versa, so they concluded "a man who is hostile toward one minority group is very likely to be hostile against a wide variety of others."[16] Their goal in building the F-scale was to compile a battery "that could yield a valid estimate of prejudicial and antidemocratic tendencies at the personality level."[17] Their initial effort contained thirty-eight items but their subsequent tinkering included numerous additions and subtractions.[18]

In terms of measuring the degree to which a person has an authoritarian personality, several problems attend AFLS's F-scale. First, many of the items assess worldview rather than personality—that is, they ask about desires for societal, not personal life. Rather than asking purely personal items such as whether respondents enjoy being under the influence of a powerful person or whether they work better when left to their own self-direction, AFLS included societal-level items such as "what this country needs, more than laws and agencies, is courageous, tireless, devoted leaders in whom the people can put their faith" and "America is getting so far from the true American way of life that force may be necessary to restore it." To be sure, some of the F-scale items come closer to personality—for example, "some things are too intimate and personal to talk about even with one's closest friends" and "leisure is a fine thing but good hard work makes life interesting and worthwhile"—but the majority of items deal with worldview. As a whole, answers to these items may suggest something about the respondent's personality but they do not cleanly address personal tendencies. A better title for the book may have been *The Authoritarian Worldview*.

A second problem is that AFLS included an entire gamut of tangential items such as whether respondents believed that "astrology can explain a lot of things," that "wild and dangerous things happen in the world," that people's fate was mystically determined, that the imaginative and tender-minded are problematic, that "no sane, normal, decent person could ever think of hurting a close relative," that "the sex orgies of the old Greeks and Romans were tame compared to some of the goings-on in this country," that "wars and social troubles may someday be ended by an earthquake or flood that will destroy the whole world," that "we should return to a more red-blooded, active way of life," that "the business man is more important than the professor," and that "familiarity breeds contempt." These items often leave the literal meaning of authoritarianism far behind. Instead of preferences for structure and submission, we find items on attitudes toward earthquakes, Roman sex, mysticism, and "red-blooded ways of life." Reflecting their sprawling conceptualization of authoritarianism, AFLS believed it included nine sub-clusters: conventionalism, authoritarian submission, authoritarian aggression, anti-intraception, superstition and stereotypy, power and toughness, destructiveness and cynicism, projectivity, and sex.

Another important problem with *The Authoritarian Personality* is that the individuals selected to participate in the surveys and subsequent intensive procedures were not representative of people in the country as a whole.[19] Lacking the resources to recruit nationally representative samples, the authors instead administered mimeographed surveys to miscellaneous groups, including students at the University of California, students at the University of Oregon, students at the University of Southern California, students at George Washington University, students at the Merchant Marine Academy, members of the United Electrical Workers Union, longshoremen, members of service organizations such as the Kiwanis, Lions, and Rotary Clubs, nurses, members of PTAs, "professional women," psychiatric patients, and even 110 inmates at the San Quentin State Prison. With more than 2,000 total survey participants, overall numbers were more than satisfactory for drawing meaningful conclusions but the representativeness of the participants was not. Thus we can only say that, though the results and interpretations offered in *The Authoritarian Personality* may describe the views of an eclectic mix of mostly young and mostly West Coast individuals, we cannot be confident they represent the views of the inhabitants of the United States in general.

A final problem with *The Authoritarian Personality* may seem trivial to non-social science readers but is actually quite important. Survey researchers have long known that when answering questions, many respondents display an acquiescence bias. This means that regardless of their actual sentiment, they are more likely to agree than to disagree with any statement presented to them. This bias is easy to uncover by including contradictory statements at various points of a survey. A respondent who agrees that "defense spending should be increased" and then, in a later item, that "current levels of defense spending are too high" could well be displaying acquiescence bias. AFLS made a serious error by phrasing all F-scale statements in such a way that agreement is consistent with an authoritarian personality. The result, as has been pointed out frequently,[20] is that people may appear to be authoritarian when in reality they merely have acquiescent tendencies.[21] Rather than asking only whether survey respondents agreed with authoritarian statements such as "obedience and respect for authority are the most important virtues children should learn," they should also have asked whether respondents agreed with non-authoritarian statements such as "creativity and independence of thought are the most important virtues children should learn."[22]

The Findings of The Authoritarian Personality

Checking in at nearly 1,000 pages, *The Authoritarian Personality* is richly detailed, punctilious, and sometimes pedantic. Despite the attention subsequent scholars lavished on the F-scale, descriptions of the intensive studies, especially the clinical interviews, take up most of the book. Lengthy direct quotes fill page after page. Many of the comments participants made when asked about their attitudes toward minorities are chilling. Consider these examples: "The Negro, however, should be kept with his own people.

I would not want my niece marrying a Negro and I would not want Negro neighbors. . . . Actually, they should have a separate state."[23] When attention turned to members of the Jewish faith, attitudes were no better, as the following two quotes, from different individuals, indicate. "My relations with the Jews have been anything but pleasant. . . . [T]hey are aggressive, clannish, and money-minded. . . . [T]hey are practically taking over the country. They are getting into everything. It is not that they are smarter, but they work so hard to get control. They are all alike."[24] Then there is this: "I don't blame the Nazis at all for what they did to the Jews."[25]

Sobering as these comments may be—and they are not atypical—the explanation AFLS offer for the existence of the authoritarian personality is the central point. Why do certain individuals score so high on the F-scale and hold attitudes that lead them to make racist and anti-Semitic comments? AFLS's answer rests on a large number of questionable Freudian inferences. Their core argument is that people display authoritarian personalities because when they were children, a parent, probably their father, was insecure about his status in life and responded to this insecurity by engaging in excessively harsh and punitive parenting which in turn caused his children to fear the parent's disapproval so much that they were driven to revere all authority figures and to revile those perceived as lower in the social hierarchy. Social psychologist Roger Brown puts this line of thought well: "Status anxiety produces authoritarian discipline which produces repression of faults and shortcomings and aggression" which is then projected onto minorities and outsiders to such an extent that generalized prejudice becomes a structured aspect of the individual's personality.[26] This being the case, AFLS's prescription for ending fascism is simple: "All that is really essential is that children be genuinely loved."[27] In so saying, they ignore the fact that authoritarian parenting could lead children to be particularly sympathetic toward those who are vulnerable to the bullying of powerful figures, having felt this weight themselves. The very conditions that AFLS claim lead to authoritarianism could just as easily be the progenitors of empathy, rebelliousness, and anti-authoritarianism.

In Frankfurt School fashion, the ultimate causes of parental misconduct were traced to issues of capitalist economics. Following psychoanalyst Erich Fromm, AFLS claimed that classic family angst has become much more common because modern industrialized capitalism generates empty frustrations among the workers whose dissatisfaction is then visited upon their children, who go on to develop authoritarian personalities.[28] This logic is set forth most clearly in The Authoritarian Personality's preface, where Adorno's Frankfurt School colleague Max Horkheimer opines that the new anthropological species arose because "highly industrialized society" creates the status anxieties and malcontented parents that in turn create the authoritarian, anti-democratic, ethnocentric personality.[29] Primitive, non-capitalistic societies were thought to be innocent of the authoritarian personality, a point Adorno stressed repeatedly in his later writings.[30]

Focused as they were on psychoanalytical speculation, AFLS pay almost no attention to other potential correlates of authoritarian personalities. Are males more likely than females to have an authoritarian personality? Older individuals more likely than younger? Religious than non-religious? Whites than minorities? Poor than rich? Educated than less educated? Even though AFLS's surveys provided a full battery of variables, with two exceptions, they present no data or speculation on any of these matters. The first exception is that AFLS include a brief chapter on the relationship between authoritarianism and intelligence—thanks to the fact that three of their participant groups had previously collected IQ data on their members. The authors are surprised to find that, compared to non-authoritarians, ethnocentric people are only very slightly lower in both intelligence and education. AFLS conclude that their results "contradict seriously one of the commonly held theories of prejudice and fascism; namely, that these attitudes are supported out of simple stupidity, ignorance, or confusion."[31] The second exception is that using the 121 clinical psychiatric patients they surveyed, AFLS include a chapter on the relationship between authoritarianism and mental health. The authors were surprised with these results as well because they revealed that relatively few psychotics were in the high F-scale quartile while numerous neurotics were in the low F-scale quartile, just the opposite of their expectations.[32]

AFLS may not have been able to report that authoritarian, ethnocentric people are stupid or mentally infirm but that did not stop them from painting a decidedly unflattering picture. They concluded that an individual with an authoritarian personality lives "in constant fear of not being like all the others"[33] and is characterized by "conventionality, rigidity, repressive denial, weakness, fear, dependency," not to mention "a desperate clinging to what appears to be strong and a disdainful rejection of whatever is relegated to the bottom."[34] The authoritarian personality is "inclined to submit blindly to power and authority," is fond of a "dichotomous conception of sex roles and moral values," and is prone to forming stereotypes and exaggerating "ingroup-outgroup cleavages."[35] In case the contrast is not yet clear, they add that those low on the F-scale are "affectionate . . . egalitarian . . . flexible" and have the potential "for more genuine satisfaction."[36] Authoritarians bad; non-authoritarians good.

Authoritarianism and Conservatism

The acknowledged problems with the F-scale led to many attempts at improving the way authoritarianism is measured. The best known belongs to Bob Altemeyer.[37] He constructed a widely used battery designed to tap what he calls Right-Wing Authoritarianism (commonly known as RWA). In so doing, he overtly recognized that authoritarianism and right-wing political beliefs are unavoidably intertwined, he balanced the pro and con items so that acquiescence bias would no longer be an issue, and he condensed AFLS's nine sub-dimensions into just three (submission, conventionalism, and aggression).[38] A related but distinct battery that improves on the F-scale, called Social Dominance Orientation or SDO, taps individual-level variation in desires for group relations and dominance.[39]

To an even greater extent than the F-scale, these newer measurement approaches focus on worldview or social arrangements rather than personality.[40] In addition, given the structure of the items, conservatives are automatically going to score higher than liberals do. For example, one of the Altemeyer RWA items reads: "You have to admire those who challenged the law by protesting for women's abortion rights, for animal rights, or to abolish school prayer." By invoking controversial issues such as abortion and school prayer, the method guarantees that compared to those on the left, those on the political right will score higher on the authoritarian scale.[41] In a similar vein, one of the SDO items asks respondents to agree or disagree with this statement: "We should strive to make incomes as equal as possible." Valuable as these batteries are, they do not measure a generic, non-ideological tendency toward authoritarian personality traits.[42] Somewhere along the way, work on the authoritarian personality ceased being about either authority or personality.

In response to these problems, a series of scholars have advocated measuring authoritarianism separately from political matters.[43] They accomplish this clever feat by returning the concept of authoritarianism to its familial roots and asking respondents which traits they believe are most important to imbue in children. A short, commonly used collection of items has resulted: One asks respondents to choose between "independence" and "respect for elders"; a second, between "obedience" and "self-reliance"; a third, between "curiosity" and "good manners"; and a fourth, between "being considerate" and "being well-behaved."[44] Empirical analysis shows that some people are more likely than others to value respect for elders, obedience, good manners, and proper behavior and that these people could reasonably be labeled authoritarian.[45] Preference for how children should be raised is still not quite a personality tendency but it comes closer and has the important advantage of not being larded with overt political content.[46]

The Evolving Meaning of Authoritarianism

With the background described, we can now return to ardent Trump supporters. Numerous observers of the modern political scene have dusted off their copies of Adorno's classic book, and its descendants, and made the claim that Trump supporters are the embodiment of *The Authoritarian Personality*. In fact, the Trump phenomenon, along with the successes of nationalist, nativist leaders around the globe has renewed interest in the book and concept. Recent essays have appeared with titles such as "If You Want to Understand the Age of Trump, Read the Frankfurt School," "The Frankfurt School Knew Trump Was Coming," "Adorno's Uncanny Analysis of Trump's Authoritarian Personality," "Reading Adorno in the Age of Trump," "The Best Predictor of Trump Support Isn't Income, Education, or Age; It's Authoritarianism," "America's Authoritarian Spring," "Group Based Dominance and Authoritarian Aggression Predict Support for Donald Trump," "Trump's America and the Rise of the Authoritarian Personality," "Childrearing Beliefs Were Best Predictor of Trump Support," and "The Rise of American Authoritarianism."[47] Watergate alum John Dean wrote that "Bob Altemeyer saw Donald Trump coming."[48] Altemeyer himself got into the act, commenting during the 2016 campaign that he "would not say that all of the people trying to surge Donald Trump into the White House are authoritarian followers but they almost certainly compose his hard core base."[49]

Attaching the label of authoritarian to Trump supporters is indeed seductive. Analysts who do so often are reacting to the willingness of Trump supporters to follow him at the expense of basic democratic principles and values, bringing to mind the supporters of autocratic, populist leaders throughout the ages. A listener to Joe Walsh's radio show called in with a comment that perfectly illustrates this point. He said, "I don't give a damn if Trump acts like a king. I don't give a damn if he steps all over the Constitution. I want him to do what he has to do to build that wall."[50]

Though I fully agree that many of Trump's strong supporters have only the most casual attachment to essential democratic principles, is being cavalier toward democracy the same as being an authoritarian? Is it the same thing as preferring to be bossed around by an authoritarian leader? Is it the same thing as being conventional? Is it the same thing as being aggressive? In fact, I believe that once their powerful desire for security is brought into the mix, none of the three components of authoritarianism—submissiveness, conventionalism, and aggression—accurately describes Trump's most enthusiastic followers. I will briefly address each of these three in turn, beginning with submissiveness.

Altemeyer argues that authoritarians will follow any "established and legitimate authority" because they believe "officials know best" and have an "inherent right" to rule.[51] My alternative claim is that fervent Trump supporters will not follow just any established authority but rather only those authorities who share their securitarian predispositions. A leader who does not, no matter how established and legitimate, will not be followed and, indeed, will be denigrated. Far from indiscriminately following leaders because leaders must know best, securitarians are actually quite discerning. Whether established or not, to earn securitarian support, a leader must be viscerally committed to protecting insiders from outsiders. Submissiveness is the result of a leader's policy positions, not legitimacy.

This attitude carries through to democratic values. People, such as ardent Trump supporters, who value vigilance and security in the face of outsider threats are situational democrats. If they are convinced democratic arrangements foster security, they will embrace those arrangements, particularly since securitarians appear to have an instinctive dislike of strong power bases that can make them vulnerable. If they believe that the messiness of democracy and the requirement that democracy pay attention to non-securitarian citizens compromise securitarian strategies, they will turn on democracy in an instant.[52] The reverse is also true, however. Just as securitarians are situational democrats, they are situational authoritarians. They support powerful executives who share their securitarian values but positively despise executives who do not (think Barack Obama). The desire for policies that lessen people's vulnerability and allow them to be secure is far different from the desire to submit to every powerful leader, regardless of message, simply because strong leaders simplify and provide direction to people's lives. Trump's intense followers were attracted to him not because they would follow any authoritarian leader and he happened to be handy but rather because he shared their no-nonsense securitarian predispositions.

Trump supporters frequently claim to like him because he is not politically correct and says what is on his mind. The impression left is that what matters is rhetorical style rather than political substance. In truth, political correctness is all about outsiders versus insiders. Fervent Trump supporters like that his language does not kowtow to outsiders such as minorities, gays, and the parade of identity groups. If his unfiltered direct speech and tweets compromised insiders and lifted outsiders, his base would turn on him in an instant. Security from outsider threats is the goal of Trump's core supporters and political correctness compromises that goal.

A parallel argument can be made for the claim that Trump's supporters conform to societal conventions and norms, the second feature in the revised meaning of authoritarianism. Ardent Trump supporters do not seem inclined to follow each and every societal convention; instead, they only conform to those norms they believe will protect them and their fellow insiders from outsider threats. They are situational conformists. Claiming that they abide by any norm that is "legitimate" only begs the question. Who gets to decide which norms and leaders are legitimate and which are not? As with submissiveness, I argue that the key is not whether a convention is legitimate, whatever that means, but whether it fosters security.

The Bible provides a good example. Virtually all strong Trump supporters believe both the New and Old Testaments of the Bible are legitimate; yet, they are clearly more comfortable with the norms contained in the Old Testament than the New. In fact, they frequently tie themselves in knots dismissing "turn the other cheek" but promoting "an eye for an eye" even though "turn the other cheek" came from the mouth of Jesus Christ himself so can hardly be passed off as illegitimate. From the point of view of fervid Trump supporters, the problem with the phrase is not its lack of legitimacy but its lack of comportment with securitarian sentiments.

Another example of securitarians minimizing an established, legitimate norm is separation of church and state and its accomplice freedom of religion. From Madison and Jefferson on, this concept is woven into the fabric of America, yet it is not a securitarian's kind of norm because a diversity of religions diminishes insider unity and strength. Many Trump supporters (and Trump himself) are not deeply, doctrinally Christian so much as they value the existence of Christianity as a core touchstone for insiders. They may not go to church often but that does not prevent them from becoming livid at the very thought of Christianity being under attack,[53] a character trait that Bill O'Reilly has leveraged to sell millions of books.[54] Securitarians are in their element when they believe they are under siege.

A final example of a "legitimate" norm that securitarians wish would disappear is engraved on one of our great national symbols: the Statue of Liberty. The inscription reads: "Give me your tired, your poor, your huddled masses yearning to breathe free, the wretched refuse of your teeming shore. Send these, the homeless, tempest-tossed to me, I lift my lamp beside the golden door!"[55] Do intense Trump supporters subscribe to this established, legitimate American convention that echoes our undeniable status as a nation of immigrants? Hardly. Like "turn the other cheek" and real freedom of religion, welcoming the world's "wretched refuse" is hardly an idea that warms the heart of Donald Trump and his followers. They conform to conventions that foster security against outsiders while dismissing conventions that hinder security—no matter how established and legitimate the conventions might be.

The third component of authoritarianism, as revised, is aggression or a "predisposition to cause harm to someone."[56] According to the literature, authority figures have the power "to direct the hostility of authoritarians against almost any target"[57] but the claim that the target of authoritarian aggression "could be anybody" is open to question. To be sure, if the Trump years taught us anything, it is that securitarians are remarkably plastic in their perception of friends and enemies. Under Trump, many conservatives quickly switched gears and viewed favorably the remnants of the "evil empire," along with its autocratic leader, Vladimir Putin. Does this not indicate that securitarians will shift allegiances in any fashion a leader encourages? I think not. By 2019, Russia was no threat to invade the United States and only had designs on countries that American securitarians did not care about (such as Ukraine). It had a GDP no bigger than South Korea and was led by a person who spoke their language, despised Hillary Clinton, and helped elect Donald Trump. For securitarians, what was not to like? Their attitude would have been quite different toward a country they believed to be a physical threat to the security of American insiders.

The questionable applicability of authoritarianism to fervent Trump supporters is apparent not only in casual observation but also in the empirical literature. I will present my own findings in Chapter 6 but two important previous works are relevant here. Using a large (N = 1,444) original survey, a team of psychologists led by Steven Ludeke found no relationship between Trump support and either submission or conventionalism (in fact, the signs were in the opposite direction and in one formulation significantly so) and, when ideology was included, the overall RWA battery was not significantly related to Trump support. They did find a modest positive relationship between authoritarian aggression and Trump support but this was probably due only to the way aggression was measured (more on this in Chapter 6).[58] In fact, with regard to aggression, these scholars make the perfect qualification by recognizing the relevance of security. They write that Trump supporters have "relatively positive attitudes about the use of aggression in the service of in-group goals."[59] That is exactly right. A second valuable study was conducted by Jake Womick and several other psychologists.[60] Their results, based on three large convenience samples, confirm Ludeke et al.'s conclusion that there is no relationship between Trump support and either authoritarian submission or conventionalism.

Conclusion: *Why* The Authoritarian Personality *Is So Controversial*

Why did *The Authoritarian Personality* kick up such a fuss? Even though ideological biases, methodological problems, and outdated Freudian dogma suffuse the book, the primary target for critics was AFLS's assertion that distinct, politically relevant personalities, types, or even sub-species, exist in the population. The suggestion that powerful predispositions prevent people from arriving at their political beliefs by careful, rational, de novo reflection on the information to which they have been exposed is apparently more off-putting than the notion that people's political and societal views are determined by whether their weak egos prevented synthesis, thereby resulting in a "failure of superego internalization."[61]

Many writers have been strident in their opposition to AFLS's depiction of a discrete, relatively fixed political predisposition. For example, in an essay written for the fiftieth anniversary of the book's publication, sociologist John Levi Martin claimed "the fundamental weakness of *The Authoritarian Personality* came from its attempt to empirically validate a typology that made categorical distinctions between types of persons."[62] In a similar vein, intellectual historian Peter E. Gordon dismissed the possibility that there are relatively fixed types: "Psychological character itself is conditioned upon historically variant social and cultural forms." He went on to assert that authoritarian tendencies are most definitely not a "determinate form of psychological character" and to apply that same belief to the modern era: "Trumpism is not anchored in a specific species of personality that can be distinguished from other personalities."[63] Adorno himself, reflecting his continuing ambivalence toward the central theme of his own book, seemed to agree. In originally unpublished remarks, he stated, "The ultimate source of prejudice has to be sought in social factors which are incomparably stronger than the psyche of any one individual."[64] The claim that what matters most are events rather than personalities is popular and appealing. AFLS stressed upbringing during childhood; Altemeyer stressed post-childhood social experiences; and all of us would like to believe that humans are flexible and rationally responsive to important societal occurrences. It is more comforting to view people as blank slates than as collections of persistent dispositions.

Truth be told, critics of the notion of politically relevant types protest too much and provide too little evidence. Of course, virtually all human variation is continuous rather than discrete but the fact remains that people's personality types and political orientations are relatively constant[65] and distributed, not smoothly and evenly, but in clusters that could accurately be referred to as types.

Their numerous, vocal opponents notwithstanding, the authors of *The Authoritarian Personality* were correct. A growing corpus of research provides evidence that political differences are not just superficial and malleable but rather attached to stable psychological, physiological, and possibly even genetic variations.[66] And you do not have to believe academic researchers: Even the most casual exposure to the modern political climate offers painfully clear confirmation. After observing intense Trump supporters interacting with equally intense Trump opponents it is impossible to conclude that they are cut from the same cloth but just happen to disagree temporarily on one issue or another. Political differences run incredibly deep and interlocutors have very little chance of effecting meaningful change in those with whom they fundamentally disagree. If you think that vocal Trump supporters and their most strident opponents are the same, you need to get out more. Ardent Trump supporters and equally ardent Trump opponents, for all intents and purposes, are distinct sub-species.

Theodor Adorno and his co-authors were correct in categorizing people into stable, meaningful political types. The problem is that when it comes to providing an understanding of the intense supporters of Donald Trump and similar nativist, nationalistic leaders around the world and across the centuries, they pointed us to the wrong type.

CHAPTER 4 | The Phorgotten Phenotype

I N CONTRAST TO conventional wisdom, many ardent Trump supporters are not economically marginalized, not religious, not submissive, not conventional, and not prototypically conservative. So what are they? I have suggested they are securitarian and briefly described that concept. Now I go into detail, initially by referencing parallel behavioral tendencies in non-human animals.

Outfoxed

Trofim Lysenko dominated life sciences in the Soviet Union for a quarter of a century and decimated it for much longer. In the wake of unfavorable weather conditions and the unmitigated failure of collectivized agriculture in the 1920s, the USSR experienced widespread famine. Millions of people perished and the search for solutions was on. Enter Lysenko, an obscure agronomist and rabid ideologue from hearty peasant stock. He rejected the concept of natural selection and believed genetics was irrelevant to the traits of all living organisms. Applying behaviorist psychological precepts to botany, Lysenko was convinced the characteristics of a plant were entirely a function of the conditions under which that plant was raised. He even asserted that weeds could be transformed into wheat merely by savvy adjustment of the environment.[1] One of his favorite strategies was to expose seeds to cool, moist conditions before planting.[2]

Setting aside the fact that he was wholly incorrect, Lysenko was the right person with the right message at the right time. For a regime that revered the noble wisdom of the peasant and believed abidingly in the powers of re-education, Lysenkoism was perfect. Not only could citizens be re-programmed but in a parallel fashion so could wheat. Genetics was the science of defeated retrograde fascists; environmental conditioning was the science of victorious enlightened revolutionaries. Lysenko once gave a speech in which he claimed that to oppose his theories was to oppose Marxism. Stalin was in attendance and is reported to have risen quickly in applause;[3] the rest of the audience wisely followed suit. In the wake of Lysenko's assent, thousands of mainstream biologists were fired, sent to prison, and in some cases executed. In 1948, genetics was officially declared a "pseudoscience." Scientists seeking favor or even just hoping to survive had no choice but to falsify their data so that the results conformed to those desired by Leninist doctrines.

Mainstream geneticist Dmitry Belyaev struggled to navigate these rocky scientific seas. Despite being a wounded, decorated World War II veteran and respected Soviet scientist, Belyaev's sympathy for outlawed Mendelian genetics resulted in his dismissal from the Department of Animal Fur Breeding at Moscow's Central Research Laboratory. It could have been worse: Belyaev's older brother, also a prominent geneticist, perished in a gulag. Belyaev was unbowed though cautious. He continued his scientific efforts but packaged them as studies of animal physiology, not genetics, and shifted his studies away from the politically charged climes of Moscow. Conditions for the scientific community improved marginally with Stalin's death in 1953 and his ultimate replacement by Nikita Khruschchev. By 1959, Belyaev was director of the Institute of Cytology and Genetics in Novosibirsk in southern Siberia, not far from the Kazakhstan frontier.[4]

Though more open-minded than Stalin, Khrushchev's attitude toward Mendelian genetics was hardly enthusiastic. Lysenko had lost a good bit of his clout but was still capable of marshalling powerful rearguard action, especially against an institute with "Genetics" in its name. Belyaev's assent to the directorship came because, after a personal visit to Novosibirsk, Khrushchev registered his displeasure with the Institute by sacking the previous director. One account has the Institute saved by the personal intervention of Khrushchev's daughter, then a prominent journalist.[5]

The status of the Institute had passed from perilous to ambiguous, leaving the intrepid Belyaev just enough room to pursue his true research interest: domestication. As they had Darwin, the cross-species similarities of domesticated animals fascinated Belyaev. Compared to their wild counterparts, domesticates such as pigs, cats, sheep, donkeys, and rabbits are all characterized by a common set of physiological features: short jawbones, reshaped ears, small brains, pie-baldness, and curly (or no) tails. Why these physical changes accompanied behavioral shifts toward docility was a mystery but almost certainly related to genetics. Belyaev intuited that many answers would present themselves if he could observe a species becoming domesticated—a seemingly absurd proposition since the biological consensus was that this process required hundreds of generations and thousands of years. Wolves did not become dogs overnight, after all. Belyaev was convinced the process was not nearly as ponderous as all that and his position and location gave him access to a breed that would be perfect for experimentation: the silver fox. Farms scattered throughout Russia were raising these remarkable creatures en masse. Their pelts were beautiful and much desired in an age when fur coats did not have the stigma they do today. As a result, fur farms served as a valued source of revenue for the cash-strapped Soviet Union.

Belyaev was fortunate to recruit a talented and deeply committed assistant named Lyudmilla Trut who in turn was able to convince one fox farm to tolerate the strange requests of the Belyaev lab. The plan was to pen off a small number of the foxes: thirty males and 100 vixens.[6] Belyaev and Trut designed a protocol by which they would identify the tamest of these foxes with the intent of breeding them to each other, then taking the tamest offspring of these unions and breeding them. They repeated this process for the next generation and so on. The only criterion used in this artificial selection, save for efforts to avoid inbreeding, was the score of each fox on various tests devised to assess docility in the presence of humans, the central element of domestication.

It quickly became apparent that Belyaev was right. After just eight to ten generations, noticeable alterations in both the behavior and physiology of the domesticated line were obvious. The animals acquired white chests and paws, distinctively shaped ears, smaller heads, shortened mandibles, and a dog-like demeanor. The tame foxes clearly craved human companionship as evidenced by licking, panting, and playful submissiveness.

Belyaev's powerful research design has now been applied to other species. Belyaev and Trut themselves worked with river otters; Frank Albert, in his lab at the Max Planck Institute, concentrated on rats. Scientific interest was not always focused on domestication, and labs have looked into the obverse. If animals can be bred to be docile, can they also be bred to be vicious? The answer of course is yes, to the point that Albert acknowledged needing to take special care that the hyper-aggressive rats his breeding experiments produced did not escape into the sewers of Leipzig.[7]

The story of Belyaev's pathbreaking experiments is well known. I repeat it here to set up a point that is not well known. Trut's description of the foxes' response to human presence actually identifies not two phenotypes but three.[8] She noted that the majority of foxes reacted aggressively when she approached and especially when she placed a stick in the cage. She was convinced these foxes wanted to rip her arm off. They became the progenitors of the hyper-aggressive line. A second and much smaller group was composed of the foxes that stayed calm and sometimes approached her; they became the domesticated line that eventually produced creatures much in demand as pets. Only in passing did she note a third group. These foxes retreated to the rear of the cage; some would cower but many just watched her intently, warily observing every move. We know less about this group because the lab saw its distinguishing behavioral pattern as nothing more than an uninteresting admixture of viciousness and tameness. The Belyaev lab made no effort to breed members of this group with each other though they were occasionally used for crossbreeding.

The research decision to focus on the docile and hyper-aggressive lines was perfectly reasonable but at the same time rendered it impossible to address questions that very much merit attention. What if attending to a threat is actually a distinct phenotype rather than a halfway point between attacking ferociously and approaching submissively? In all the talk about friendly foxes and fierce foxes, little attention was given to the foxes that neither provoked nor prostrated, neither pounced nor purred. Little attention was given to the foxes that believed the only appropriate and prudent response was to monitor, preferably from a safe distance, the large, strange, furless, two-legged creatures coming near their cages. Little attention was given to the wary, vigilant, attentive foxes. Little attention was given to the securitarians.

If the securitarian foxes were capable of reflection, the behavior of the docile foxes would have seemed horribly naïve, even reckless. Why would any self-respecting fox open itself to potentially serious trouble by being submissive before even determining what the humans were about? A conscientious fox surely would play it safe, moving to high ground while carefully scouting for an indication—any indication—that the potential threat had become overt. The behavior of the violent foxes would be equally puzzling to the securitarian foxes. Claws and teeth are valuable fox weapons but to fly into battle without a full understanding of the capabilities of an adversary five times taller and ten times heavier is precipitous and imprudent.

The appropriate securitarian response is neither fight nor flight but sight and might. The cowering behavior that Trut observed may not seem to fit with the bluster characteristic of human securitarians but is no doubt attributable to the fact that in this instance the securitarian foxes found themselves locked in a small cage and thus denied their normal response pattern. In fact, a foundational securitarian strategy is to do everything possible to avoid being caged, being vulnerable, being confined, being unprotected, being unfree, being insecure, being at the mercy of an outsider—especially an unfamiliar outsider. Regardless of species, when forced so far out of their comfort zone, the reaction of securitarians is bound to be unbecoming.

Securitarians are not the first to initiate a fight and they are not the first to cavort with strangers. They are, however, the first to minimize their vulnerability by assiduously following deterrence strategies, by assessing and diligently attending to possible threats and by taking all possible precautions should deterrence strategies fail. Trump supporters are not eager to commence military action around the world; they are eager to build walls.[9]

Escape Tunnels and Gun Rights

Oldfield mice eat seeds and insects and love the sandy soil of the American Southeast in part because it is the soil that best allows them to dig burrows in which they can relax, watch *Simpsons* reruns, and raise their litters of three to four offspring. These burrows consist of a tunnel that slopes down to a nest chamber and then, on the other side of the nest, an escape tunnel that climbs up to within just a few centimeters of the surface. In case of danger—for example, a snake appearing at the entrance tunnel—the mice scurry up the escape tunnel, burst through the sand, and run to safety.

Deer mice, though a separate species, are similar enough to interbreed with oldfield mice. Despite the physical similarities, the two species display significant behavioral differences. The most relevant for our purposes is that, unlike oldfield mice, deer mice do not attach escape tunnels to their burrows—ever.

Intrigued by this difference, Harvard biologist Hopi Hoekstra and her colleagues set out to investigate the reasons mice build the particular burrows they do. The Hoekstra team began by noting that no matter how long the mice spent in glass cages that denied them burrow building opportunities, when they were eventually provided with those opportunities, the mice immediately began building burrows consistent with their species' proclivities even though they had never see any other mice building burrows. The researchers crossbred oldfield and deer mice and observed the burrow-building behavior of the offspring. Surprise number one was that every single one of these offspring built burrows with escape tunnels, suggesting that building escape tunnels is likely traceable to a very small number of genes—perhaps just one—and that the version of the gene correlating with building escape tunnels is dominant over the version for not building escape tunnels. Hoekstra et al. next crossed the heterozygote mice with deer mice in an effort to secure variation in escape-tunnel-building behavior, and in this they were successful. This variation allowed insights into the genetic differences between the mice that did and the mice that did not build escape tunnels, which turned out to be a very small segment of DNA on Chromosome 5. The fact that such a small region of DNA could have such a large influence on a complex behavior such as burrow building is noteworthy. The painstaking work of identifying the genes themselves and the precise chemical function they serve is ongoing and promises to be even more revealing.[10] In the meantime, this important study gives us a great deal to ponder.

Compared to their non-escape-tunnel-building colleagues, escape-tunnel-building mice do not appear to be more fearful, anxious, neurotic, pessimistic, or threatened. In fact, if anything, they are less anxious.[11] Neither is there any evidence that escape-tunnel-building mice have experienced an inordinate number of close encounters with snakes or other predators. Escape-tunnel-building mice prepare for outsider threats not because of greater innate fear or because of environmental conditioning; they prepare for outsider threats because that is how they are programmed to behave.

Many people resist the notion that complex behaviors such as burrow building can be shaped by genetics but the Hoekstra result and many like it are impossible to explain without reference to genetics. People especially resist that notion when it is applied to humans but even though environmental factors are without a doubt vitally important there is no reason to believe that genetics is completely irrelevant to complex human behaviors, especially when those behaviors are conceptualized at the level of basic evolutionary forces and not highly contextualized issues of the day.[12] Mice do not enter the world as blank slates and neither do humans.[13] We are not born securitarian or unitarian but we are born with tendencies one way or the other that subsequent environmental factors may or may not override.

Homo sapiens typically do not build escape tunnels onto their homes but they can prepare for outsider threats by keeping ostensible predators at a distance, promoting group unity and values, purchasing a gun, becoming self-sufficient, supporting "defend the castle" and "stand your ground" laws, stockpiling provisions, and building defensive perimeters. Like escape-tunnel-building mice, human securitarians behave the way they do, not because they were surrounded by threats as children, had a domineering parent, or are habitually more neurotic. Human securitarians advocate building prophylactic walls on the southern border for the same reason escape-tunnel-building mice build escape tunnels: they are predisposed to do so.

As a thought experiment, imagine what would happen if St. Patrick came to the southeastern United States and drove out every single snake. What would escape-tunnel-building mice do when presented with clear evidence that no snakes will ever attack them? The answer is that they would continue to attach escape tunnels to every single burrow they dug. They would do so because the calculated likelihood of attack is not really the reason they build escape tunnels.

Human securitarians are no different. Sure, they will glom onto evidence suggesting outsider threats are rampant but evidence of the total elimination of the danger would not alter their behavior—even if that evidence were wholly credible. Securitarian strategies are not data driven; securitarian strategies are not fear driven; securitarian strategies simply are.

Before securitarians become incensed over being compared to mice, I should note that unitarians have no reason to be smug. The door swings both ways. Irrefutable evidence that snake attacks are at epidemic levels will not prod non-escape-tunnel-building mice to commence building escape tunnels; similarly, evidence that threats to human safety are rampant is unlikely to turn unitarians into securitarians. Like securitarians, unitarians are also largely impervious to data and experiences. What would the rate of immigrant crime have to be before committed liberals began actively agitating for the removal of all immigrants? When it comes to matters of groups, identity, and security, political orientations run deep and, in the long-term, they are largely unaffected by data and experiences. Americans' widely described and perfectly understandable shift to the right in the wake of the 9-11-2001 terrorist attacks turned out to be short-lived.[14] We all have our dispositional set points to which we tend to return after ephemeral, environmentally influenced disruptions. Securitarians have theirs; unitarians have theirs. The problem is that the two groups' set points are very different and close to immutable.

As another thought experiment, imagine that researchers allowed the oldfield mice to gambol in sandy soil but somehow prevented them from attaching escape tunnels to their burrows. My hunch is that these mice would feel agitated, naked, distraught, and out-of-sorts, just like the securitarian foxes locked in cages. On the other side, if researchers somehow forced deer mice to build escape tunnels, it would not go well. Their tunnel building behavior would likely be half-hearted and patently ineffective. Now apply that same line of thought to politically active humans. Prohibiting a securitarian from taking steps to be secure is just about the worst thing that could be done to them. They would feel exposed, infuriated, and unfulfilled.

Conversely, coercing unitarian humans to take the same relentlessly defensive and security-conscious steps as securitarians would be a recipe for disaster. Their efforts would be as ineffectual and comical as Michael Dukakis sticking his head out of a tank. "Type" is difficult to alter . . . and to fake.

Securitarians are not endemically more fearful. Compared to unitarians, they typically do not report being more threatened by anything other than outsiders. They gave no appearance of being more threatened by the coronavirus and they are not known for being concerned about manmade climate change and environmental collapse. Even when it comes to outsiders, they do not need to be threatened to behave the way they do. Oh, they will paint a negative image of immigrants if they believe doing so might convince unitarians to shape up but securitarians are likely to oppose immigration regardless because the particular traits and qualities of outsiders are not that relevant.[15] Securitarians do not need to think of outsiders as inferior or threatening in order to want them to stay away. The fact that they are outsiders is quite enough, thank you.

Foxes and mice provide hints of a securitarian phenotype that attends to outsider threats without necessarily being threatened but to this point the applicability to humans I have outlined is entirely conjecture. Is there evidence?

Attention Must Be Paid

An eyetracker is a device that makes it possible to determine the exact parts of an image that have drawn the attention of the viewer. A few years ago, my colleagues and I conducted a study in which we first constructed several collages.[16] Each collage had four, equally sized images, at least one of which was pleasant (e.g., a beautiful sunset or a cuddly animal) and at least one of which was unpleasant (e.g., a wrecked car or a hand holding a very large knife). We asked our participants to look at each collage for eight seconds and we recorded the precise length of time each participant's attention "dwelled" on the individual images within each collage. The results indicated that, compared to liberals, conservatives spent significantly more time looking at the unpleasant, often threatening, images.

The eyetracking results fit with a large number of studies on the deep psychological and even biological differences between liberals and conservatives. These studies show that conservatives are more likely to spot negative faces in a crowd,[17] to be drawn to negative stimuli,[18] to remember negative images,[19] to process negative information more readily,[20] to have elevated physiological responses to negative material,[21] and to have distinct neurological responses to unexpected,[22] risky,[23] and negative situations.[24] This remarkably broad and diverse evidence connecting conservatives to the negative and problematic elements of life leads many observers to conclude that conservatives' political stances are driven by fear of the negative.[25]

Though understandable, the "fearful conservative" thesis is an inappropriate inference based on these existing findings. An individual can give priority to negative stimuli without fearing them. Just because, in relative terms, conservatives, spot, identify, attend to, process, and respond to negative information does not necessarily mean that they fear the negative more than liberals do. The eyetracker results are particularly informative in this regard. If conservatives are merely fearful, would they not avoid troubling images, choosing to look at pictures of floppy-eared bunnies, fruit baskets, beach balls, and natural beauty rather than vulnerable kayakers, large spiders, and pending knife attacks? The fact that conservatives spend more time than liberals dwelling on the negative is consistent with the interpretation that conservatives do not so much fear threats as attend to them. We can say the same for the findings that conservatives are more likely than liberals to remember and to process negative information. Even the neuroimaging research is consistent with an attention interpretation. One of the brain regions found to be more active in conservatives than in liberals when viewing mutilation images was the anterior cingulate cortex, which is involved in identifying situations that require high-level consideration rather than habituated response.[26]

In fact, the only finding in this research stream that does not fit particularly well with the notion that conservatives attend to rather than fear negative situations is that conservatives have an elevated physiological or sympathetic nervous system (SNS) response. Changes in electrodermal activity (skin conductance) are the most widely used measure of SNS activity, colloquially known as the "fight or flight" response. Though attention relates to this response, it is not at its core. In fact, when divorced from stress, focused concentration and attention may even reduce rather than increase SNS response.[27] Seen in this light, what would be the explanation for the finding that conservatives have an elevated SNS response to negative stimuli? There may be no need for an explanation because the physiological finding is not replicating consistently.[28] A lack of confidence in that result only strengthens the case that conservatives and liberals differ less in fear of threats than in attention to them.

Scholars conducted all these studies, including the one utilizing the eyetracker, before the rise of Trump so the participants of interest were conservatives generally rather than Trump supporters specifically. Moreover, the studies looked at generic negativity rather than outsider negativity. If the comparison had been between Trump supporters and everyone else and if the focus had been on outsider threats specifically, the differences found in the non-physiological research are likely to have been even greater.[29]

Psychologists often contrast approach behavior and avoidance behavior.[30] As was the case with the behavior of the silver fox, empirical research on humans indicates there is an important third option. Many people neither approach nor avoid potential threats: they attend to them. These people are securitarians and many strong Trump supporters are quintessential securitarians. They do not ignore threats; they do not attack threats; they do not submit to threats; they peruse, they posture, and they prepare. The securitarian phenotype is not structured to be afraid of outsider threats; it is structured to be ready for them.

I Feel Good Just Like I Knew I Would

When it comes to politics, observers tend to focus on negative emotions such as fear, anger, anxiety, and resentment while overlooking positive emotions such as hope, happiness, satisfaction, contentment, and fulfillment. This is understandable but unfortunate since some of the biggest differences between avid Trump supporters and their opponents may involve positive rather than negative emotions.[31] I contend that intense Trump supporters are vigilant against outsider threats less because of fear, anxiety, anger, and bitterness than because, usually without their even being aware of it, vigilance allows them to feel satisfied, content, virtuous, and fulfilled. Strong Trump supporters, like all securitarians, enjoy the feeling they get when they take steps to protect themselves and their loved ones from threats posed by outsiders. They strive for protection more out of duty than fear. Note that, if correct, this assertion does not mean Trump supporters are more virtuous than if they were motivated by unadulterated fear—palpable unease when it comes to outsiders is still palpable unease when it comes to outsiders—but it does make their motivations markedly different from what is typically averred. Norris and Inglehart assert that "the authoritarian culture is a rational response to perceived tribal threats,"[32] but it may be that perceiving outsiders as threats helps securitarians to rationalize their pre-existing instinct to distance themselves as far as possible from immigrants and other outsiders.[33]

Those who stridently opposed Donald Trump—that is, those who can be described as unitarians rather than securitarians—also want to be secure from threats but they do not derive the same satisfaction from being secure and they certainly are not focused on outsider threats. In fact, even thinking of people in insider and outsider terms bothers them. Security from outsiders is something they would rather not have to contemplate. They are eager to pursue more interesting aspects of life and, when needed, they are even ready to root out those insiders who are powerful enough to be threats to outsiders.

If this account is accurate, it explains a surprising feature of conservatives generally and quite probably intense Trump supporters specifically. Research consistently shows that conservatives score higher than liberals on social well-being, a term referring to a sense of belonging, social inclusion, contentment, and even happiness.[34] In the context of the claims about conservatives being more fearful, anxious, angry, threat sensitive, and bitter, the "happy conservative" phenomenon seems baffling, even incredible. How could those who are fearful and angry, anxious and beset by threats, also be happy? Scholars have tried to explain the conservative happiness advantage by reference to religion, income, survey response tendencies, and other psychological constructs, but a gap generally persists even after incorporating these factors.[35]

I believe conservatives' greater sense of social well-being is not merely a function of money or religious faith but rather the satisfied feelings they derive when they parry outsider threats. Shifting the focus from the negative feelings produced by being threatened to the positive feelings produced by countering threats renders the relatively high level of social well-being among conservatives much less surprising.[36] This argument also fits nicely with cross-national research showing that the greater the external threats facing a country, the greater the relative happiness of conservatives in that country.[37]

Drilling down to strong Trump supporters might make the gap in social well-being even more pronounced given that they comprise the subset of conservatives most focused on contravening outsider threats.[38] If indeed passionate Trump supporters turn out to score higher than others on positive emotionality, as I expect they will, it does not mean there is something wrong with non-Trump-supporters because life is much more than a contest to see who can attain the highest level of self-reported social well-being.

Deplorable?

During an event in New York on September 9, 2016, Hillary Clinton made a widely discussed observation about Trump supporters. Similar to the comment Barack Obama had made eight years earlier about rural conservatives, she said half of Donald Trump's followers were financially insecure so were casting about for answers or promises that would lessen their financial anxieties. She said she could understand the frustrations of these individuals and felt sorry for them. Then she turned her attention to the other half. She said she had no tolerance for them and that they could be put in a basket of deplorables: "racist, sexist, homophobic, xenophobic, Islamophobic—you name it." She went on to say that Trump had lifted up and given voice to such people: "he tweets and retweets their offensive hateful mean-spirited rhetoric . . . they are irredeemable."[39] Outrage ensued and Clinton quickly apologized for saying half of Trump's followers were deplorable. Upon reflection, she thought the fraction was somewhat smaller but she did not apologize for asserting that an important segment of Trump's followers held decidedly negative views of minorities, gays, and immigrants. She even decried then vice presidential candidate Mike Pence for his refusal to call David Duke "deplorable."

So what about it? Are intense Trump supporters racist, sexist, homophobic, xenophobic, and Islamaphobic? Are they deplorable? A common and growing belief in the academic community is that Trump won in 2016 not because of declining manufacturing jobs but rather because of race and culture.[40] As one observer put it, "Trump Won Because of Racial Resentment."[41] Is that what drives Trump's most impassioned followers?[42]

This may be the place to remind those readers who fervently oppose Trump and his followers that my goal here is not to excuse racist behavior but rather to try to explain to you how Trump and his followers can believe they are not racist. If at the end of that description you conclude that the beliefs described fit your definition of racist, as I am quite certain you will, have at it. Still, I continue to believe that, regardless of the label applied, it is useful to know what Trump's base is thinking on race. This is my best shot.

As journalist David Goodhart notes, many activists on the left prefer an extremely wide and loose definition due to their "mistaken belief that this somehow contributes to the elimination of racism."[43] In fact, calling people racist typically does nothing to improve their behavior. Without understanding the reasons behind ostensibly racist behavior, the chances for eradicating that behavior dwindle.[44] Explaining is not excusing but it can facilitate change. By understanding the attitudes of Trump's most ardent supporters concerning race, group, and security, a more accurate sense of societal divides—and the best strategies for improving the behaviors causing those divides—will be possible.

In an interesting experiment, political psychologists Matthew Luttig, Christopher Federico, and Howard Lavine demonstrated that if Trump supporters are asked by a black man to consider support for a housing assistance program they are much more opposed to the policy and are more likely to blame the prospective beneficiaries for needing housing assistance than if the request for consideration came from a white man. In contrast, opponents of Donald Trump showed the opposite pattern and actually were more favorable to the policy if the request came from a black rather than a white man.[45]

Non-Trump supporters see this fascinating result as a clear indication that Trump supporters are prejudiced against black people. After all, the mere fact that the request came from a black person led to negativity toward the housing program. Trump supporters, however, see this result as an indication that non-Trump supporters are prejudiced against white people. After all, the mere fact that the request came from a black man led non-Trump supporters to be more favorable toward the housing program. Who is being racist here? The answer depends on who is asked. Many non-Trump supporters believe it is impossible by definition to be racist toward a majority population that has controlled the institutions of power throughout our country's history. Trump supporters, on the other hand, believe it is possible to be prejudiced toward any group of people, whether it is a majority or a minority group. The real distinction highlighted by this experiment is that some people are predisposed against outsiders and some against insiders—a classic securitarian/unitarian division.

One reason that Trump supporters do not believe they are racists is that their central interest is more in enhancing insider security than derogating other groups and races.[46] Their belief is that if people of other countries and races feel demeaned, that is merely collateral damage. Ardent Trump supporters and securitarians everywhere tend to have an extremely restrictive definition of insiders. From their perspective, the fewer unfamiliar people they have to deal with and the more homogeneity they can obtain, the stronger and more secure they and their fellow insiders will be. This orientation means they are unwelcoming to people who have not already proven themselves to be contributing insiders. Intense Trump supporters see only a downside to diversity since it diminishes the unity and strength of insiders.

A comment from Trump devotee Michelle Malkin at the 2019 Conservative Political Action Conference (CPAC) meetings illustrates this point nicely: "Diversity is not our strength. Unity is. Our common purpose is the common defense of our nation. Good people make America great. Good people stand up and fight." In case you missed the implication, a few moments later she said, "the most important issue we face is immigration."[47] US Representative Steve King (R-IA) and Hungarian prime minister Viktor Orban have made remarkably similar statements about the negative effects of diversity. To Trump supporters and their counterparts around the world, wariness of people from other races, countries, and groups is not so much racist as common sense.

Strong Trump supporters observe that non-Trump supporters—even those on the far left—rarely advocate completely open immigration/borders. As such, Trump supporters assert that liberals, like conservatives, also accord insiders a privileged status vis-à-vis outsiders. From the perspective of vocal Trump supporters, the difference in attitudes is merely a matter of degree.[48]

In the minds of many fierce Trump supporters, security is so fragile and vigilance so essential that anyone failing to demonstrate a commitment to the welfare of narrowly defined insiders also should be kept at arm's length.[49] In other words, those who have not clearly shown that they belong to and are willing to help defend insiders are suspect. Members of minority groups, criminals, welfare recipients, and immigrants have to prove their devotion to the in-group before full acceptance. The onus is on them. As political scientist Elizabeth Theiss-Morse puts it, "No leeway is given to marginalized ingroup members. In fact, marginalized group members are expected to live up to the group norms even more faithfully than prototypical members."[50] Political scientists Donald Kinder and Cindy Kam go even further when they write that from the perspective of individuals with ethnocentric tendencies, "members of out-groups (until they prove otherwise) are thought to be unfriendly, uncooperative, unworthy of trust, dangerous, and more."[51] The basic securitarian query is "Does the person in question make insiders stronger and more secure?" If the answer is no, they do not want to welcome such a person, let alone treat him or her as a full-fledged insider. In the minds of securitarians, defense and cohesion are precarious and crucial; unknown, unfamiliar, uncommitted people jeopardize both.

From the perspective of securitarians, those who are not insiders probably have the interests of their own group at heart—at least, if they have any common sense they do. Trump supporters do not blame people from other countries for placing their own country first. In fact, this is how Trump and his supporters believe the world should work. In September 2019, Trump gave his third annual address to the General Assembly of the United Nations. In a remarkable speech, particularly in light of the organization to which it was given, he asserted that all nations should "exert their sovereignty, protect their borders, and reject any mutual and international cooperation that doesn't put their country's interests first."[52]

As they envision refugees, immigrants, and asylum seekers, strong Trump supporters are likely to think, "Sorry your country is a mess but you need to stay home and fix it and not expect foreign aid—and for God's sake, do not go caravanning across Mexico in hopes of infiltrating our precious country."

To committed Trump supporters, attitudes of this sort are not racist and xenophobic but necessary for the preservation of insiders. They recognize that in the course of firing up and unifying insiders, their fellow securitarians sometimes overdo it and endorse decidedly uncharitable visions of outsiders but, though it is incomprehensible to unitarians, securitarians see those overstatements as mere trash talking rather than dangerous xenophobia. Observers often allege that intense Trump supporters are white supremacists and, while this label is obviously applicable to some, Trump supporters are more likely to be white nationalists. For them, the superiority or inferiority of other peoples is not as important as the simple fact that they are different.

Though securitarians are perfectly comfortable with the attitudes just described, most unitarians find them appallingly ethnocentric. Unitarians are convinced that being leery of outsiders to the point of wanting to minimize exposure to them is deeply wrong. From the perspective of unitarians, making preservation of insiders a primary life objective is impossible without denigrating outsiders in a fashion that is tantamount to racism or at least outsider-ism. For non-securitarians, just as for Belyaev's docile foxes, there is nothing wrong with assuming the best of those who are different even if doing so might increase vulnerability. Concepts such as insiders, blind patriotism, unity, purity, and whitewashed accounts of national history give unitarians the willies. Strong Trump supporters should quit trying to explain to unitarians how important it is to preserve the safety and cohesion of insiders because unitarians are no more likely to be persuaded of this than a deer mouse is to be persuaded to build an escape tunnel. This difference in orientation to security in the face of outsiders constitutes the most fundamental divide in political systems around the world, now and always.

Many strong Trump supporters have convinced themselves that they cannot be bigoted because they get along well with an acquaintance who is black, Jewish, gay, Islamic, or foreign. In a similar vein, they maintain that Trump himself must be okay on race because a black employee at Mar-a-Lago likes him or because he nominated Ben Carson to be secretary of Housing and Urban Development. Their belief is that people reveal bigotry, xenophobia, and racism not by their policy preferences and broad social attitudes but by personal actions and relationships—and Trump supporters typically give themselves high marks on this count. To demonstrate that he was not racist, an attendee at a Trump rally in 2019 explained to a reporter that just the day before he had given $20 to a stranger who needed help taking care of his black foster child. Another attendee pointed out that he had done missionary work with impoverished people in Thailand for fifteen years.[53]

By this logic, securitarians believe they can push for ending immigration, axing foreign aid, splitting amnesty-seeking families, and enacting Muslim travel bans without being xenophobic, racist, or even mean-spirited. Though non-securitarians regard it as extraordinarily facile, this ability to separate racism from policy preferences while attaching it to personal relationships makes perfect sense to securitarians. Isolated personal encounters and friendships are mostly irrelevant to the security of insiders so securitarians are safe in pursuing them. When it comes to matters they believe actually impinge on security, however, such as immigration policies, they cut outsiders no slack.[54]

One challenge to my theory involves the distribution of securitarians within various racial and ethnic groups. Taking blacks as an example, if securitarianism is the key to the enthusiastic support Trump inspires and if vanishingly few Trump supporters are black, the logical inference is that the proportion of black securitarians is much lower than the proportion of white securitarians. I can think of no obvious evolutionary reason why this should be the case. My explanation for this conundrum parallels Hetherington and Weiler's reasoning regarding the racial distribution of what they call "fixed" types.[55] I suspect that just as many racial and ethnic minorities as whites are securitarians; however, not being a member of the majority group in society changes everything. Part of being a white securitarian is a reluctance to acknowledge that minorities are automatically full-fledged members of the in-group. The policies flowing from this reluctance are often deeply bothersome to members of minority groups. If blacks constituted a historically dominant majority in US society, variations in securitarian impulses among blacks would predict support for a black Donald Trump just as it currently does for whites. In other words, many members of racial minority groups desire security and behave in the vigilant and vulnerability-averse manner typical of securitarians but those predispositions are not enough to cause them to support leaders who treat them as outsiders in their own country.

Moving beyond racial and ethnic distinctions, why do securitarians often adopt negative attitudes on gender equality and gay rights? Securitarians see insiders as hard-working, law-abiding, white male straight Christians, with anyone not in that group being at least a bit of an outsider. Seen in this light, securitarians need to be convinced that gays and women contribute tangibly to the security of insiders and do not reduce the unity that they believe is a vital source of insider strength. Of course, the fact that securitarians oppose allowing women in combat roles and gays and transgender individuals in the military at all makes it impossible for members of these particular groups to demonstrate that they have the ability to contribute to security.

For securitarians, however, it is the height of folly to roll the dice on matters of security. Because they perceive members of other races, residents of other countries, women, and gays as not contributing much to the core mission of enhancing security and strengthening the unity, position, and status of the insiders, securitarians are reluctant to accord them full respect.

Even though the securitarian mindset is reluctant to see females as complete equals with males, as we will see later, a surprising number of females are securitarian. The National Rifle Association (NRA) claims that the fastest growing group of gun owners in America is unmarried women[56] and it is likely that a large portion of them supported Trump. Political scientists Mark Setzler and Alixandra Yanus present data from the American National Election Studies (ANES) indicating that "many women fear that outsider groups may be altering the political landscape" and suggest it is a mistake to assume that concerns over security and in-filtration of the in-group are entirely the purview of angry white males. A substantial number of women (though certainly fewer than men), in classic securitarian fashion, worry that traditional American orientations and values are weakening.[57]

Having said this, securitarians have an easier time accepting women and members of the gay, lesbian, bisexual, transgender, and questioning (GLBTQ) community than they do immigrants and racial minorities. Public opinion around the world has moved to the left on many social issues, including gay rights, religious diversity, gender equity, and tolerance of diversity,[58] and there is sometimes the sense that this drift is equally applicable to all topics and groups. As Eric Kaufmann points out, however, "We should not auto-matically expect attitudes to immigration to liberalize over time the way views on women's roles, religion, sexual mores, homosexuals, or even racism have."[59] Secular nationalism is different from social issues. To a securitarian, immigrants (and, I would add, racial minorities) are more clearly and irre-deemably outsiders than women and gays. Securitarians will slowly warm to women and gays with the passage of the years but foreigners, immigrants, and racial minorities will be quite another story.

Give Me Liberty or Give Me . . . Authority?

If, as we are told, they prefer "obedience over liberty,"[60] authoritarians are the polar opposites of libertarians. People can either live under a strong authority figure who provides structure and certainty by controlling their lives or they can enjoy unfettered freedom to do and think as they wish; they cannot have it both ways. If authoritarians are at one pole and libertarians at the other, where, exactly, do securitarians fit?

Authoritarianism is a cluster of values often alleged to be driven by fear, that lead people to prioritize collective security for the group at the expense of liberal autonomy for the individual.[61] These authoritarian values include conformity, authority, loyalty, and a preference for strict moral sanctions that encourage people to close ranks behind tribal leaders.[62] Authoritarians are proto-fascists. Adorno and colleagues, after all, used an f(ascism)-scale to identify those individuals who have authoritarian personalities. Scores of articles claim to enumerate the fascist qualities of Trump and his followers.[63]

Fascism entails centralized autocratic government, severe economic and social regimentation, and, at its extreme, the complete submersion of the individual into the state. Fascism gives people something to venerate, something bigger than themselves, something to die for. It does so by elevating nation and possibly race above the individual. A classic Nazi slogan is "You are nothing; your people is everything" and of course the fascist leader is the embodiment of the people. Fascists take to the next level authoritarians' desire to follow the instructions of a strong authority figure.

Does all this sound anything like Trump supporters? Are passionate Trump supporters eager to subjugate themselves to an all-powerful state? Are they conformists who love to follow rules? Do they crave being told what to do? Do they relish being the same as everyone else? Do they happily fall in line with the existing strictures of polite society? Do they see themselves as nothing more than replaceable cogs in a big monolithic machine? Substantial anecdotal evidence suggests that the standard traits of authoritarians cum fascists are not at all those of fervent Trump supporters. Under many circumstances, Trump supporters recoil from the thought of an all-powerful state, are intent on avoiding subjugation, are individualistic, resist conformity, and hate to be told what to do, what to say, and how to live their lives.

So does this mean Trump supporters are libertarians, the antithesis of authoritarians? Observers are of two minds on this matter. A 2018 article in the official publication of the Libertarian Party states, "Trump is the opposite of a libertarian." Reflecting the preference of many libertarians for the legalization of drugs, the article went on to assert that "the danger that Trump and [then Attorney General Jeff] Sessions pose to peaceful adults who choose to recreate with drugs is no joke. It is certainly not libertarian."[64] The intellectual branch of the libertarian movement, including the Niskanen Center and the CATO Institute tended to be decidedly anti-Trump. Ilya Somin of the CATO Institute wrote "blood and soil nationalism . . . is utterly inimical to the libertarian tradition."[65] Big money libertarians, such as the Koch Brothers, steered clear of Trump in part because they look favorably upon immigrants, DACA youth, and drug legalization. Psychologist Matthew Iyer and colleagues accurately note that "libertarians are likely to join with liberals in opposing projects and legislation that are aimed at strengthening national identity."[66] This opposition means libertarians will often be at odds with securitarians. Moreover, some evidence suggests that, compared to other Republicans, strong Trump supporters are more supportive of economic redistribution and therefore are distinctly non-libertarian.[67]

On the other hand, Paul Krugman writes of "Trump's Big Libertarian Experiment,"[68] Jonathan Chait argues that libertarians largely came around to supporting Trump,[69] and Rand Paul, who fancies himself a libertarian, consistently voted with Trump and was one of the most enthusiastic supporters of Trump's abrupt decision in October 2019 to bring US forces home from Syria where they had served as a buffer for our erstwhile allies, the Kurds. During his visit to the large libertarian gathering known as FreedomFest, the remarkable diversity of libertarians impressed *New York Times* writer Ross Douthat. He estimated that half of the crowd supported Trump.[70] What explains this halting relationship between libertarians and Trump-supporting securitarians?

Securitarians are not particularly trusting of anything, even the military. They are happy to support strong military and police presences—after all, doing so is better than feeling insecure—but they are innately suspicious of any entity capable of impinging on their ability to protect themselves and their in-group. Enthusiastic Trump supporters respect the military, engage in patriotic displays, and applaud large defense budgets, but for many of them nothing can replace the feeling they get from defending themselves and their culture. Strong Trump supporters often are not satisfied with the kind of security provided by an all-powerful central apparatus. Think of how quickly they turned on the US intelligence community when whistleblowers and others within that community created difficulties for their champion.

In an attempt to explain to non-gun-carrying people why it is so important for gun owners to be able to carry weapons on their person, David French, a writer for the *National Review*, nicely captures the libertarian inclination of some securitarians:

> Those individuals who "carry" do so because they do not want to belong to the class of citizens that is inherently helpless—totally reliant upon the state to protect not just themselves but their family, friends, and neighbors. If the choice is between protectors and protected, they

choose to be protectors. . . . There is no set of government policies that can eliminate from human society the need for immediate protection. People can and will try to hurt others and it strikes us as utterly reckless to be unprepared for this reality. . . . The protected class is a dependent class—not economically dependent of course, but dependent on the state in perhaps a more fundamental way (for their very lives).[71]

Securitarians want to be protected. If that means being protected by somebody else, so be it, but their first choice is to protect themselves. Securitarians prefer to be active participants in their own security. This desire might lead to organized military service but more often, it entails individualized steps to ensure personal safety in the face of outsider threats. A key goal of securitarians is to avoid feeling helpless by avoiding total reliance on others—even the military—for something as central as security.

The desire for personal agency in one's own security leads many securitarians not just to own firearms but to undertake actions that promote self-sufficiency, even to the point of joining survivalist-oriented groups such as those affiliated with the "prepper" movement—groups that are surprisingly popular with blacks as well as whites.[72] Preppers see the rest of society as mired in "mindless complacency." One reported that after seeing a movie depicting a fictional crime, he promptly decided to "learn everything possible to prevent that situation from occurring to him,"[73] a behavioral response that perfectly illustrates the securitarian approach to life. To many securitarians, and even some non-securitarians, the novel coronovirus pandemic starting in early 2020 only confirmed the value of self-sufficiency as well as separation from outsiders.

Securitarians often have difficulty understanding how non-securitarians are able to look at themselves in the mirror. Those who are not protectors are by definition dependent. True securitarians cannot stand being dependent, so they have difficulty fathoming how others can. As French puts it, "The problem is . . . the protected person's very sense of themselves."[74] How can they shirk their most basic duty and have any semblance of self-respect?

Michelle Malkin asks, "To whom shall we entrust the existential responsibility of securing the greatness of America?" Her answer is not the military; it is not the police; it is not the Republican Party; it is not a greater-than-the-sum-of-its-parts national entity that has fused people and leader. Tellingly, her answer is that this responsibility falls to those she refers to as the "disruptors," people who are willing to take on a system that securitarians believe all-too-often does not have the true interests of real America at heart.[75]

The desire to play the role of protector gives securitarian attitudes a libertarian flavor but still leaves them some distance from classic libertarianism which is frequently couched in economic terms (small government, low taxes), sometimes in social terms (legalized gambling, drugs, gay marriage, and abortion), but rarely in security terms (eliminate the military and law enforcement). In fact, as much as they oppose granting government a role in anything, traditional libertarians typically recognize the necessity of a governmental presence in military and police matters. The type of society libertarians prefer is, as one trope goes, "anarchy with a constable."

Securitarians begin with the desire to be in a position to protect their personal and their group's security. They adopt libertarian attitudes advocating a minimalist role for government not because of an abiding belief that governments are not up to the task of managing the economy[76] but because of a deep-seated fear that government can insinuate itself into securitarians' ability to mount their own effective defense against infiltration by criminals, freeloaders, immigrants, and other outsiders. A government that can put fluoride in our water and ethanol in our gas; a government that can ban plastic bags from our grocery stores, corrugated cardboard from our garbage dumps, and incandescent bulbs from our floor lamps certainly is a threat to prevent us from defending ourselves. Securitarians back into libertarianism by way of their intense desire to prevent anyone or anything from hindering their ability to fend for themselves. Conspiracy theories are sometimes a natural outgrowth of this mindset and are seldom far from the thoughts of many fervent Trump supporters.[77]

In 2015–16, Francesco Duina conducted a series of interviews with Americans who were extremely poor yet still extraordinarily patriotic, a puzzling combination of traits. When asked what they liked best about the United States, their most common response was freedom. Some were homeless, yet they saw their situation in positive terms. They were delighted with their freedom to be physically isolated, to be "out of anyone's reach," to have nothing looming overhead, not even a roof.[78] One summarized her feelings this way: "I don't wanna be told what I can and can't do."[79] These interviews occurred before Donald Trump became president so we do not know whether Duina's interviewees were Trump supporters or even politically engaged, but we do know that a remarkable number of their comments come straight out of a securitarian, aversion-to-vulnerability playbook.

Pause to note how far these attitudes are from fascism. For fascists, the military is a central part of a national monolith and the notion that individuals can construct stand-alone defense capabilities, remain detached, pursue separate agendas, and delight in not being told what to do by anyone is incomprehensible. Note also how far these attitudes have come from authoritarianism. True authoritarians fear the very disruptors that Malkin lauds. After all, disruptors challenge vital norms, weaken legitimate sources of power, and imperil the civil order. Authoritarians are conformists; securitarians, on the other hand, are ready to shake up the system if that is what it takes to preserve insider security. An important reason his followers were attracted to Trump was that they saw him as an agent of change, as an outsider, as an anti-authoritarian.

Securitarians' authoritarian-libertarian tension can be summarized this way. They want a leader who is strong enough to protect their right to defend themselves but not strong enough to take away that right. Securitarians recognize the difficulty of threading this needle. James Madison's solution, embodied in the US Constitution, was to create multiple institutions that neutralized the ability of any single institution to acquire inordinate power. Securitarians, however, are unimpressed with Madisonian niceties. Their preferred solution is to be extremely careful in vetting possible leaders. Securitarians only support leaders they know in their bones to be fellow securitarians. They do not like having to trust leaders so it is essential that they avoid mistakes. Leaders who merely mouth securitarian words will not do; they must ooze securitarianism. Few leaders can do this but when securitarians find one who does, the bond is powerful. Securitarians do not want a defense hawk like John McCain; they do not want a libertarian like Rand Paul; they do not want an internationalist like Jeb Bush; they want a securitarian like Donald J. Trump.

I have given the issue of gun rights a prominent role and as a result my description of securitarians may seem too US-centric and not all that applicable to the rest of the world, where gun control laws tend to be strong and popular. In truth, securitarians are everywhere. People in most countries deny their citizens a particular way of feeling secure that happens to be wildly popular among securitarians in the United States and a few other countries—owning a gun. Most securitarians in other countries would own a gun if it was legal and many of them own a gun even when it is not. Quite apart from guns, however, outlets for securitarian inclinations abound.

Securitarians in the United Kingdom bristled at the very thought of being forced to obey edicts from Brussels; securitarians in the Philippines were thankful for Duterte's support for vigilantism and harsh punishments for drug dealers; securitarians in France and Hungary refused to accept immigrants from Syria and Turkey; securitarians in Denmark were convinced their culture and cherished social welfare system were under attack; securitarians in India defended their country and Kashmir against the Islamic threat emanating from neighboring Pakistan; securitarians in Mexico, lacking trust in the police, formed their own neighborhood watches, defensive perimeters, and security details; and securitarians in Afghanistan threw in with the local warlord to protect family and traditions. In sum, though the nature of outsider threats and means to counter those threats vary from country to country, securitarians are everywhere.

Communitarians and Populists

On the basis of his long-term interactions with them, sociologist Robert Wuthnow concluded that the denizens of rural America, most of whom, according to statistics, are conservatives who were avid supporters of Donald Trump, are remarkably community oriented. He writes, "They may be rugged individualists but they are not fundamentally that."[80] Maybe so, but it would be a mistake to think that Wuthnow's rural citizens generally, let alone securitarian Trump supporters specifically, are misty-eyed communitarians who believe the concept of community is imbued with enriching, elevating, and emergent properties.[81]

The orientation to community evident in Wuthnow's interviews is practical, even utilitarian. The people he describes crave the familiarity of small towns because they see them as places of safety where they can know everybody and feel a sense of being in control.[82] More ominously, it was apparent to Wuthnow that one of the ways these individuals kept their sense of identity and familiarity was by excluding others.[83] If he is correct about this, then small town life joins seamlessly with securitarianism. People desiring protection from outsiders can do no better than the manageable, recognizable, bounded, relatively homogeneous environs of small town life. The fewer unknown, unfamiliar people the better.

It is true that many small town residents feel an obligation to their town, but they tend to believe this obligation is fulfilled by taking care of one's own family and concerns and expecting everybody else in town to do the same. A frequently stated goal is to avoid "being a burden on one's neighbors."[84] This form of communitarianism is quite distinct from that found in the scholarly literature.[85] The rural communitarians Wuthnow describes do not believe "it takes a village";[86] they believe it takes individuals who each do their part on their own. Many would agree with former United Kingdom Prime Minister Margaret Thatcher's famous assertion that "there is no such thing as society—only individual men, women, and families."

If not communitarians, are fervent Trump supporters populists? Populism is a concept that is "notoriously difficult to pin down."[87] Norris and Inglehart see it as a style of rhetoric devoid of substance. However, a more common and literal sense of the term is that it is a preference for giving political influence to the people rather than to elites and authorities.[88] One source of confusion is that perceptions of the political value of elites/authorities do not necessarily correlate inversely with perceptions of the political value of the people. In a recent survey, my colleagues and I found that many Americans have extremely negative views of the capabilities of the American people (believing that they are not intelligent and that they lack both good judgment and common sense) but still want to give those ordinary people additional political influence by expanding the number of ballot initiatives and referenda. The reason for this odd combination seems to be that as poorly as respondents view the American people, they have an even more negative view of the political capabilities of elites/authorities.[89] Many Americans are anti-elitists without being populists.

Is the same true of fervid Trump supporters? Writers often call Donald Trump a populist leader, which would mean his followers must want a populist.[90] I have doubts about that label. Of course Trump claims to speak for the people. This is a favorite ploy of nationalist, nativist leaders, but they are not alone. Politicians across the political spectrum and around the world assert that they have some special sense of what "the people" want. Trump may be especially inclined to this approach but he certainly does not have the market cornered on it. Just as securitarians are situational authoritarians and situational libertarians, they are also situational populists. If invoking "the people" fosters insider unity and personal security, they will do so. If the people fail to appreciate the pressing need for security and patriotism, securitarians will ignore them. Like authoritarianism and libertarianism, communitarianism and populism do not capture the essential motivation of intense Trump supporters. That motivation is not authority, not liberty, not community, and not people power; it is physical and cultural security.

Conclusion

Political scientists Matt Grossman and David Hopkins wrote an important book.[91] In it, they point out that the Democratic and Republican parties, far from being two sides of the same coin, are fundamentally different. They write that the Republican Party is an ideological party whereas the Democratic Party is merely a collection of disparate groups that is "not united by devotion to a common political creed."[92] Grossman and Hopkins detail the many ways this asymmetry manifests itself—from campaign themes and strategies to fundraising and electoral coalitions and from rhetoric and policy proposals to governing strategies and visions for the country. I agree that the structure of the two parties is wildly dissimilar and I accept all their evidence; however, I believe the asymmetries in fact spring from a perfect symmetry: Democrats are the party of including outsiders; Republicans the party of excluding outsiders.

The Republican Party is the party of patriotic, security-conscious, straight white Christian Americans. Before they will be accepted, all others must prove themselves contributors to insider security or at least must provide evidence they are not a threat to that security. Democrats, on the other hand, accept everyone except, of course, those they believe are acting in an exclusionary fashion. It is easy to espouse a relatively homogeneous ideology when being exclusionary but Democrats do not have that luxury. As a result, they appear to lack a focused ideology even though they have one: help outsiders in the face of insider threats.

Political scientists tend to misunderstand ideology, treating it as something that is esoteric, issue-based, and primarily economic (e.g., socialism or capitalism). One scholar even went so far as to posit that people cannot have ideologies unless they are able to provide a sophisticated definition of what it means to be a liberal or a conservative.[93] Psychologists (and laypeople) are more likely to view ideology as a subterranean aspect of life orientations that extends well beyond politics.[94] From this deeper and more realistic perspective, an orientation toward either including or excluding outsiders clearly qualifies as an ideology. In fact, whether an individual's orientations grow out of genetics or the psychological instantiation of life's various experiences, these two options for the treatment of outsiders form the basis of the central ideologies structuring political systems.

Grossman and Hopkins are completely correct in their description of the massive differences in the orientations of the Democratic and Republican parties, but this does not mean one party is ideological and one is not. It means that if your ideology is to welcome all diverse outsider groups, the resultant policy tenets will be amorphous, even unruly; conversely, if your ideology is built around the security of a narrow collection of similar-looking and similar-thinking individuals, the particular policy tenets of that ideology are likely to be focused, even resolute.[95]

The core political divide in all societies is between securitarians, whose central goal is for insiders to be protected from outsider threats, and unitarians, whose central goal is for outsiders to be protected from insider threats. Outsiders themselves naturally are attracted to the unitarian side of the divide, thus making that side much more heterogeneous. In the American context, the arrangement means that on the left you have white unitarians forming a coalition with blacks, Latinxs, Asian Americans, Native Americans, members of the GLBTQ community, atheists, and so on. They are opposed on the right by mostly white securitarians.[96] It seems like an unfair fight—and it might well be in the long run—but remember that, as Grossman and Hopkins point out, on balance, the forces on the left are less motivated and unified.

Though a great many of Trump's strong supporters are not even aware of it,[97] security concerns are the primary reason they are attracted to him just as security concerns are the primary reason certain individuals are attracted to nativist leaders around the world. Securitarians are built to expect outsider threats to their person and culture. They prepare for outsider threats. They attend to outsider threats. Securitarians are in their element when outsider threats are in the offing—and for securitarians, outsider threats are always in the offing. Securitarians' mission in life is not only to be secure but also to pursue security. Liberals seem to believe that if intense Trump supporters would only look at the data on immigrant crime rates, they would come to their senses and soften their opposition to immigration. In truth, avid Trump supporters will never stop attending to outsider threats and strategizing about how to mitigate those threats. Security from outsiders is an ongoing mission for them rather than something that will one day be achieved. The only thing that will change—and this is not trivial—is their perception of who is and is not an outsider.

The divide between securitarians and unitarians makes it difficult for human societies to function amicably. Wary silver foxes do not care about the behavior of docile silver foxes, and oldfield mice do not care whether deer mice attach escape tunnels to their burrows. For these species, when it comes to security, to each his own. In homo sapiens' highly developed social life, however, one person's decisions affect other people. We pass laws; we impose sanctions; and these collective decisions signal a society that is focused either on insider security or the welfare of outsiders.

CHAPTER 5 | The Trump Venerator Next Door

A S OF APRIL 2019, 38% of all American adults "supported" Donald
Trump, 33% said they would be with him in the 2020 Republican
primaries no matter who the challengers were, 32% said they would proudly
wear a hat or display a sticker with the "Make America Great Again" logo on
it, and 29% said they believed him to be one of the best presidents ever (see
Figure 5.1).[1] As the items became more demanding, some drop-off occurs
but surprisingly little: 77.4% of those supporting Trump also believe him to
be one of the best presidents ever. When it comes to Trump, in for a penny,
in for a pound.

Trump support closely paralleled people's self-identification as either a
conservative or a Republican. Though hardly news, the fact that so very few
conservatives and Republicans failed to support Trump is notable, especially
in light of his polarizing personal style and willingness to take on Republican
and conservative orthodoxy. To provide numbers, Table 5.1 shows that 84%
of conservatives supported Trump and 72% of them labeled themselves
strong supporters. Dividing the political landscape by identification with a
party rather than an ideology provides a similar story. Very few Democrats
supported Trump (9.8%) but even fewer Republicans opposed him (6.5%).
More than two years into his term, despite Trump's bitter 2016 primary fight
with establishment Republicans, despite his tweets and bombast, despite
his attacks on free trade, and despite the well-publicized defections of notable conservatives such as George Will, David Brooks, Ana Navarro, George
Conway, and William Kristol, rank-and-file conservatives and Republicans
were nearly all in his corner. If the claim that we are a politically "sorted"
country needs further evidence, this is it.[2]

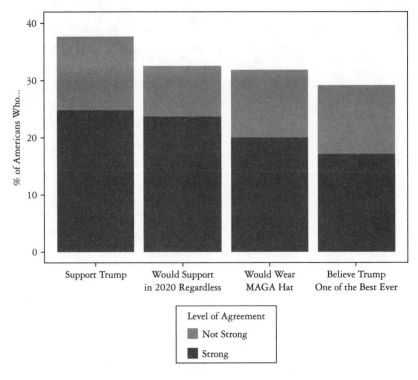

FIGURE 5.1 Attitudes toward Donald Trump

TABLE 5.1 Ideology, Party Identification, and Trump Support

	Liberals	Moderates	Conservatives
Support Trump	9	26	84
Neutral	5	16	7
Oppose Trump	86	58	9
	100	100	100
(% of sample)	(32)	(33)	(35)
	Democrats	Independents	Republicans
Support Trump	10	34	87
Neutral	5	17	7
Oppose Trump	85	49	6
	100	100	100
(% of sample)	(39)	(31)	(30)

Note: Total N = 888 (some respondents did not report an ideology)

If anything, in the two years he had been president, those who strongly supported Donald Trump became *less* distinct from others on the political right. I asked the Republicans in the sample not just whether they currently supported Trump but also whether they supported him in the 2016 primaries. This type of recall item can be unreliable because people forget or selectively remember but it is still noteworthy that 61% said they supported Trump both in April 2019 and back in the 2016 Republican primaries. Only 10% of Republicans opposed him at both time points, meaning opinions toward Trump changed for 29% of Republicans, with 26% going from opposing him in 2016 to supporting him in 2019 and just 3%(!) going from supporting him in 2016 to opposing him in 2019. In other words, 90% of the Republicans switching positions on Trump moved from opposition to support. Trump's conduct as president turned off remarkably few Republicans and the same is true for conservatives. As the years wore on, the Trump base became less distinct from the Republican Party and from rank-and-file conservatives.

Though the high degree of overlap between Trump supporters and conservatives makes it more challenging, my central goal is to provide a detailed description of Trump's most ardent defenders primarily by distinguishing them from conservatives who do not place Trump on a pedestal. The "best ever" question provides an opportunity to accomplish this feat. As can be seen in Figure 5.2, 49% of American adults strongly disagreed that Trump was one of the very best presidents ever; 7% merely disagreed, 15% could not decide, 12% agreed, and 17% strongly agreed. Those strongly agreeing that Donald Trump was one of the best presidents in the history of

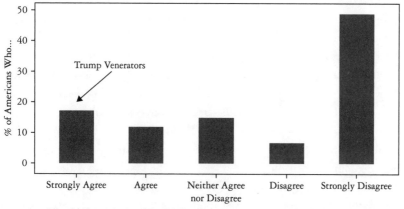

"Donald Trump is one of the very best presidents in the entire history of our country"

FIGURE 5.2 Perceptions of Donald Trump's Place in History

the country constitute his most earnest followers, I will focus on them and call them Trump venerators.

Not all conservatives were willing to go this far, however. "Only" 41% of self-identified conservatives strongly agreed that Trump was one of the very best presidents ever, meaning 59% of conservatives stopped short. The fact that a large number of conservatives did not strongly agree—that is, were not Trump venerators—provides the analytical leverage needed to determine what was unique about Trump's core supporters.[3]

Before turning to the results, a caveat. Any single survey is merely a snapshot of the targeted population at a given time. Especially when it comes to politics, events and attitudes change quickly so it is important to consider the context at the time the survey was in the field. Donald Trump was elected in November of 2016 and assumed the mantle of the presidency in January of 2017. Many observers analyzed the 2016 and 2020 Trump electoral coalitions. My objective is different in that I want to scrutinize strong Trump supporters outside of the context of an election. I am less interested in describing who is more likely to prefer Trump in comparison to a particular Democratic nominee, such as Hillary Clinton or Joe Biden, than taking the measure of those who adore Donald Trump. The best time to do this is after people have had a couple of years to observe him as president but before the descent into full campaign mode against a named Democratic opponent.

Thus, the survey was conducted more than two years into his term yet still eighteen months before the 2020 election. At that time, people knew what they were getting with Donald Trump and their evaluations are based on something more than campaign promises and wishful thinking. Shining a light on intense Trump supporters will make it possible to become better acquainted with a political phenotype that is ubiquitous and fundamental—a political phenotype that will affect politics long after Trump has left the political scene.

I divide respondents into four ideological groups: those identifying as liberals; those identifying as moderates; those identifying as conservatives but who do not strongly agree that Trump is one of the very best presidents ever, and finally those who strongly agree that Trump is one of the best presidents ever—the group I label Trump venerators. This approach has the disadvantage of excluding respondents who cannot or will not specify their ideological position (about 11%)[4] but the good news is that those who do report an ideology are spread across the four categories fairly evenly (approximately 31% liberals, 29% moderates, 21% non-Trump-venerating conservatives, and 19% Trump venerators). In this chapter, I focus on the demographic and personal traits that distinguish Trump venerators from the other three groups and then in the next chapter I home in on the evidence that Trump venerators are securitarian rather than authoritarian.

Trump Venerators' Demographic Traits

The standard narrative holds that Trump's most intense supporters are overwhelmingly old, white, poor, uneducated, male, rural, and religious.[5] In Chapter 2, we looked at the demographic profile of those who voted for Trump in 2016. Now we look at the profile of those who venerated Trump in 2019. I present the first results in Table 5.2. This table includes a great many numbers so a brief explanation is in order, especially since many of the tables to follow are structurally similar. The first four columns of numbers are straightforward enough. They contain the means (or averages) for various traits across the four key categories employed. To use the first row as an example, as of April of 2019, 68% of liberals in the United States were white, 66% of moderates were white, 73% of non-Trump-venerating conservatives (labeled "NTV Conservatives" in the table) were white, and 78% of Trump venerators were white. Overall, there seems to be an upward or whitening trend as attention shifts from liberals to moderates to conservatives and then to Trump venerators but the increase is only 10 percentage points. Is that a meaningful difference?

Readers averse to statistics may want to skip the next four paragraphs and will have to trust that what I say in the text is accurate but relatively simple procedures make it possible to determine whether numerical differences can be taken seriously and these procedures require brief explanation. A correlation is a summary number that captures the degree to which two variables—in this case, percent white and the four-part ideological classification scheme—are related. I present these correlations in the fifth column of numbers in Table 5.2 (labeled "Overall Correlation"). Here we see that the correlation for percentage white is +.08. Since correlations can range from +1.0 to −1.0 with +1.0 indicating the variables move together perfectly and −1.0 indicating they move in exactly opposite directions (and 0 indicating no relationship at all), a correlation of .08 suggests a weak positive relationship. Whiteness increases from left to right—but not by much.

It is possible to test correlations for whether they meet the standards of statistical significance and those that do are more meaningful because the odds are small that the difference is merely the result of chance. In this case, because the relationship meets the standard tests of significance, two asterisks

TABLE 5.2 Demographics and Trump Venerators

Demographics	Liberals	Moderates	NTV Conservatives	Trump Venerators	Overall Correlation	NTVCs/TVs Correlation
% white	68	66	73	78	.08**	NS
% above $50,000 annual income	45	50	56	52	NS	NS
% with at least some college	68	68	65	55	-.09**	-.11**
% rural or small town	26	29	37	38	.11**	NS
% attend church twice/month	22	34	54	46	.22**	NS
% saying they are born again	12	26	51	48	.32**	NS
% female	52	54	54	47	NS	NS
Mean age in years	46.5	46.9	50.3	56.9	.20**	.20**

Note:

N=888

*=sign (p<.10) **=sign (p<.05) NS=not significant (p>.10)

NTV Conservatives = non-Trump-venerating conservatives

Overall Correlation = the bivariate correlation between the item and the four categories

NTVCs/TVs Correlation = the bivariate correlation between non-Trump-venerating conservatives and Trump venerators

The numbers in the first four columns are the percentage agreeing with each item.

follow the coefficient. Correlations not meeting significance standards are indicated by the letters NS (for "not significant") and, based on the data available, we cannot be confident these relationships are real.[6]

It is widely known, however, that liberals are more racially heterogeneous than conservatives so the "Overall Correlation" does not contribute much beyond previous knowledge. Besides, it assumes linearity by placing Trump venerators farther than non-Trump-venerating conservatives from liberals and this assumption may not be valid. My major interest is in the traits that distinguish Trump venerators from conservatives who do not venerate him and we can glean this information first by comparing the numbers in the third and fourth columns. In the case of percentage white, we see that Trump venerators are slightly whiter than non-Trump-venerating conservatives (78% to 73%).

In addition, the column of numbers on the far right of the table (labeled "NTVCs/TVs Correlation") reports the correlation between the non-Trump-venerating conservatives and Trump venerators. The same test of statistical significance was conducted for this correlation and with just two categories we do not have to worry about mis-ordering them. A positive correlation means that compared to conservatives who did not venerate Trump, Trump venerators tended to score higher on that trait; a negative number indicates Trump venerators scored lower; and, as before, NS means the correlation was not statistically significant. To continue with the top row as an example, the correlation between the racial composition of non-Trump-venerating conservatives and Trump venerators is not significant, meaning that, given the number of respondents, we cannot be confident the difference in whiteness is real rather than the result of chance perturbations. Whether they do or do not venerate Trump, conservatives in general share many features and attitudes; therefore, most of the correlations in the NTVCs/TVs column likely will be "NS" for not significant.[7] It will be a challenge to find traits on which Trump venerators are different from non-Trump-venerating conservatives. Those correlations that do attain significance should be given special attention as they involve traits that distinguish Trump venerators from conservatives who do not venerate him.

With these statistical matters out of the way, we can proceed quickly through the results. They suggest that as we move across these four groups, from left to right, the percentage of people who live in rural domiciles, who are religious (more likely to attend church and more likely to classify themselves as "born again"), and who are older, all increase significantly but the percentage of people who have attended at least some college decreases. Contrary to conventional wisdom, clear trends do not appear for either income or gender.[8] Compared to liberals, Trump venerators are only slightly more likely to be male than female and, if anything, are more well-to-do.

With the expected demographic contours of the left-right divide generally confirmed, we are ready to zero in on the traits that distinguish Trump venerators from conservatives who do not venerate him. Here, among all the variables, the numbers reveal only two solid relationships. Compared to non-Trump-venerating conservatives, Trump venerators are significantly older (mean age of 56.9 compared to 50.3) and less educated (only 55% had ever set foot in a college classroom while 65% of non-Trump-venerating conservatives had at least some college experience). Several other traits show differences but differences that, at least based on these data, are too slight to generate confidence.

For the most part, demographic variables are not powerful predictors of whether an individual is a Trump venerator or a conservative who does not venerate Donald Trump. The relationships are usually modest and many fail to meet even forgiving levels of statistical significance. A surprising number of Trump venerators are not poor, not uneducated, not rural (62% live in cities or suburbs), not religious (54% attend church services only a few times a year or less), not old (one-third are under 50), and not male (47% of all those who are convinced Donald Trump is one of the very best presidents ever are females).

For those readers preferring pictures, I include a figure to illustrate selected patterns. In Figure 5.3, I present a line graph for education, income, church attendance, and rural residence. Differences across the four groups are

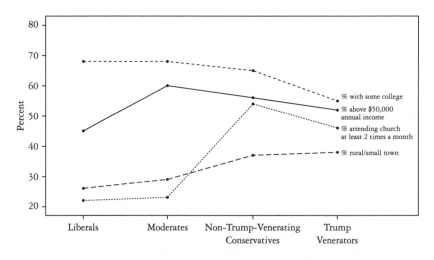

FIGURE 5.3 Selected Demographics and Political Orientation

usually modest except that conservatives go to church much more frequently than moderates and especially liberals. The similarity of Trump venerators and non-Trump-venerating conservatives is the most relevant feature of the figure. Many of the average demographics for these two groups are not identical but they are not much different, either.

Trump Venerators' Personality Traits

Perhaps personality traits do better at identifying the unique features of Trump venerators. The 2019 survey assessed eight personality-like characteristics by presenting respondents with two items concerning each trait, one worded positively and one worded negatively. Psychologists refer to the first personality traits I will discuss as the "Big Five," reflecting scholarly consensus regarding the traits that are the most consistently visible across a wide variety of cultural contexts.[9] They are extraversion, agreeableness, conscientiousness, neuroticism, and openness to new experiences. What are expectations? A consistent finding in the literature is that people on the political right are higher on conscientiousness while people on the political left are more open to new experiences so we might expect that Trump venerators, being on the right, would be relatively high in conscientiousness and relatively low in openness.[10] Scholars have found the other three Big Five traits to be less predictive of ideological differences. In other words, neither liberals nor conservatives are consistently higher than their counterparts when it comes to agreeableness, neuroticism, and extraversion.

Not all conservatives are the same, however. What about possible differences between Trump venerators and non-Trump-venerating conservatives?[11] Table 5.3 reports the results utilizing the general format introduced in Table 5.2 with traits analyzed across the same four categories: liberals, moderates, non-Trump-venerating conservatives, and Trump venerators. One difference is that since I now measure each trait with two items, they are added together to make an index running from 0 to 8 (rather than percentages) with higher numbers indicating a greater degree of the personality trait in question. The first four columns of numbers are the mean scores of each group on the various two-item indices. Two columns of coefficients then follow the means, the first pertaining to all four ideologically based categories and the second only to non-Trump-venerating conservatives and Trump venerators. In the table, I also provide the significance level of these coefficients.[12]

TABLE 5.3 Personality Traits and Trump Venerators

Trait	Liberals	Moderates	NTV Conservatives	Trump Venerators	Overall Correlation	NTVCs/TVs Correlation
Extraverted	3.6	3.5	3.5	3.9	NS	.13*
Agreeable	5.2	5.2	5.3	5.6	.09*	NS
Conscientious	5.5	5.6	5.7	6.0	.12**	.14**
Neurotic	3.3	3.3	3.0	2.5	-.16**	-.15**
Open to new experiences	5.4	5.2	4.7	5.1	-.11**	.13*
Dogmatic	4.6	4.6	4.8	4.8	NS	NS
Prefer closure	3.4	4.0	4.5	4.4	.28**	NS
Prefer consensus	3.6	3.7	4.4	4.3	.22**	NS

Note:

N=450 (personality battery only asked to half the sample)

*=sign (p<.10) **=sign (p<.05) NS=not significant (p>.10)

NTV Conservatives = non-Trump-venerating conservatives

Overall Correlation = the bivariate correlation between the item and the four categories

NTVCs/TVs Correlation = the bivariate correlation between non-Trump-venerating conservatives and Trump venerators

The numbers in the first four columns are the scores on a 0 to 8 index for each trait.

The results confirm previously discovered patterns, with people on the right being significantly more conscientious (r = .12) but significantly less open to new experiences (r = –.11). In addition, the data suggest that people on the right are more agreeable (r = .09) and less neurotic (r = –16).[13] The group averages indicate that the reason these two correlations are statistically significant is my practice of breaking out Trump venerators and placing them outside of other conservatives, allowing their relatively high score on agreeableness (5.6) and relatively low score on neuroticism (2.5) to bolster the correlations across all four categories.

Focusing exclusively on the differences between non-Trump-venerating conservatives and Trump venerators, we see that Trump venerators are significantly more extraverted, conscientious, and open to new experiences, and significantly less neurotic.[14] Given the seemingly boisterous nature of some Trump supporters, the high extraversion scores may not be surprising—especially since Fortunato et al.'s study of Trump's 2016 primary supporters finds precisely the same pattern. Trump venerators' relatively high score on openness to new experiences is also notable, though remember that this is only in relation to non-Trump-venerating conservatives and that the mean score on openness for Trump venerators (5.1) is lower than the mean openness of liberals (5.4). Nonetheless, on four of the Big 5 personality traits, Trump venerators are not your typical conservatives.

The Big Five does not cover the entire waterfront of personality traits and the survey contained pairs of counterbalanced items designed to tap three others: dogmatism, a preference for closure, and a preference for consensus.[15] The results indicate that dogmatism (e.g., "I am set in my ways"), preference for closure (e.g., "I like problems with many correct answers"—reverse coded), and preference for consensus (e.g., "I prefer to be around people who share my beliefs") all increase as attention shifts from the political left to the political right (significantly so for the latter two) but that there is no real difference between Trump venerators and non-Trump-venerating conservatives for any of the three.

Figure 5.4 presents a sampling of the "Big 5" results in line graph form. The specific survey items included are "I see myself as someone who is extraverted and enthusiastic," "I see myself as someone who is open to new experiences and complex," and "I see myself as someone who is calm and emotionally stable."[16] The figure shows that most everyone reports being calmer and more open than extraverted but the differences between Trump venerators and liberals are surprisingly muted (never more than eight points), though, interestingly, compared to non-Trump-venerating conservatives, Trump venerators do report being both more extraverted and open to new experiences.

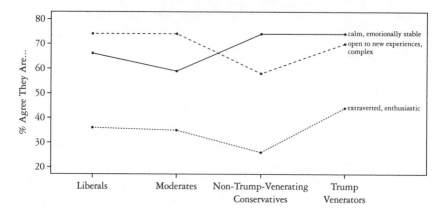

FIGURE 5.4 Personality Traits and Political Orientation

Are Trump Venerators Emotional?

As explained in Chapter 2, a common assertion is that Trump's base is composed of bitter, resentful, angry, disgust-sensitive people. Is it really the case
that people who feel they are surrounded by a world that is frustrating, con-
fusing, and wrong tend to be attracted to Donald Trump? Analysis of the
items in Table 5.4 provides answers. These items all happened to be worded
positively so I present them individually. This arrangement means that, in
this particular case, acquiescence bias could be a factor; nonetheless, the
results are revealing.

Are ardent Trump supporters, as we so often hear, bitter about their place
in the world? One item in the 2019 survey directly addresses this matter. It
reads "I admit to being somewhat bitter about the way that people like me
are viewed and treated." The results suggest that conventional wisdom is
quite badly incorrect. Of the four groups, Trump venerators are actually the
least likely to agree—10 percentage points lower than liberals (33% to 43%).
A roughly similar story is apparent with the "I am angry and frustrated about
my status in the world" item: Trump venerators are 14 percentage points less
likely than liberals to agree with this statement. A third item posed a statement that is more similar to the personality items in the previous table: "I
see myself as someone who is angry and frustrated." It is encouraging to see
that most people do not agree with this statement (less than one in five of the
overall population) but note that, even in relative terms, Trump venerators
do not generally see themselves as angry and frustrated. In fact, their agreement is lowest among the four groups (just 12%) and is significantly lower
than non-Trump-venerating conservatives (r = −.12).

TABLE 5.4 Negative Emotions and Trump Venerators

Items	Liberals	Moderates	NTV Conservatives	Trump Venerators	Overall Correlation	NTVCs/TVs Correlation
I feel bitter about the treatment of people like me.	43	41	47	33	-.09**	-.16**
I am angry and frustrated about my status.	46	36	23	32	-.13**	NS
I see myself as angry and frustrated.	20	22	21	12	NS	-.12*
I resent wealthy people who don't have to work.	38	38	30	20	-.26**	NS
I resent educated people who live in coastal cities.	14	11	21	12	NS	-.20**
I see myself as socially unfulfilled.	42	23	22	19	-.18**	NS
It would bother me to drink flyswatter stirred soup.	67	68	74	78	.10*	NS
It would bother me to see a glass eye removed.	42	50	46	54	NS	NS

Note:

$N=888$

*=sign ($p<.10$) **=sign ($p<.05$) NS=not significant ($p>.10$)

NTV Conservatives = non-Trump-venerating conservatives

Overall Correlation = the bivariate correlation between the item and the four categories

NTVCs/TVs Correlation = the bivariate correlation between non-Trump-venerating conservatives and Trump venerators

The numbers in the first four columns are the percentage agreeing with each item.

If they are not particularly bitter or angry, perhaps Trump venerators are resentful of wealthy, white-collar, overeducated, city-dwellers—the rural resentment we have heard so much about. It turns out that this aspect of the standard narrative does not withstand analysis either, as the next two items in the table demonstrate. On average, Trump venerators are easily the least likely to resent wealthy people who "do not have to do physical labor"— 18 percentage points less likely than liberals. The other item asked for a response to the following statement: "I sort of resent those who have lots of education and live in cities on the coasts." Just 15% of the entire sample agreed with this statement and more to the point, there is no appreciable difference as attention shifts from liberals to moderates to non-Trump-venerating conservatives and then to Trump venerators, though Trump venerators actually were significantly less likely to agree with this statement than non-Trump-venerating conservatives. On the whole, the level of resentment among Trump venerators is remarkably low.[17]

Are Trump venerators socially adrift in their isolated rural enclaves? It would not appear so. When confronted with the item "I see myself as someone who is socially unfulfilled and in need of a better support system," the group that was by far the most likely to agree was liberals (42%) with Trump venerators being the least likely (just 19%) and this relationship (r = −.18) was statistically significant.[18] The assertion that people deeply devoted to Donald Trump are socially unfulfilled receives no confirmation in the data. The vast majority of Trump venerators feel comfortable with their social network and circle of friends.[19] If we are going to be concerned about any group on this point, it should be liberals, though it is likely that Trump's presidency led liberals—many of whom are vitriolic Trump opponents—to feel particularly angry, bitter, resentful, and perhaps even dissatisfied with their social support system (more on these points shortly).

Next, we turn to the issue of disgust. Previous research finds that people on the right of the political spectrum are more likely to be disgust-sensitive. Does this pattern apply to Trump venerators? Items assessing disgust-sensitivity are a little different from the other items in Table 5.4.[20] They specify a particular situation and ask respondents to indicate whether they agree or disagree that they would be bothered if they found themselves in that situation. The items included in Table 5.4 are, would it bother you "to drink a bowl of your favorite soup that had been stirred with a used but thoroughly washed fly swatter" and would it bother you "to see a person with a glass eye remove the eye from the socket?" Overall, the prospect of drinking the flyswatter-stirred soup bothers people more than witnessing removal of a glass eye but there was surprisingly little variation across political groups. We do see some evidence of the pattern established in previous research: compared to liberals and moderates, respondents on the political right seem slightly more disgust-sensitive. The differences are modest, however, and though their disgust-sensitivity is marginally higher, Trump venerators are not significantly more likely than non-Trump-venerating conservatives to agree that they would be bothered by either hypothetical situation.[21]

As with previous tables, I single out a few items to present graphically (in Figure 5.5). The results illustrate that of the four groups, Trump venerators are the least bitter, the least resentful, and the least socially unfulfilled. Most notably, the differences between Trump venerators and non-Trump-venerating conservatives are substantial, with Trump venerators 14 points lower on bitterness and 9 points lower on resentment.

Many readers will find these patterns initially surprising and may have already formulated an explanation: Trump himself. The generally positive emotions evinced by Trump venerators are likely attributable in part to the fact that at the time of the survey the object of their veneration was firmly ensconced in the White House. It may well be that Trump venerators are only out of sorts when they do not like the current occupant of the White House. If true, as I suspect it is, two important points follow.

First, politics plays an important role in influencing people's emotional well-being—apparently, even satisfaction with their social support network. At the time of the survey, Trump had been notably unsuccessful at bringing manufacturing jobs back, at stemming the opioid crisis, at reducing the influx of immigrants into the United States, at promoting law and order, at

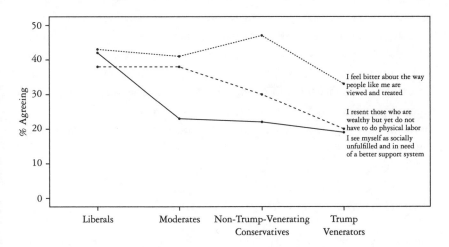

FIGURE 5.5 Negative Emotions and Political Orientation

negotiating more favorable trade agreements, and at improving the farm economy—all issues that were supposed to be vital to Trump's base—yet that base barely wavered. Merely having a president who shared their values may have been enough to improve the emotional health of Trump venerators just as having a president who opposed those values may have been enough to diminish the emotional health of many liberals. It appears that politics is not merely "a sideshow in the great circus of life," as political theorist Robert Dahl so famously described it.[22] For many, it now occupies the center ring.[23]

Second, if it is the case that the political climate is sufficiently powerful to affect emotional health, this pattern is directly at odds with the conventional wisdom holding that conservatives and, more specifically, unwavering Trump supporters are chronically bitter, angry, resentful, socially frustrated, and disgust-sensitive people. (Note that none of these items references politics, so respondents needed to bring that element into their answer on their own.) The apparently powerful influence of political context on emotional well-being stands in contrast to the common assertion that the people who compose Trump's base are endemically grumpy. They may only report negative emotions when they do not like those in control of the levers of political power.

Liberals may be inclined to resist results indicating that intense Trump supporters are relatively low in anxiety and high in social well-being, but they shouldn't. With apologies to Bobby McFerrin, "Don't worry; be happy," is not necessarily the best guiding life principle. In fact, many liberals may believe it is wrong to be happy when there is so much suffering and socioeconomic injustice in the world (remember, Adorno could not fathom writing poetry in the wake of Auschwitz). If a person's primary mission in life is to connect emotionally and helpfully with all outsiders, being upbeat is going to be a challenge. Being vigilant against outsiders gives Trump venerators worth and purpose, whereas doing battle against powerful and long-standing sources of mass oppression and rampant inequality often makes liberals feel spent and frustrated (though some liberals may view the situation as an ennobling obligation). In short, those whose mission it is to secure protection from outsiders are more likely to possess a positive emotional profile—especially if the very process of striving for that protection is rewarding to them.

People Behaving Badly

The survey also included 10 items assessing not personality traits, not emotions felt, but actual behaviors. The specific behaviors measured are smoking/vaping tobacco, enjoying pornography, having received more than four traffic citations, averaging at least four alcoholic drinks a week, regularly buying lottery tickets, gambling for stakes over $20, telling inappropriate jokes, owning a firearm, traveling outside the United States (within the last five years), and either hunting or fishing (also within the last five years).

The overall percentage of the population engaging in these diverse behaviors (see Table 5.5) is remarkably consistent, ranging between 18% to 30% with two exceptions: 36% of adult Americans tell off-color or in-appropriate jokes and 52% have an immediate family member who owns a gun.[24] As to patterns across the four groups, four were statistically significant. Compared to respondents on the left, those on the political right are more likely to have received numerous traffic citations, to regularly play the lottery, and (not surprisingly) to own a firearm, but are less likely to report that they enjoy pornography. The correlation for gun ownership is the largest though even 39% of liberals belong to a family with a gun.

When I restrict the analysis to differences between Trump venerators and non-Trump-venerating conservatives, Trump venerators display modest tendencies to watch more porn, get more traffic citations, and tell inappropriate jokes but none of these differences is statistically significant. As a further indication that stereotypes are not always on target, Trump venerators are marginally *less* likely than non-Trump-venerating conservatives (and especially moderates) to report having hunted or fished in the last five years. In fact, Trump venerators are more likely to travel overseas (33%) than to hunt or fish (29%). Most of those guns are not being used for hunting.

Who Feels Threatened by What?

Much of the literature implies that conservatives and by extension Trump venerators are more concerned about all threats no matter whether they take the form of a vicious dog, a windstorm, a criminal, or a crashed grid. The claim is that conservatives focus on the negative and threatening aspects of life and that this is why they are eager to take precautions in their personal lives and to enact protective policies at the societal level. As I described in Chapter 2, however, some research finds that felt threat varies with the nature of the threat, such that conservatives are indeed more threatened by certain things but that liberals are more threatened by others.

The results from the April 2019 survey come down firmly in support of the claim that the type of threat is crucial in determining who feels

TABLE 5.5 Personal Behaviors and Trump Venerators

Behavior	Liberals	Moderates	NTV Conservatives	Trump Venerators	Overall Correlation	NTVCs/TVs Correlation
smoke tobacco (22)	18	20	29	23	NS	NS
watch porn (29)	36	26	22	28	-.13**	NS
numerous traffic citations (18)	15	16	17	26	.08*	NS
at least 4 drinks/week (21)	20	24	21	15	NS	NS
play the lottery (20)	16	18	23	26	.08*	NS
gamble for higher stakes (24)	28	22	23	24	NS	NS
tell off-color jokes (36)	36	35	33	42	NS	NS
own a firearm (52)	39	49	65	63	.30**	NS
travel outside the U.S. (28)	31	32	27	33	NS	NS
hunt or fish (30)	21	33	30	29	NS	NS

Note:

N=450 (behavior battery only asked to half the sample)

*=sign (p<.10) **=sign (p<.05) NS=not significant (p>.10)

NTV Conservatives = non-Trump-venerating conservatives

Overall Correlation = the bivariate correlation between the item and the four categories

NTVCs/TVs Correlation = the bivariate correlation between non-Trump-venerating conservatives and Trump venerators

The numbers in the first four columns are the percentage agreeing with each item.

The numbers in parentheses are the overall percentage of the sample agreeing that they would engage in the behavior.

threatened. As can be seen in Table 5.6, those who venerate Trump are not more threat-sensitive across the board but only when it comes to threats from those they view as outsiders.

The first items in the table constitute a battery in which respondents were given the opportunity to strongly disagree, disagree, neither agree nor disagree, agree, or strongly agree that they feel threatened by each of eleven individual entities. The first six items—China, criminals, immigrants, terrorist attacks, the federal government, and liberals—are all more threatening to non-Trump-venerating conservatives and Trump venerators than to moderates and especially liberals. In fact, some of the differences are dramatic. Seven percent of liberals report feeling threatened by immigrants whereas 75% of Trump venerators do; 31% of liberals feel threatened by terrorist attacks whereas 82% of Trump venerators do; 29% of liberals feel threatened by "the military and economic strength of other countries such as China" whereas 70% of Trump venerators do; and 6% of liberals feel threatened by liberals (an interesting 6%) whereas 74% of Trump venerators do. These patterns produce some of the largest overall correlations that we have seen to this point: .36 for feeling threatened by terrorist attacks, .40 for criminals, .60 for immigrants, and .63 for liberals. Ideology is clearly related to feeling threatened by outsiders.

Limiting the analysis only to Trump venerators and conservatives who do not venerate Donald Trump generates equally revealing results. Trump venerators are distinguished from non-Trump-venerating conservatives by the fact that they feel significantly more threatened by China, criminals, immigrants, terrorist attacks, and liberals but the difference is especially notable for immigrants. Compared to non-Trump-venerating conservatives, Trump venerators are 9 points more likely to feel threatened by China, 3 points more likely to feel threatened by criminals, 12 points more likely to feel threatened by terrorist attacks, and 2 points more likely to feel threatened by the federal government but they are 35 points more likely to feel threatened by immigrants. As a factor distinguishing Trump venerators from non-Trump-venerating conservatives, perceiving immigrants as threats (.37) is the most important variable of any analyzed to this point.

No doubt part of the reason for the influence of this concept is that Trump made immigration and the wall along the southern border such salient issues. Some may simply be following his lead. On the other hand, if I am correct that securitarians such as most Trump venerators are psychologically predisposed to feel threatened by outsiders, then the reason for seeing immigrants as threats runs deeper than Trumpian rhetoric. In sum, Trump venerators are threatened by outsiders such as foreign powers, criminals, immigrants,

TABLE 5.6 Felt Threats and Trump Venerators

I feel threatened by . . .	Liberals	Moderates	NTV Conservatives	Trump Venerators	Overall Correlation	NTVCs/TVs Correlation
countries like China.	29	56	61	70	.33**	.19**
criminals.	39	60	76	79	.40**	.12*
immigrants.	7	22	40	75	.60**	.37**
terrorist attacks.	31	50	70	82	.36**	.18**
the federal government.	34	47	67	69	.32**	NS
liberals.	6	21	62	74	.63**	.17**
the growing income gap.	80	64	42	37	-.43**	NS
people without health care.	68	53	32	32	-.31**	NS
racists.	80	50	41	40	-.33**	NS
conservatives.	69	36	9	15	-.53**	NS
natural disasters.	58	61	57	54	NS	NS
Belief in a dangerous world						
Any day, chaos and anarchy will erupt all around.	37	36	47	57	.18**	NS

					Overall Correlation	NTVCs/TVs Correlation
Things seem to be getting more dangerous but they aren't.	40	30	25	18	-.17**	-.14*
The world is big, beautiful, and not dangerous.	47	35	33	24	-.16**	-.18**

Note:

N=450 (threat battery only asked to half the sample)

*=sign (p<.10) **=sign (p<.05) NS=not significant (p>.10)

NTV Conservatives = non-Trump-venerating conservatives

Overall Correlation = the bivariate correlation between the item and the four categories

NTVCs/TVs Correlation = the bivariate correlation between non-Trump-venerating conservatives and Trump venerators

The numbers in the first four columns are the percentage agreeing with each item.

terrorists, and those insiders who undermine the real Americans who are ready and willing to do whatever it takes to enhance security.

Conservatives and in particular Trump venerators do not feel universally threatened, however. No meaningful difference appears in the degree to which liberals, moderates, non-Trump-venerating conservatives, and Trump venerators feel threatened by "storms, earthquakes, and other natural disasters" and if my survey had gone to the field in April of 2020 instead of April of 2019 and had included items on the coronavirus, I am confident it would have shown that Trump venerators were not more threatened than other groups by the virus itself but were more convinced that an outside entity was responsible.

Not surprisingly, compared to liberals, conservatives are significantly less threatened by non-outsider threats such as the growing income gap between rich and poor, by the number of people who do not have health care, by racists, and by conservatives. Again, some of the differences are striking: 80% of liberals agree that they feel threatened by racists whereas only 40% of Trump venerators do; 80% of liberals feel threatened by the income gap whereas only 37% of Trump venerators do; and 69% of liberals feel threatened by conservatives whereas only 15% of Trump venerators do.

Most Trump venerators (and many non-Trump-venerating conservatives) do not feel threatened by the income gap, deficiencies in health care, and even racists because they are not convinced these situations or groups threaten insiders. In fact, in the securitarian mindset, those people who are taking advantage of insiders—for example, by accepting benefits they have not earned—are part of the problem. As such, securitarians fear that policies designed to redistribute income or to provide the needy with health care will benefit outsiders and weaken insiders.[25] Recall the dust-up in August of 2019 when the Trump administration proposed banning those immigrants likely to receive government benefits. Director of US Citizen and Immigration Services Ken Cuccinelli explained that the administration wanted to amend the words on the Statue of Liberty so they read "Give me your tired and your poor *who can stand on their own two feet and who will not become a public charge.*"[26] Trump venerators are not sensitive to all threats; they are sensitive to threats posed by outsiders and by those who provide comfort and encouragement to outsiders.

Table 5.6 concludes with three items that are not part of the "I feel threatened by . . ." battery but that tap respondents' "belief in a dangerous world."[27] Taken together, the results generated by these three items could be interpreted as providing evidence that non-Trump-venerating conservatives and especially Trump venerators are more likely than others to be universally threatened. After all, compared to liberals, they are significantly more likely to agree that "any day now chaos and anarchy will erupt all around us" and

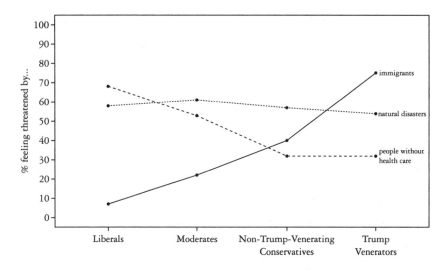

FIGURE 5.6 Felt Threat and Political Orientation

they are significantly less likely to agree that the world isn't getting more dangerous and that "the world is a beautiful place to explore." I maintain, however, that respondents are likely to interpret the "belief in a dangerous world" items such that the danger emanates primarily from outsiders. In their minds, outsiders are the source of chaos and anarchy. Imagine that belief in a dangerous world was measured with items such as "any day now the most influential and established elites of society will acquire so much power and wealth that our country will be hopelessly corrupted and endangered." It is likely that response patterns across the four groups would look much different.[28]

In Figure 5.6, I single out three of the potential sources of felt threat from Table 5.6: immigrants, health care availability, and natural disasters. The figure shows that Trump venerators and non-Trump-venerating conservatives are amazingly similar in terms of the extent to which they feel threatened by natural disasters and by the prospect of people not having health care. Contrast these results with the belief that immigrants are threatening: 40% of non-Trump-venerating conservatives feel threatened by immigrants, a fairly high percentage compared to moderates and especially liberals, but nothing in comparison to Trump venerators where we see that three out of every four feel threatened by immigrants, the quintessential outsiders. To the extent that Trump venerators feel threatened, it is by human outsiders specifically, not amorphous and disembodied threats such as accidents, climate change, viruses, and income inequality.

Given the central role that immigrants play in Trump venerators' view of the world, I give the topic additional attention. A closer look suggests the key is less the degree to which Trump venerators feel threatened by immigration than their policy positions even when they do not feel threatened. My argument is that most Trump venerators are securitarians and that securitarians feel it is their duty to pursue protection from outsiders regardless. If I am correct, securitarians do not need to feel threatened by immigrants in order to want them to stay away. The data from the survey make it possible to test this thesis.

I regressed respondents' attitudes toward reducing immigration (4 = strongly agree with reducing immigration; 0 = strongly disagree) on the degree to which they felt threatened by immigrants (4 = strongly agree that I feel threatened; 0 = strongly disagree). Regression produces a line of best fit that nicely captures a relationship and in the top half of Figure 5.7 I present these lines for liberals, for moderates, for non-Trump-venerating conservatives, and for Trump venerators.

The lines of best fit for the four groups show that when people feel threatened by immigrants it does not much matter whether they are liberals, moderates, conservatives, or Trump venerators. A glance at the right-hand side of the figure reveals that regardless of ideology, everyone who feels threatened by immigrants wants to reduce immigration. Support for re-ducing immigration ranges only between 3.13 for liberals to 3.76 for Trump venerators—a difference of just 0.63. For those who strongly disagree that they feel threatened by immigrants (the left-hand side of the figure), the range is all the way from 0.52 for liberals to 2.55 for Trump venerators—a difference of 2.03. Of course, the number of Trump venerators who strongly disagreed that they feel threatened by immigrants is relatively small but the important point is that 89% of those who did, still strongly agreed that im-migration into the United States needed to be reduced.

Looking at perceptions of immigrants rather than felt threat reveals a sim-ilar dynamic. I combined two items to measure perceptions: the first states that "the percent of immigrants who engage in criminal acts is surprisingly low," and the second "immigrants more often than not make America a better place to live." A score of zero on this index means that the respondent had highly favorable perceptions of immigrants and a score of eight means the re-spondent had highly negative perceptions. Then, I replicated the procedures just described for felt threat.

The bottom half of Figure 5.7 presents these results and the same pat-tern appears. Liberals, moderates, non-Trump-venerating conservatives, and Trump venerators have nearly identical desires to reduce immigration when they have negative perceptions of immigrants but they differ greatly when they have favorable perceptions of immigrants. If they have decid-edly negative perceptions of immigrants, all four groups on average—even

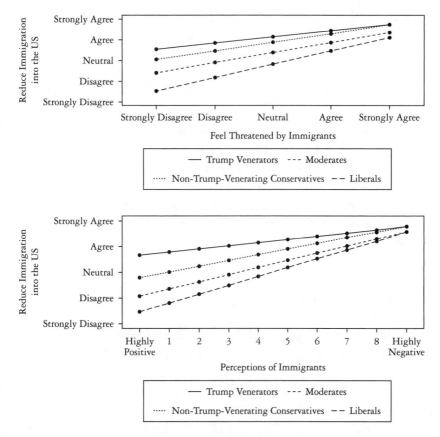

FIGURE 5.7 Attitudes toward Immigrants and the Desire to Reduce Immigration

liberals—want to reduce immigration into the United States. The difference comes among people who believe immigrants make America a better place to live and that immigrants do not commit many crimes. Liberals with positive perceptions of immigrants strongly oppose reducing immigration, but Trump venerators with those same perceptions of immigrants strongly support reducing immigration.[29] None of this negates the fact that many Trump venerators report feeling threatened by immigrants. It seems likely, however, that when Trump venerators say that immigrants are threats, they are not reflecting a belief that outsiders are criminal or economic threats so much as they are reflecting a belief that immigrants by their very presence are a threat to the strength, homogeneity, and unity of insiders.

Trump venerators want to stop immigrants from infiltrating the country even if they do not feel threatened by immigrants and even if they believe immigrants make America a better place to live and do not commit crimes.[30] The attitude seems to be, "We must keep out people we agree would be helpful." To some extent Trump venerators' tendency to report feeling threatened by immigrants may be an unwitting attempt to rationalize their pre-existing desire to exclude outsiders.

Trump venerators' attitudes toward outsiders are also apparent in the lack of trust they place in them. This attitude can be glimpsed in Trump's own statement in August of 2019 that "in my world, in this world, I think nobody can be trusted."[31] One survey item stated that "it is best to assume outsiders probably tend to do us harm even if that later proves not to be the case." Just 11% of liberals agreed with that statement but 57% of Trump venerators did—a figure that was also significantly higher than that for non-Trump-venerating conservatives ("only" 38% of them agreed). For Trump venerators, the default is to be wary of outsiders. From a securitarian point of view, this is only prudent; from a unitarian point of view, this is unvarnished ethnocentrism.

Racist and Sexist?

As I discussed earlier, to securitarians, race is an obvious indicator of outsider status, making racial attitudes of particular interest to any analysis of Trump's strongest supporters. I can address this topic with the April 2019 survey data. The items on race deal specifically with blacks so an investigation of attitudes toward Latinxs, Asians, and other racial groups will have to wait, though note that previous research, dating back to Adorno, reports that individuals who are prejudiced toward one minority racial group are almost always prejudiced toward others.[32]

Agreement with some items indicates greater sensitivity to blacks and agreement with other items indicates less sensitivity. In fact, I paired pro and con items for three separate aspects of racial attitudes: the perceived causes of racial disparities, differences in perceived deservingness across black-white lines, and overt racism. The first of the two items pertaining to the causes of racial disparities reads, "It's really a matter of some people not trying hard enough; if blacks would only try harder they could be just as well off as whites," and the second, "There still is a great deal of discrimination against blacks in the United States today and this limits their chances of getting ahead." The first item on deservingness reads, "Over the past few years, blacks have gotten less than they deserve," and the second, "Over the past few years, blacks have gotten more economically than they deserve." Finally, the first overt racism item reads "Truth be told, for the most part, blacks are not as talented and capable as whites," and the second, "The notion that blacks are less able than whites is deeply wrong and offensive."

Reverse coding one of the items in each pair and adding the responses together produces a 0 to 8 index with larger numbers indicating responses less favorable to blacks. The top half of Table 5.7 reports the results for the six individual items on race as well as for the three two-item indices. The top panel of Figure 5.8 presents the patterns for the three two-item indices.

Regarding both the reasons for racial disparities in the United States (lack of effort or discrimination) and the degree to which blacks are getting what they deserve, the differences from liberals to moderates to non-Trump-venerating conservatives to Trump venerators are readily apparent. Liberals generally agree that blacks are not getting what they deserve and that the reason has a great deal to do with discrimination. Moderates and especially conservatives are more likely to agree that blacks get what they deserve and to the extent they do not, it is because they are not trying. Trump venerators are the most likely to agree with these latter claims. The overall correlation for the "perceived causes" index is .60 and for "deservingness" index is .56 and the difference between non-Trump-venerating conservatives and Trump venerators is significant for both (.24 and .17, respectively). Trump venerators are more likely than any other group analyzed to believe that blacks are getting what they deserve and that, if they want more, they merely need to make a greater effort.

This pattern continues for overt racism—the belief that, compared to whites, blacks are less skilled and able. Not surprisingly, respondents overall are substantially less likely to endorse this sentiment but, parallel to the results for the other two racial measures, the belief that blacks are inferior increases significantly as attention shifts from the political left to the political right. Seven percent of liberals agree that "blacks are not as talented and capable as whites" as do 12% of moderates and 10% of non-Trump-venerating conservatives. Among Trump venerators, however, the figure jumps to 22%. Though a majority of Trump's ardent supporters do not admit to believing that blacks are inferior to whites, somewhere between a fifth and a fourth of them do.[33]

Turning to attitudes toward females, the research approach is consistent with that for race but the results are not. I employed six counterbalanced items tapping three separate but related concepts. An index addressing perceptions of the current status of females consists of the following two items: "When it comes to giving women equal rights with men, the country has gone too far" and "Men still have it much easier in our country these days." An index on "benevolent sexism" is built from "Women should be cherished and protected by men" and "In a disaster, women should NOT be rescued before men." Finally, two items tap overt sexism: "Women are not as

TABLE 5.7 Racial and Gender Attitudes and Trump Venerators

	Liberals	Moderates	NTV Conservatives	Trump Venerators	Overall Correlation	NTVCs/TVs Correlation
Race items						
Blacks just need to try harder.	7	26	45	62	.56**	.27**
Discrimination keeps blacks from getting ahead.	80	53	27	19	-.50**	NS
Two-item cause of disparity index					.60**	.24**
Blacks get less than they deserve.	70	36	21	19	-.48**	NS
Blacks get more economically than they deserve.	4	15	24	40	.44**	.16**
Two-item deservingness index					.56**	.17**
Blacks are not as talented as whites.	7	12	10	22	.22**	.20**
The notion that blacks are less able is wrong.	82	72	82	74	-.12**	NS
Two-item overt racism index					.20**	.17**
Gender Items						
We have gone too far on women's rights.	4	14	23	33	.46**	NS
Men still have it much easier than women.	80	50	33	40	-.35**	NS
Two-item current status index					49**	NS
Women should NOT be rescued first.	19	19	17	20	NS	NS
Women should be cherished and protected.	34	60	79	74	.31**	NS
Two-item benevolent sexism index					.27**	NS
Women are not as talented as men.	4	16	14	20	.25**	.19**
The notion that women are less able is wrong.	85	65	61	69	-.29**	NS
Two-item overt sexism index					.33**	NS

Note:

N=450 (race and sex items only asked to half the sample)

*=sign (p<.10) **=sign (p<.05) NS=not significant (p>.10)

NTV Conservatives = non-Trump-venerating conservatives

Overall Correlation = the bivariate correlation between the item and the four categories

NTVCs/TVs Correlation = the bivariate correlation between non-Trump-venerating conservatives and Trump venerators

The numbers in the first four columns are the percent agreeing with each item.

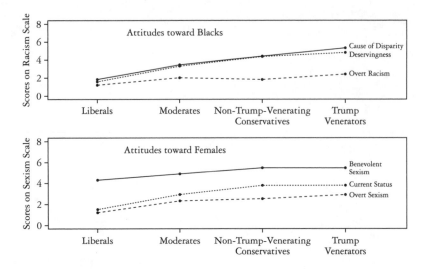

FIGURE 5.8 Race, Sex, and Political Orientation

talented and capable as men," and "The notion that women are less able than men is deeply wrong and offensive."

I present the results in the bottom halves of Table 5.7 and Figure 5.8. Here we see that benevolent sexism is quite common across all four groups but goes up markedly as attention shifts to the right: 34% of liberals, 60% of moderates, 79% of non-Trump-venerating conservatives, and 74% of Trump venerators agree that women should be protected and cherished by men. The two-item index is positive (.27) and significant. Still bigger upward shifts are apparent for the other two indices, especially perceptions of the current status of women (r = .49): 80% of liberals but only 40% of Trump venerators agree that "men still have it much easier than women." The pattern for overt sexism is also significant, with Trump venerators being more likely (but still not very likely) to agree that women are inferior. Though the overall patterns from left to right are statistically significant, the difference between non-Trump-venerating conservatives and Trump venerators is not for any of the three sex-status indices (though the difference for overt sexism comes close).

In sum, consistent with earlier speculation that if securitarians are ever going to cease using race as a marker of outsider status, it is going to take a long time, all three racial indices show significant differences between non-Trump-venerating conservatives and Trump venerators but none of the gender indices does. Compared to non-Trump-venerating conservatives, Trump venerators give significantly less favorable responses to blacks but not to women. It appears that Trump venerators are more likely to see blacks than females as outsiders.

Conclusion

Trump's strongest supporters are overwhelmingly conservative and overwhelmingly Republican, making it a challenge to tease out the distinguishing features of the Trump base. Whether the topic is demographics, personalities, emotions, personal behaviors, perceived threats, or racial and gender attitudes, the differences between liberals and conservatives are large and not all that surprising. The differences between Trump venerators and conservatives who do not venerate Trump, however, are more limited, subtle, intriguing, and informative.

On demographics, compared to non-Trump-venerating conservatives, Trump venerators are more likely to be white, less well off, less educated, rural, male, and old but, with the exception of age and education, the differences are more modest than is typically averred. The large percentage of Trump venerators who are financially well-to-do, college educated, suburban, female, religiously inactive, and under forty-five means that the Trump base should not be dismissed as merely a bunch of old, uneducated, fundamentalist, rural males.

Turning to personality, the consistent finding in the existing literature is that, compared to liberals, conservatives are more conscientious, more dogmatic, more likely to prefer closure and consensus, and less likely to be open to new experiences but that on extraversion, agreeableness, and neuroticism, liberals and conservatives are not very different. For the most part, these patterns are apparent in the results analyzed here but some interesting differences emerge when I compare Trump venerators to non-Trump-venerating conservatives. Trump's most enthusiastic supporters see themselves as significantly more extraverted, agreeable, and conscientious than liberals, moderates, and non-Trump-venerating conservatives—and significantly less neurotic. They also see themselves as more conscientious and more "open" than conservatives who do not venerate Trump. When it comes to personality, Trump venerators give themselves favorable marks.

The findings for emotionality might be even more surprising. Trump venerators are significantly less likely than all other groups to feel "bitter about the way people like them are viewed and treated," to be "angry and frustrated about their status in the world these days," to "resent those who are wealthy and yet don't have to do physical labor," and to see themselves as being "social unfulfilled and in need of a better support network." In some political contexts, the people who are Trump's most enthusiastic supporters may be angry, bitter, frustrated, resentful, and socially adrift but we now know that in some contexts (such as when Trump was in the White House) they are not. Their alleged negative emotionality is a state, not a trait.

In terms of personal behaviors, the real surprise is the degree to which behaviors are similar across the four groups employed in this analysis. Differences in tobacco usage, alcohol consumption, telling off-color jokes, and gambling are remarkably modest. Trump venerators are not less likely than the other three groups to travel overseas and are only slightly more likely to hunt or fish. The only difference of any size is that Trump venerators are more likely to own a firearm (67% of Trump venerators compared to 39% of liberals).

Trump's ardent supporters are more likely than others to feel threatened but even here only by outsiders and those who support outsiders. Liberals are significantly more threatened than Trump venerators by income inequality, racists, and problems relating to health care access, and maybe even by natural disasters. The threats that concern Trump venerators, even when compared to non-Trump-venerating conservatives, are quite tightly defined and center on outsiders: immigrants, terrorists, criminals, and foreign powers, as well as those who have thrown in with outsiders—namely, liberals and the government (i.e., deep state). What's more, feeling threatened by immigrants is not a prerequisite for Trump venerators to want to stop immigration

Finally, Trump venerators are significantly more likely than the other three groups, including non-Trump-venerating conservatives, to believe that blacks are not getting less than they deserve, that to do better all blacks need is to try harder, and that blacks are innately inferior to whites. When it comes to gender attitudes, conservatives in general score significantly higher than moderates and especially liberals on overt sexism, benevolent sexism, and perceptions that the current status of women in society is good; however, Trump venerators are no different from non-Trump-venerating conservatives on these indices. Trump venerators are different from non-Trump-venerating conservatives in their attitudes toward blacks but not women.

The point of all this is not to paint Trump venerators as either wonderful or despicable human beings. The point instead is to show that many of the pat explanations of Trump venerators' motivations—for example, financial stress and emotional negativity—are not accurate. If we are to come to grips with why members of the Trump base have the attitudes they do, we must dig deeper than the conventional wisdom on demographics and personality; we must look at their attitudes toward authority and security.

CHAPTER 6 | Better Secure than Submissive

W ITH REGARD TO demographics, personality, negative emotions, felt threat, personal behaviors, and racial attitudes, Trump's most committed supporters are about as likely to violate the standard narrative as to conform to it. Now, we turn to the degree to which Trump's base is authoritarian—a central claim of scores of previous works.

As detailed in Chapter 3, the modern conceptualization of authoritarianism has evolved well beyond its original meaning into something that we are told is "more involved, more dynamic, and psychologically more powerful than simple submission to an authority."[1] Unfortunately, it is also more theoretically muddled. At the core of the new meaning is still the idea that authoritarians prefer to submit to the authority of someone else but modern academic treatments append two other concepts. The first is conventionalism— a tendency to abide by societal traditions and conventions—and the second is aggression—the tendency to treat with hostile aggression whatever entities the relevant authority figure wants targeted.

One problem with the evolving meaning of authoritarianism is well known. Current measures of authoritarianism merge personality with political worldview; in other words, they conflate desires for personal life with desires for societal arrangements and structures. For example, one of the items in the best known of these measurement approaches, "Right-Wing-Authoritarianism" (RWA), reads, "You have to admire those who challenged the law and the majority's view by protesting for women's abortion rights, animal rights, or to abolish school prayer."[2] Other items in that same battery reference atheists, feminists, homosexuals, and "Godless immoral people."

Asking about attitudes toward atheists, feminists, homosexuals, Godless immoral people, abortions, and school prayer is quite different from asking about whether people see themselves as neurotic, conscientious, or open to new experiences.[3] If the goal is a measure that correlates strongly with political views, this is a great approach, but if the goal is to understand what is really going on with people at the personal level and how personal and societal preferences map onto each other, it is much less useful. All it tells us is that political beliefs correlate with political beliefs, a tautology.

A second problem—and one that is especially relevant to this book—is that the survey items typically employed prevent analysts from separating desires for authority from desires for security. People may give answers that appear to indicate desires for authority and obedience to social norms when their true motivation is a unified and therefore less vulnerable in-group. In other words, rather than indicating that prospective followers are eager to submit to anyone with a modicum of authority, a desire for mighty leaders might indicate a belief that authorities are the ticket to greater security from outside threats. In order to determine whether people are driven by a desire for security rather than authority, individual survey items must deal with one concept or the other but not both.

In the analysis to follow, I will take care to separate people's preferences for personal life from their preferences for societal structures and to separate people's preferences for authority from their preferences for security. The result should be a truer picture of motivations and especially the motivations of fervent Trump supporters. I believe such an analysis will show that intense Trump supporters are not distinguished by generic authoritarianism but rather by a desire to empower only those authority figures and societal conventions that they believe foster both security against outsiders and the preservation of insiders.[4] As we will now see, data from the 2019 survey back up my claims. We will begin at the personality level, then move to political issues, and then conclude at the level of broader worldview (preferences for general societal operations).

Authoritarian Personalities?

True authoritarian followers would be eager to submit to any authority figure because they find it pleasing when someone else is in charge and therefore providing direction to their lives. This is literally the definition of the concept. Like goslings following whatever happens to be present shortly after they hatch, authoritarian followers do not much care who or what they follow. They simply find it psychologically rewarding to follow. In certain cases (Charles Manson, Adolf Hitler, the Reverend Jim Jones), authoritarian followers have committed atrocities merely because an authoritarian leader told them to do so. If Trump venerators have authoritarian personalities, as so much recent writing asserts, they should want to leave key decisions in their lives to others—no matter who those others are.

Two items in my survey most directly address this psychological tendency toward submission: one is worded positively and one negatively. The items are: "I like it when others shape my life and make decisions for me" and "I prefer to be independent of others and largely self-sufficient." No survey item is perfect but these two avoid the acquiescence bias and tap a psychological orientation toward submission without bringing politics into it. How do the authoritarian tendencies of Trump's strongest supporters compare to others? The answer is found in Table 6.1 which is formatted in the same fashion as the tables in Chapter 5.

The first finding of note is that Americans in general are not very submissive. Only 15% of the national sample like it when others make decisions for them and about 75% agree that they prefer to be independent of others and largely self-sufficient. The topic of primary interest, however, is the pattern in submissiveness across the four categories of respondents. Here, contrary to popular belief but consistent with my argument, we see a *decline* in submissiveness as attention shifts from the political left to the political right. Though the differences are quite modest, liberals are the most likely (18%) and Trump venerators the least likely (12%) to be comfortable when others make decisions for them just as liberals are the least likely (70%) and Trump venerators the most likely (82%) to prefer to be independent of others and largely self-sufficient. The relationship between an additive index of these two items and the four political categories is negative (r = −.13) and statistically significant, meaning that, if anything, conservatives are less likely than liberals to display submissive personality tendencies.

Of even more relevance is the pattern between the two groups of respondents on the right side of the political spectrum. Trump venerators are quite similar to non-Trump-venerating conservatives but if they are different at all, they are slightly more averse to the idea of letting somebody else make decisions for them and slightly more likely to prefer to be independent of others. When the two items are combined, a significant relationship appears in the direction of Trump venerators being *less* submissive than non-Trump-venerating conservatives. In Figure 6.1, I present this information pictorially. The line shows the level of submissiveness (measured here as the difference

TABLE 6.1 Authoritarian Personality

	Liberals	Moderates	NTV Conservatives	Trump Venerators	Overall Correlation	NTVCs/TVs Correlation
Submissiveness items						
I like it when others make decisions for me	18	15	14	12	-.06*	NS
I prefer to be independent of others	70	71	78	82	.11**	NS
Submissiveness index					-.13**	-.14**
Conventionalism items						
I enjoy ruffling society's feathers	46	41	35	39	-.11**	NS
I see myself as living life by the book	37	38	54	57	.19**	NS
Conventionalism index					.21**	NS
Aggression items						
I have been in a physical fight	18	27	32	38	.16**	NS
I frequently lose my temper	26	25	30	37	.09*	NS
Aggression index					.15**	NS

Note:

N=888

*=sign (p<.10); **=sign (p<.05); NS=not significant (p>.10)

NTV Conservatives = non-Trump-venerating conservatives

Overall Correlation = the bivariate correlation between the item and the four categories

NTVCs/TVs Correlation = the bivariate correlation between non-Trump-venerating conservatives and Trump venerators

The numbers other than the correlations are the percentage agreeing with each statement.

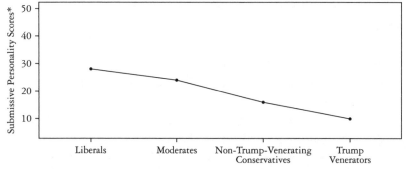

*Scores are the percentage preferring others to decide minus the percentage preferring to make decisions themselves (plus 80 to make the number positive)

FIGURE 6.1 Submissive Personality Tendencies and Political Orientation

in the degree to which decisions by others are preferred to self-decisions) for each group, with Trump venerators clearly being the least submissive. The central element of authoritarian personality tendencies—being eager to submit to someone else—not only fails to distinguish Trump venerators, it actually is a significant predictor of not being a Trump venerator. At least by this measure, liberals, moderates, and non-Trump-venerating conservatives all have more submissive personalities than Trump venerators do.[5]

Of course, by definition, Trump venerators venerate Donald Trump but it may well be a mistake to conclude that this reverence springs from a deep psychological desire to take instructions from anyone in authority. It seems more likely that Trump venerators only submit to a very particular type of authority figure: one believed to be as serious as they are about securing insiders from outsider threats. To Trump venerators, all other authorities (e.g., Barack Obama, Nancy Pelosi, and even John McCain) are misguided and thus a source of threat rather than solace.[6] This is hardly the stuff of an authoritarian personality.

So much for submissiveness. What about the other two legs of the modern version of authoritarianism? Does an intense desire to conform to norms and conventions distinguish Trump venerators? We know that, compared to people on the left, those on the right are more eager to abide by societal customs and, since Trump venerators are on the right, logic suggests they will score high on conventionalism.[7] On the other hand, Trump devotees often project an image that betokens an indifferent or even hostile relationship with norms and conventions—many of which they view as pandering to the priests of political correctness. Moreover, previous work on Trump followers finds no support for the claim that they are high on conventionalism so there is reason for doubt.[8] To the evidence.

As with submissiveness, we again have two counterbalanced items, one in which agreement indicates conventionalism ("I see myself as someone who mostly lives life 'by the book'") and one in which it indicates the opposite ("Sometimes I enjoy ruffling the feathers of 'proper' society"). As the middle part of Table 6.1 indicates, the expected overall ideological pattern is apparent this time. As attention shifts from those on the left to those on the right, the percentage of respondents agreeing that they like to "ruffle society's feathers" decreases and the percent agreeing that they "live life by the book" increases. It would have been surprising if these patterns had not appeared given that scholars frequently view an aversion to change as an integral and even definitional part of conservatism.[9]

The question of interest, though, is whether Trump venerators are more conventional than conservatives who are not Trump venerators and the answer is no. Compared to others on the right, Trump venerators appear to be neither more nor less conventional. They are slightly more likely than non-Trump-venerating conservatives to see themselves as living life by the book (57% to 54%) but, contrary to conventional wisdom, slightly more likely to say they enjoy ruffling society's feathers (39% to 35%). These differences, however, are small and do not achieve significance either alone or in combination (see the far right column in Table 6.1). Referring to individuals scoring high on his measure of right-wing authoritarianism, Altemeyer observed that "unconventionality and lack of respectability disturb them."[10] Whether or not this assertion is true, Trump venerators are not distinguished from garden-variety conservatives by their overall devotion to society's norms. It is quite possible they endorse those conventions they believe make the in-group more secure and spurn those they believe do not.

The final leg of redesigned authoritarianism is aggression—an extremely difficult concept to measure directly because most people avoid describing themselves as aggressive. Previous measurement efforts have muddied the water by naming only a particular type of group toward which the aggression is targeted. Consider this example, again from the right-wing authoritarianism (RWA) battery: "The biggest threat to our freedom comes from the Communists and their kind, who are out to destroy religion, ridicule patriotism, corrupt the youth and in general undermine our whole way of life."[11] This item does not refer to aggression but does gratuitously mention communists, those who destroy religion, and those who ridicule patriotism— groups that all happen to be enemies of the political right.

What would happen if the item had read: "The biggest threat to our freedom comes from the greedy businesspeople and their kind, who are out to line the pockets of their wealthy friends, corrupt the entire political system with illicit donations, ridicule the needy, and in general undermine our whole way of life"?[12] The targets mentioned in the actual RWA items are those viewed by securitarians as outsider threats to country and culture so cannot adjudicate between authoritarianism and securitarianism. Altemeyer should have realized that the mention of other target groups would generate quite different response patterns since he reports that those scoring high on authoritarianism were less likely to want to punish a police officer for abusing a prisoner than the prisoner himself just as they were less willing to seek punishment for an accountant charged with assaulting a hippie than a hippie charged with assaulting an accountant.[13] The standard measures of aggression are less about aggression than whether the target is an insider or an outsider.[14]

If the goal is to assess who does and who does not have aggressive personality tendencies, the prudent thing to do is to ask about actual aggressive personality features without introducing particular categories of target groups. In the 2019 survey, I asked respondents if as an adult they had been involved in "at least one physical fight." Likewise, I asked if they frequently lost their temper in discussions/arguments. These items are not perfect but do a better job of soliciting generic aggression than an item suggesting that "communists are a threat to our way of life." When employing these less loaded items, we find that Trump venerators may be more aggressive than others.

The percentage of American adults who have been in a physical fight is surprisingly high—at least to someone who has spent his entire adult life surrounded by bookish nerds in the ivory tower of academia: between a fourth and a third of adults (28%) report having been in a physical fight. Does a proclivity for fisticuffs vary with political orientation? Yes. Just 18% of liberals have been in a fight whereas 32% of non-Trump-venerating conservatives and 38% of Trump venerators have. Though the difference between Trump venerators and non-Trump-venerating conservatives does not achieve significance, the overall pattern does (see the bottom portion of Table 6.1). Trump venerators are not significantly more likely than non-Trump-venerating conservatives to have been in a fight but they are significantly more likely than moderates and liberals.

The pattern is similar for temper. As attention shifts from left to right politically, there is a general but modest increase. Trump venerators are somewhat more likely than those in the other three political groups to report frequently losing their temper in discussions. These differences are not significant though they would have been if the entire sample (rather than only half) had answered this particular item. When I combine the two aggression items into a single index, the overall correlation is significant but not the correlation for the difference between Trump venerators and non-Trump-venerating conservatives. As such, these measures of aggression indicate that people on the political right are marginally more generically aggressive than people on the political left but that Trump venerators are about the same as (or only slightly more aggressive than) non-Trump-venerating conservatives.[15]

The political right may be more conventional and more aggressive than the left, but the Trumpian right is not significantly more conventional and aggressive than the non-Trumpian right. The results for the central element of authoritarianism—submissiveness—are even more noteworthy. Though the differences are substantively small, if anything, Trump venerators actually are *less* submissive than people with other political orientations. Trump venerators like to be independent of others and prefer to make decisions for themselves. All told, removing sociopolitical content from the items and keeping the focus on personal behaviors and attitudes leads to the conclusion that an authoritarian personality is not what distinguishes Trump venerators from non-Trump-venerating conservatives.

Preferences for Child-Rearing

As mentioned in Chapter 3, a creative, alternative way of assessing authoritarianism without incorporating overt political content, such as respondents' reactions to communism and capitalism, atheism and school prayer, abortion and capital punishment, is to ask people how they think children should be raised. Scholars typically measure child-rearing attitudes with four items: "Do you think children should be raised to respect elders rather than to be independent," "Do you think they should be raised to be obedient rather than self-reliant," "Do you think they should be raised to have good manners rather than to be curious," and "Do you think they should be raised to be well-behaved rather than to be considerate?" Results indicate that, if forced to choose, the American public thinks children should be raised to respect their elders more than be independent; to be self-reliant more than obedient, to have good manners more than be curious, and to be considerate rather than well-behaved. The key issue, though, is the degree to which people's views vary with their political orientations and especially with whether or not they venerate one Donald J. Trump.

As can be seen in the first four items in Table 6.2, conservatives are more likely than moderates and especially liberals to state a preference for

TABLE 6.2 Child-Rearing Preferences

Children should be raised to . . .	Liberals	Moderates	NTV Conservatives	Trump Venerators	Overall Correlation	NTVCs/TVs Correlation
respect elders rather than be independent.	47	72	76	77	.23**	NS
be obedient rather than self-reliant.	17	37	41	37	.17**	NS
have good manners rather than be curious.	39	64	67	72	.24**	NS
be well-behaved rather than considerate.	18	37	37	38	.16**	NS
live by conventions rather than stand up to them.	26	57	68	67	.31**	NS
follow authority rather than challenge it.	34	62	72	74	.30**	NS
work for change quietly rather than aggressively.	72	78	75	59	-.08*	-.17**
be humble and modest rather than self-confident.	64	73	69	60	NS	NS

Note:

N=441

*=sign (p<.10); **=sign (p<.05); NS=not significant (p>.10)

NTV Conservatives = non-Trump-venerating conservatives

Overall Correlation = the bivariate correlation between the item and the four categories

NTVCs/TVs Correlation = the bivariate correlation between non-Trump-venerating conservatives and Trump venerators

The numbers other than the correlations are the percentage agreeing with each statement.

"authoritarian" goals in child-rearing: respecting elders, being obedient, having good manners, and being well-behaved. All four patterns are statistically significant and the spread is occasionally substantial. For example, only 47% of liberals opt for children respecting elders rather than being independent but nearly 77% of conservatives do. Once again, however, the differences between non-Trump-venerating conservatives and Trump venerators are modest and statistically insignificant. When measured with the child-rearing items, there is no indication that Trump venerators are more authoritarian than non-Trump-venerating conservatives are.

Preferences for child-rearing are useful strategies but the standard four items do not cover all aspects of authoritarianism. In hopes of broadening the approach and making it more relevant to Trump venerators, I presented the survey respondents with four additional child-rearing choices. They are: "Do you think children should be raised to live according to societal expectations or to stand up to those expectations?," "Do you think children should be raised to challenge authority or to follow authority?," "Do you think children should be raised to be aggressive in pursuing needed change or to work quietly behind the scenes?," and "Do you think children should be raised to be humble and modest or to be highly self-confident?" The results are presented in the bottom half of Table 6.2.

On the whole, people opt for children who are raised to live by society's conventions, to follow authority, to work quietly for change, and to be humble and modest but the patterns across the four groups are occasionally fascinating. The results for two of these items are unsurprising. Liberals are the least likely to agree that children should live by society's conventions and that children should follow rather than challenge authority. The overall pattern for these two items is statistically significant, though the difference between Trump venerators and non-Trump-venerating conservatives is not.

For the final two items, however, differences from liberals to Trump venerators are smaller—just 13 points for the "work-quietly-versus-be-aggressive" item and just four points for the "be-humble-versus-be-self-confident" item. What is interesting is that, to the extent there is a pattern, it defies conventional wisdom. Trump venerators are significantly less likely than non-Trump-venerating conservatives to take the "work quietly" option. In a similar vein and perhaps reflecting the brash behavior of the object of their veneration, fervent Trump supporters are nine points less likely than non-Trump-venerating conservatives to see value in raising children to be humble and modest as opposed to highly self-confident.[16]

Securitarian Personalities?

Whether measured with the personality items in Table 6.1 or the child-rearing items in Table 6.2, the only time Trump venerators are significantly different from non-Trump-venerating conservatives—on submissiveness and on raising children to work quietly behind the scenes and possibly to be humble and modest—they turn out to be less rather than more authoritarian.[17] Shorn of inappropriate ideological content, authoritarian items provide little assistance in distinguishing between Trump venerators and non-Trump-venerating conservatives.

My central theoretical claim is that Trump venerators do not have authoritarian personalities so much as they have securitarian personalities. Their driving psychological motivation is security in the form of preserving person, family, and insider culture. The first step in testing this assertion is measuring securitarianism at the personality level. Table 6.1 included six authoritarian personality items, so to enhance comparability my measure of securitarian personality also included six items. They are "Projecting weakness is just about the worst thing a person could do"; "I think a good deal about the security of my family and country"; "I let others worry about keeping me and my family secure"; "Accidents are actually a bigger threat than evil people"; "I would rather be thought of as nice than strong"; and "'Being prepared' to face threats is the best motto for living one's life" (Table 6.3). Three are worded such that agreeing constitutes a securitarian response and three such that disagreeing constitutes a securitarian response. All six assess the degree to which respondents focus on being secure against outsider threats.[18]

Variation across the four groups is substantial for several of the securitarian personality items: 27% of liberals agree that "projecting weakness is about the worst thing a person could do" but 60% of Trump venerators do; 45% of liberals agree that they "think a good deal about security" whereas a whopping 86% of Trump venerators do; and though just 41% of liberals agree that "being prepared is the best motto for living one's life," 80% of Trump venerators do. Variation across groups on the negatively worded items is not nearly as great. For example, almost nobody, regardless of ideological group, agrees that they let others worry about keeping their family safe. When the six items are combined into an overall index, securitarian personality tendencies correlate nicely (.38) with movement from liberals to moderates to non-Trump-venerating conservatives to Trump venerators. To provide context, the highest comparable correlations for the Big 5 personality indices are only −.15 for neuroticism and .14 for conscientiousness.

TABLE 6.3 Securitarian Personality

Securitarian items	Liberals	Moderates	NTV Conservatives	Trump Venerators	Overall Correlation	NTVCs/TVs Correlation
Worst for a person to project weakness	27	37	42	60	.22**	.17**
I think a good deal about security	45	61	78	86	.32**	.10**
I let others worry about keeping me secure	15	13	10	14	NS	NS
Accidents are a bigger threat then evil people	40	30	26	21	-.15**	NS
I'd rather be seen as nice than strong	43	36	33	36	-.07**	NS
Being prepared for threats is the best life motto	41	57	71	80	.29**	.10**
Securitarian index					.38**	.15**

Note:

N=888

*=sign (p<.10); **=sign (p<.05); NS=not significant (p>.10)

NTV Conservatives = non-Trump-venerating conservatives

Overall Correlation = the bivariate correlation between the item and the four categories

NTVCs/TVs Correlation = the bivariate correlation between non-Trump-venerating conservatives and Trump venerators

The numbers other than the correlations are the percentage agreeing with each statement.

Focusing exclusively on the political right, unlike the authoritarian personality items where the only significant coefficients were in the direction contrary to traditional wisdom, securitarian personality items are quite useful in distinguishing Trump venerators from non-Trump-venerating conservatives. Compared to non-Trump-venerating conservatives, Trump venerators are significantly more likely to see problems with a person projecting weakness and they are more likely to think a good deal about security and to see being prepared to face threats as a good way to lead life. Trump venerators make good Boy Scouts. The six-item index also correlates positively (r = .15) and significantly with whether individuals are non-Trump-venerating conservatives or Trump venerators. Compared to non-Trump-venerating conservatives, the personalities of Trump venerators clearly are oriented toward security from the threats posed by outsiders.

By focusing on four illustrative survey items, Figure 6.2 demonstrates pictorially that Trump venerators are not much different from liberals and especially from non-Trump-venerating conservatives on two central authoritarian items (the left half of the figure) but are substantially different on two securitarian items (the right half). Securitarian personality traits vary across political orientations much more than authoritarian personality traits do.

Bringing Politics In

When it comes to their personal lives, a key distinguishing feature of Trump venerators is their focus on security, not authority. Now it is time to move beyond the personal level to the political issues that are important to Trump venerators and the policies they most want enacted.

I gave respondents a list of nineteen issues and asked them to rank the four that were most important to them.[19] Table 6.4 contains the responses of the four groups. The most important issues for self-identified liberals are, in order, "racial justice, "health care," "women's rights," and "income inequality." There could be no better description of a group of people primarily concerned with the welfare of outsiders; that is, those who are not powerful, those who have traditionally been oppressed (women and racial minorities), and those who need better health care and higher incomes. Self-identified moderates list many of the same concerns though economic health makes an appearance on their list.[20] Like moderates, non-Trump-venerating conservatives list health care and economic health but instead of racial justice and income inequality they list national defense/security and immigration. Moving on to Trump venerators, unlike non-Trump-venerating

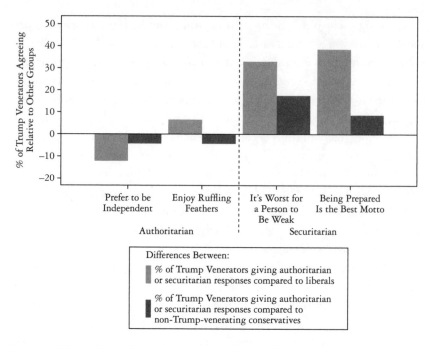

FIGURE 6.2 Authoritarian and Securitarian Personality Responses

TABLE 6.4 Political Problems Viewed as the Most Important

	Liberals	Moderates	Non-Trump-Venerating Conservatives	Trump Venerators
1.	Racial Justice	Health Care	National Defense	Immigration
2.	Health Care	Racial Justice	Immigration	National Defense
3.	Women's Rights	Economic Health	Health Care	Gun Rights
4.	Income Inequality	Income Inequality	Economic Health	Law and Order

Note:

The full list of issues from which respondents could choose was immigration, taxes, health care, the federal deficit, national defense/security, law and order, racial justice, excess government spending, income inequality, economic health, abortion, homosexuality, religious rights, women's rights, trade with other countries, lack of patriotism, welfare spending, gun rights/gun control, and government regulations on business conservatives, health care and economic health are not in their top four but guns and law and order are. In fact, just as liberals' list perfectly embodies caring for outsiders (racial minorities, women, people who are economically vulnerable) and concerns about insider power, Trump venerators' list perfectly captures concerns directed at outsider threats and preservation of insiders: immigration, national security, guns, and law and order.

By taking note of the average rankings of each group, it is possible to observe the issues for which differences in priorities are statistically significant. When this is done (results not shown), of the nineteen possible issues, Trump venerators had significantly different priorities from non-Trump-venerating conservatives on only four: Trump venerators assess health care and women's rights as significantly less important and law and order and guns as significantly more important.

It is one thing for people to identify the issues that are the most important to them; it is quite another to take a stance on what needs to be done to address each issue. Guns can be an important issue to people who want to protect gun rights but also to those who want to enact additional gun control legislation. Thus, I next turn to the portion of the survey that asked respondents to report whether they agreed or disagreed (strongly or not strongly) with twenty-one specific policy proposals (listed in Table 6.5). To ease interpretation, I have grouped these issues into three larger categories: economic issues such as reducing taxes on everyone; social issues such as legalizing gay marriage; and securitarian issues such as reducing immigration.

The large variations visible as we move from liberals to conservatives are no surprise since these differences are important parts of what it means to be a modern liberal or a conservative. Whether the issue pertains to the economy, to social norms, or to security, the differences from liberals to conservatives are typically massive, with many of the correlation coefficients over .5—a rarity in social science survey research. Seven-item indices for each of the three types of issues correlate with political orientation at between .6 and .7. Though important to note, finding that liberals are more favorable than conservatives to free college tuition, higher taxes on the rich, legalized marijuana, abortion rights, athlete protests during the national anthem, and immigration is like shooting fish in a barrel.

The more challenging question is whether issue stances are different for Trump venerators and for non-Trump-venerating conservatives. The final column of the table provides the answer. These coefficients indicate whether or not the two groups are meaningfully different from each other and the direction of any difference.

TABLE 6.5 Stances on Political Issues

	Liberals	Moderates	NTV Conservatives	Trump Venerators	Overall Correlation	NTVCs/TVs Correlation
Economic issues						
Government health care	79	48	26	15	-.57**	-.18**
Reduced welfare	12	29	63	76	.56**	.18**
Regulate business	65	40	28	15	-.44**	-.21**
Small government	20	42	71	76	.49**	NS
Lower taxes on all	36	56	80	82	.42**	NS
Higher taxes on rich	85	58	33	23	-.54**	-.13**
Free college tuition	77	50	33	21	-.52**	-.15**
Index of 7 Economic Issues					.69**	.24**
Social issues						
Abortion rights	86	58	21	26	-.54**	NS
Legalize gay marriage	82	55	24	21	-.55**	NS
Legalize marijuana	78	49	43	33	-.39**	NS
School prayer	20	44	72	80	.55**	.13**
Abstinence-only sex ed.	9	16	41	39	.43**	NS
Birth control	89	73	51	49	-.40**	NS
Legalize gambling	42	35	29	30	-.16**	NS
Index of 7 Social Issues					.62**	NS

Securitarian issues

					Overall Corr.	NTVCs/TVs Corr.
Death penalty	24	45	61	79	.44**	.22**
Reduce immigration	12	35	65	83	.61**	.23**
Protect gun rights	24	45	78	90	.58**	.24**
More defense spending	13	27	59	85	.58**	.33**
Anthem protests	74	32	15	11	-.60**	-.17***
Eavesdropping suspects	48	53	69	82	.26**	.19**
English as natl. language	37	60	85	93	.52**	.23**
Index of 7 Securitarian Issues					.70**	.35**

Note:

N=888

*=sign (p<.10); **=sign (p<.05); NS=not significant (p>.10)*

NTV Conservatives = non-Trump-venerating conservatives

Overall Correlation = the bivariate correlation between the item and the four categories

NTVCs/TVs Correlation = the bivariate correlation between non-Trump-venerating conservatives and Trump venerators

The numbers other than the correlations are the percentage agreeing with each statement.

On all seven of the economic items, Trump venerators are more conservative than non-Trump-venerating conservatives. They are more opposed to government playing a role in providing health care, more in favor of reducing welfare spending, more opposed to government regulations on business, and so on. The difference for all but two are statistically significant as is an additive index of all seven economic issues ($r = .24$; $p < .01$). Social issues are another story. Though liberals are significantly different from conservatives on classic social issues, Trump venerators are not significantly different from non-Trump-venerating conservatives. In fact, for only one of the seven issues (school prayer) is there a significant difference.

As I expected, the largest differences come in the area of securitarian issues that pertain to protection against physical or cultural intrusions—issues such as reducing immigration, protecting gun rights, and establishing English as a national language. Not only are conservatives more likely than liberals to take the securitarian position on all seven of these issues, but Trump venerators are significantly more likely than non-Trump-venerating conservatives to do so. The correlation for the index of all seven securitarian issues is .35 ($p < .01$) which is 46% larger than the correlation for the economic issues index ($r = .24$).

For readers uncomfortable with correlations, Figure 6.3 presents the average difference in issue positions between non-Trump-venerating

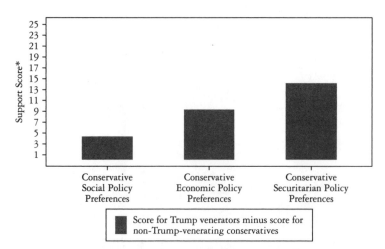

*Scores for each category range from 0 (strongly disagree with all conservative positions in the pertinent category) to 28 (strongly agree with all 7 conservative positions in the pertinent category)

FIGURE 6.3 Comparing the Issue Stances of Trump Venerators and Non-Trump-Venerating Conservatives

conservatives and Trump venerators for all three policy domains. These two groups differ only a little on social issues, more significantly on economic issues, and then dramatically on security matters. Across the seven securitarian issues, Trump venerators on average are more than 14 percentage points further to the right than conservatives who do not venerate Trump.

Yet another way to think about these relationships is that Trump venerators are more "conservative" than non-Trump-venerating conservatives on the vast majority of the twenty-one items but note the issues on which Trump venerators are more liberal, even if only by a little: abortion rights, abstinence-only sex education, and legalized gambling (legalized gay marriage and the ready availability of birth control pills are close). Relative to non-Trump-venerating conservatives, Trump venerators are significantly more conservative on economic issues where they prefer small, non-redistributive government and especially on securitarian issues where they prefer policies that prevent inroads into the cultural and physical security of insiders. They are not significantly more conservative than non-Trump-venerating conservatives on most social issues, such as abortion, sex education, and gay marriage. Security is at the core for Trump venerators both in terms of their personality (Table 6.3) and their policy preferences (Tables 6.4 and 6.5). Now it is time to look at broader sociopolitical concerns, first as they pertain to authoritarianism and then to securitarianism.

Sociopolitical (or Worldview) Authoritarianism

Traits relevant to personality take us only so far and specific political priorities and stances do not make it possible to uncover what is driving people to take those stances. Compared to non-Trump-venerating conservatives, Trump venerators do not have authoritarian personalities but do they have authoritarian preferences for organizing the social world? Regardless of their preferences on specific topics such as anthem protests, immigration, tax cuts, and school prayer, what are their deeper values, objectives, and worldviews?[21]

To find out, I analyzed items focusing not on authority in the family or in the workplace but in society overall. Instead of asking about preferences for how respondents wanted their personal lives to run, these items tap how respondents want their society to run. Unlike previous attempts that mention specific types of groups and topics such as atheists, feminists, and abortion rights, that are bound to elicit an ideologically lopsided response, I have made a conscious effort to balance the groups and issues in ways that will not render it a certainty that conservatives will appear more hostile and authoritarian. The result should be a truer assessment of general authoritarianism in worldviews.

Thus, instead of asking, as the RWA battery does, only whether the respondent believes the country needs a mighty leader who will "destroy radical new ways and sinfulness," I measure desire to submit to powerful leaders with two items: one more palatable to liberals and one more palatable to conservatives: To wit, "our country desperately needs a forceful mighty leader who will help the poor and save the Earth's environment" and "our country desperately needs a forceful mighty leader who will keep us safe from criminal elements and foreign powers." Likewise, instead of tapping aggression with items that refer to "smashing perversions" (another RWA item) I have one item that reads "drastic and aggressive action is required to protect our country from criminals, freeloaders, and threats from abroad" and a balancing item that reads "drastic and aggressive action is required to save the environment and spread this country's immense wealth around more fairly." The goal is to determine the degree to which people are fond of submitting to authority generally and not merely authority that blatantly tilts toward certain groups and actions.

It is no surprise that liberals agree on the need for a mighty, forceful leader if that leader is going to help the poor and the Earth's environment just as it is no surprise that conservatives agree on the need for a mighty, forceful leader if that leader is going to provide protection from criminal elements and foreign powers. When these items are combined into an additive index to provide some sort of ideological balance, that index is only weakly correlated ($r = .09$) with conservative views, and even this weak correlation could reflect the time the survey was conducted—when Donald Trump rather than Barack Obama was in the White House.[22]

More to the point, the difference in the two-item submissiveness index between Trump venerators and non-Trump-venerating conservatives is not significant even at a permissive level. Trump venerators may be more likely to submit to mighty leaders when those leaders provide security from outsiders but liberals are almost as likely to submit to mighty leaders who help the environment and redistribute income to the needy. The notion that Trump venerators are simply habitually more desirous of mighty leaders may not be true. They certainly were not pleased when President Obama took forceful, sometimes unilateral, executive actions. Why? Because Trump venerators were convinced Obama's policies and approaches abetted outsiders and they even harbored suspicions that Obama himself was an outsider. If Trump venerators enjoy submitting to authority—any authority—empirical research has yet to provide the evidence.

The two items assessing preferences for conventionalism at the societal level are "Society's existing norms and conventions are often misguided" and "The code of conduct passed down from olden days is badly out of place in the modern world." Table 6.6 presents the results. Both items are worded so that higher agreement indicates less support. Thus, 54% of liberals but only about 30% of conservatives agree that the code of conduct from olden days is badly out of place today. The correlations indicate that conservatives are different from liberals on each of the two items as well as the index of conventionalism but that none of the differences is significant when the analysis is restricted to Trump venerators and non-Trump-venerating conservatives. Compared to conservatives who do not venerate Donald Trump, Trump venerators appear no more and no less committed to society's conventions.

Finally, as with the submission-to-a-mighty-leader items, the societal-level aggression items were designed to counterbalance ideological biases, with one item referring to drastic and aggressive action to protect from outsider threats but the other referring to drastic and aggressive action to protect against the threats of environmental disaster and economic inequalities. The results indicate that liberals and conservatives both see a need for "drastic and aggressive" action, just for markedly different purposes: 83% of Trump venerators want drastic and aggressive action to protect from outsider threats but just 26% of Trump venerators want drastic and aggressive action to protect against insider threats such as the accumulation of too much wealth. On the other hand, only 18% of liberals agree that drastic and aggressive action is needed to protect the country from outsiders but 75% want aggressive action to save the Earth and redistribute income. Moreover, the differences between Trump venerators and non-Trump-venerating conservatives are significant, with Trump venerators being more supportive of aggressive action to protect against outsider threats but less supportive of aggressive action to address threats from income inequality. When I combine these two items, however, there is no statistically significant difference in the desire for drastic and aggressive action between non-Trump-venerating conservatives and Trump venerators.[23]

I am not satisfied with the aggression items I use, meaning conclusions should be drawn cautiously, but I will say this. Trump venerators may well be more aggressive. Previously referenced research by Ludeke, Klitgaard, and Vitriol, as well as by Womick et al. finds that they are—and remember, in Chapter 5 I picked up hints that Trump venerators were more likely to get in fights and lose their temper.[24] Moreover, on some occasions Trump rallies have included violent acts. Then again, the measures of aggression used in previous research are weak and the small number of Trump venerators who

TABLE 6.6 Authoritarian Societal Preferences

	Liberals	Moderates	NTV Conservatives	Trump Venerators	Overall Correlation	NTVCs/TVs Correlation
Submissive items						
Country needs a mighty leader to help poor	69	56	33	35	-.32*	NS
Country needs a mighty leader to keep us safe	33	39	72	84	.46**	.24**
Submissiveness index					.09*	NS
Conventionalism items						
Existing norms are often misguided	53	46	48	45	-.12**	NS
Old conduct code is out of place today	54	31	26	32	-.28**	NS
Conventionalism index					.26**	NS
Aggression items						
Aggressive action needed to protect country	18	34	63	83	.54**	.25**
Aggressive action needed to spread wealth	75	56	22	26	-.52**	-.15*
Aggression index					NS	NS

Note:

N=450

*=sign (p<.10); **=sign (p<.05); NS=not significant (p>.10)

NTV Conservatives = non-Trump-venerating conservatives

Overall Correlation = the bivariate correlation between the item and the four categories

NTVCs/TVs Correlation = the bivariate correlation between non-Trump-venerating conservatives and Trump venerators

The numbers other than the correlations are the percentage agreeing with the statement.

attend rallies may not be typical of the large number of Trump venerators who do not. In sum, I have not seen systematic documentation that Trump supporters are more aggressive once the target of the aggression is controlled but I am willing to believe they might be.

When I combine all six of these items into an overall index of authoritarian sociopolitical preferences (not shown), respondents on the right do tend to be more authoritarian but there is no significant difference between Trump venerators and non-Trump-venerating conservatives, though the coefficient is in the direction of Trump venerators being more authoritarian and is close to being significant. Pulling the evidence together, Trump venerators are not distinguished from non-Trump-venerating conservatives by authoritarian personality tendencies and only a little by authoritarian sociopolitical (or worldview) tendencies.

How Far Would You Go to Achieve Your Political Objectives?

In the survey, I presented respondents with a set of items that may or may not relate to aggression. Respondents were asked to "imagine a politician who was enacting policies that [they] believed with all [their] heart to be deeply wrong and harmful to the country" and then asked how far the respondent "would be willing to go to promote change or to register dissatisfaction?" I next presented respondents with a dozen actions and for each asked them to indicate whether they definitely would do it, probably would, probably would not, or definitely would not. I calculated the percentage of respondents who reported they would either probably or definitely engage in the act and compared these totals across the four political categories highlighted throughout this chapter. The results are in Table 6.7.

These activities run the gamut. Some (intentionally misplacing ballots and violating contribution limits) involve breaking the law, some (attending a potential riot or assisting in property damage) flirt with violence, and some (heckling and spreading false rumors) are at the least unbecoming, but others (engaging in a peaceful sit-in or communicating forcefully with officials) could be viewed as perfectly appropriate ways of registering political feelings. Still, all these items tap the concept of political action as opposed to passivity and thereby make it possible to test the belief that, compared to those with other political orientations, ardent Trump supporters are more willing to take action in order to achieve their political objectives.

TABLE 6.7 How Far Would You Go?

Act	Liberals	Moderates	NTV Conservatives	Trump Venerators	Overall Correlation	NTVCs/TVs Correlation
Curse the politician (69)	80	66	60	67	-.20**	NS
Avoid restaurant (64)	82	60	52	55	-.30**	NS
Send critical message (46)	62	40	34	44	-.21**	NS
Attend sit-in (42)	69	38	26	24	-.38**	NS
Refuse to serve (30)	47	29	16	21	-.31**	NS
Potentially violent rally (27)	36	21	21	29	-.14**	NS
Heckle the politician (24)	34	21	16	23	-.18**	NS
Spread untrue rumors (16)	18	11	16	22	NS	NS
Remove neighbor's sign (16)	17	17	13	17	NS	NS
Assist in property damage (14)	12	15	10	20	NS	.13*
Contribute over legal limit (14)	10	14	16	19	NS	NS
Purposely misplace ballots (24)	9	14	7	16	NS	NS

Disobeying a law is a mistake even if disobeying protects our country	43	33	26	30	-.18**	NS
If the choice is b/w security and democracy, go with security	13	26	46	59	.43**	.19**
Index of commitment to democracy					-.41**	-.18**

Note:

N=450

*=sign (p<.10); **=sign (p<.05); NS=not significant (p>.10)

NTV Conservatives = non-Trump-venerating conservatives

Overall Correlation = the bivariate correlation between the item and the four categories

NTVCs/TVs Correlation = the bivariate correlation between non-Trump-venerating conservatives and Trump venerators

The numbers other than the correlations are the percentage agreeing with the statement.

The numbers in parentheses are the overall percentage of the sample agreeing that they would engage in the acts.

To begin, note the overall tendency to engage in these various actions. To make this easier, the acts have been arranged, starting at the top, from those that people are most likely to engage in (privately cursing the problematic politician) to those that people are least likely to engage in (purposely misplacing a box of ballots to alter the election outcome) and the overall percentage of agreement with each act is listed in parentheses right after the act. Thus, 69% of Americans would curse a politician they thought to be deeply wrong and harmful to the country; 64% would avoid a restaurant owned by that politician, and so on. At the bottom end, only 11% report that they would purposely misplace a box of ballots. Though this is a small number, the fact that one out of nine Americans would illegally manipulate an election in this manner is noteworthy and disturbing.[25] Moving to other questionable acts, 14% would assist in property damage, 14% would make campaign contributions beyond the legal limit, and 16% would spread rumors they knew could well be false.

How does the willingness to engage in these actions vary from liberals to conservatives? As of April of 2019, conservatives were not significantly more likely than liberals to engage in any act but liberals were significantly more likely than conservatives to engage in seven of them. Relative to conservatives, liberals were especially likely to refuse to serve the problematic politician, to avoid patronizing a restaurant owned by the politician, to engage in a sit-in, and to send critical messages. If any ideological group was more action oriented toward an offending politician it was liberals.

Of course, the willingness of liberals to engage in these various acts is likely traceable to the fact that Trump was in office at the time of the survey, making it painfully easy for liberals to imagine "a politician who was enacting policies they believed with all [their] heart to be deeply wrong and harmful to the country."[26] Even if the Trump presidency is the explanation, these results still contradict the popular, authoritarian-derived argument that conservatives and especially Trump supporters are particularly inclined to engage in decisive action. The evidence instead appears to suggest that political assertiveness varies according to context, with people who feel they are on the political outside looking in being more likely to take actions.

Not all acts are equal, however, and most observers would agree that the acts toward the bottom of the list cross moral and legal lines and are inconsistent with basic democratic values. These items raise the larger issue of whether ardent Trump supporters are more likely than those in other political groups to sacrifice democratic principles in order to further their political agenda. Table 6.7 provides a hint that this might be the case. Even though less than a fifth of all Trump venerators say they would contribute money beyond the legal limit or intentionally misplace a box of ballots, they are more likely than any other group to do so. Sixteen percent of Trump venerators report that they would misplace the ballots whereas only 9% of liberals (and just 7% of non-Trump-venerating conservatives) do; 19% of Trump venerators reported that they would contribute beyond the legal limit whereas only 10% of liberals agree that they would. These differences are not statistically significant but would be with a larger sample.

Focusing specifically on the two groups of primary interest, Trump venerators on the whole are not more likely than non-Trump-venerating conservatives to engage in assertive political actions. Only one of the twelve actions generates a significant difference between those two groups (Trump venerators are significantly more likely than non-Trump-venerating conservatives to say they would "assist in inflicting minor property damage during a riot"). Trump venerators' relative endorsement of an act does appear to increase with its nastiness and illegality—a finding that is not to be trivialized since some of these actions are egregious enough that it would only take a few people—or even one person—to create serious problems.

The term "authoritarian" often refers not to someone with a desire for an all-powerful leader but rather to someone who lacks an appreciation of democratic principles. This usage is unfortunate because the two sentiments are very different and even people who do not crave strong authority figures often lack the will or knowledge to do what is necessary to maintain a system as challenging, delicate, and inconsistent with human inclinations as a democracy.[27] Being cavalier about democracy is not the same thing as wanting a domineering leader. This being said, how committed to democracy are ardent Trump supporters and how does their level of commitment compare to others?

Two survey items provide insight: "Disobeying democratic laws even if doing so protects our country from threats is a mistake" and "If a country had to choose between being secure and being democratic, being secure would probably be the way to go." These two items are balanced in that when it comes to supporting democratic principles one is worded positively and one is worded negatively. Unfortunately, they are not balanced from the standpoint of the situation being presented as the alternative to democracy. The items are designed to see whether securitarians and not unitarians can be tempted away from democracy in that both items mention protection and security.[28] It may be that unitarians are willing to sacrifice democracy in order to help the downtrodden or prevent ecological catastrophe but tests of these possibilities will have to await additional data, though political scientists Matthew Graham and Milan Svolik present evidence that a lack of support for democratic rules and norms does indeed extend to both sides of the political divide.[29]

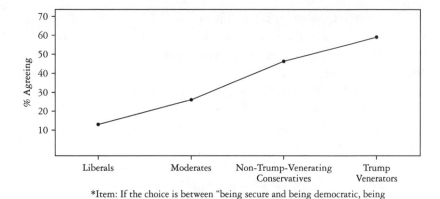

*Item: If the choice is between "being secure and being democratic, being secure would be the way to go."

FIGURE 6.4 Commitment to Democracy and Political Orientation

Table 6.7 presents the results and they indicate that when security is at issue, a remarkable number of Trump venerators are willing to trade in democracy. For example, 59% of Trump venerators agree that "a country should choose security over democracy" but only 13% of liberals do—and Trump venerators' level of agreement on this item is significantly higher (13 percentage points higher) than non-Trump-venerating conservatives (see Figure 6.4).

Trump venerators are also significantly less likely than liberals to say democratic laws that might weaken the country's security should still be obeyed (though in this regard they are little different from moderates and non-Trump-venerating conservatives). An additive index of these two items, structured so that higher values indicate a commitment to democracy in the face of security threats indicates clearly that Trump venerators score significantly lower, even than non-Trump-venerating conservatives. These results do not allow us to say that Trump venerators are less committed to democracy than liberals are; however, they do allow us to say that a strong majority of Trump venerators would sacrifice democratic values in a heartbeat if doing so led to greater security.[30]

Securitarian Societal Dispositions and Veneration of Donald Trump

When it comes to structuring society in an authoritarian fashion, the desires of Trump venerators are not much different from those of non-Trump-venerating conservatives (see Table 6.6), but I predict there will be more substantial differences in desires to structure society in a securitarian fashion. Six survey items test a securitarian worldview—three are worded positively and three negatively: "There are many better ways for our government to spend money than on defense," "A central goal for our country is to become so strong that outsiders will realize it does not make sense to attack us," "The biggest danger to our society is not criminals and foreign countries but economic inequality and the concentration of power in the hands of a few," "If we are not vigilant we will quickly become victimized by criminals, immigrants, and the power of foreign countries," "Just about the worst thing for a country is to be perceived as weak," and "It is possible for a country to be truly great without being militarily strong." These items capture respondents' desires for their country to be vigilant and powerful in order to deter outsider threats. The battery touches only lightly on policies (these were covered in Table 6.5) and focuses on broader, societal principles such as a country being strong, being vigilant, and being prepared—anything to prevent insiders from being in a vulnerable posture.

These items correlate strongly with ideological orientations and do an excellent job of distinguishing between Trump venerators and conservatives who are not Trump venerators. Consider the item stating, "If we are not vigilant we will quickly become victimized by criminals, immigrants, and foreign countries." Only 18% of liberals agree, but 88% of Trump supporters do—a throw of 70 percentage points. These results fit perfectly with what I posit to be the core, politically relevant division of human beings: Some think society needs to be vigilant in order to prevent the cultural or physical intrusion of outsiders such as criminals, immigrants, and foreign potentates; others do not see outsiders as threats and in fact are more concerned about securing protections from powerful insiders who have too much wealth and influence.

Relative to liberals and moderates, conservatives overall are on board with securitarianism but note that all six of the items in Table 6.8 also distinguish Trump venerators from non-Trump-venerating conservatives. As can be seen in Figure 6.5, Trump venerators are 16 percentage points more likely than non-Trump-venerating conservatives to agree that "if we are not vigilant we will quickly be victimized" by outsiders, 15 percentage points more likely to agree that "a central goal for our country should be to become so strong" that we deter outsiders, and 12 percentage points more likely to agree that "just about the worst thing for a country is to be perceived as weak." The index of all six items generates the highest coefficients we have seen (r = .30) for distinguishing between Trump venerators and non-Trump-venerating conservatives. This is no mean accomplishment since non-Trump-venerating conservatives are hardly unsympathetic to security concerns.

TABLE 6.8 Securitarian Societal Preferences

Securitarian items	Liberals	Moderates	NTV Conservatives	Trump Venerators	Overall Correlation	NTVCs/TVs Correlation
Better ways for country to spend than defense	76	49	22	14	-.54**	-.19**
Country's central goal should be strength	29	50	73	88	.50**	.25**
Biggest threat not outsiders but inequality	81	56	35	31	-.47**	-.10*
If we are not vigilant we will be victims	18	36	72	88	.58**	.23**
Worst for a country to be seen as weak	32	48	76	88	.45**	.19**
Country can be great w/o military strength	65	41	31	21	-.42**	-.18**
Index of securitarian items					.68**	.30**

Note:

N=888

*=sign (p<.10); **=sign (p<.05); NS=not significant (p>.10)

NTV Conservatives = non-Trump-venerating conservatives

Overall Correlation = the bivariate correlation between the item and the four categories

NTVCs/TVs Correlation = the bivariate correlation between non-Trump-venerating conservatives and Trump venerators

The numbers other than the correlations are the percentage agreeing with the statement.

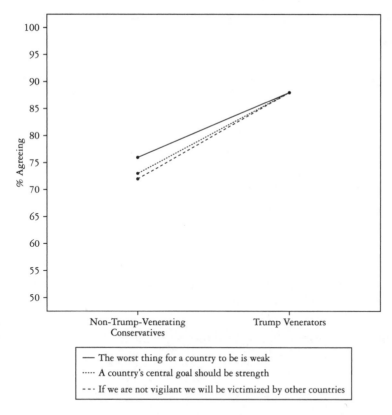

FIGURE 6.5 Securitarian Worldview Items and Political Orientation

Putting Securitarianism in Context

Before concluding this chapter, two final empirical points are in order. First, Adorno and his colleagues set out to study a personality trait, but more and more, the focus of the research stream they started has been on societal rather than personal preferences. Instead of only personal items such as "I see myself as someone who is open to new experiences," most batteries also include many items asking how respondents feel about society's treatment of, for example, atheists, feminists, and animal rights advocates. In contrast, the authoritarian and securitarian items used here are either clearly personal (e.g., "I would rather be thought of as nice than strong") or clearly societal ("a central goal for our country should be to become so strong that outsiders will realize it does not make sense to attack us").

One of the benefits of this approach is that it makes it possible to determine the extent to which people's personalities connect to their societal preferences. Are the people who are most concerned about security against outsiders in their personal lives the same ones who are most eager for society as a whole to be secure in the face of outsider threats or do people separate their personal preferences from their societal preferences? In order to be a societal securitarian is it necessary to be a personal securitarian?

To find out, I correlated the compilation of the six securitarian personality items in Table 6.3 with the six securitarian societal items in Table 6.8. The coefficient is .56, indicating that these two concepts are strongly and positively related but that they are far from identical. It is possible for a person who does not take personal security all that seriously to place a great deal of importance on societal security. Not surprisingly, people's political orientation correlates more strongly with societal preferences ($r = .67$) than with personal traits ($r = .38$), but note that even the purely personal traits have a great deal to do with ideological orientation and Trump veneration.[31]

Because their wording is nearly parallel, a particular pair of items allows for an even more direct test of the relationship between personal and societal preferences. The personality item is "Projecting weakness is just about the worst thing a person could do," and the societal item is "Just about the worst thing for a country is to be perceived as weak." These items correlate with each other at .48 and, again, the societal item correlates more strongly with ideological orientation ($r = .45$) than does the personal item ($r = .27$).[32] When they are used to differentiate Trump venerators from non-Trump-venerating conservatives, however, the personal item actually is just as powerful ($r = .21$ for personal and $r = .19$ for societal). Relative to other conservatives, Trump venerators are distinguished by a belief that national weakness is bad but the more interesting finding is that they are distinguished from other conservatives to an even great extent by a belief that personal weakness is bad. In most cases, societal preferences are much more likely than personal preferences to map onto political ideology so the fact that personal strength is so important to Trump venerators is an important illustration of the personal affecting the political. Concerns about personal weakness and strength translate into Trump support to a degree that far outstrips the connection of most personal concerns to political orientations and fit nicely with Trump's own fixation on projecting personal strength and dominance.

The second empirical point is that the analyses so far have looked at only two variables at a time, making it impossible to know whether effects hold up when many of them are analyzed together. For example, we have found that Trump venerators are older than non-Trump-venerating conservatives and also that they score higher on an index of securitarian personality traits such as "being prepared for threats is the best life motto," but maybe older people are more likely to have securitarian personalities, making age the key variable and securitarianism merely spurious—or maybe both effects go away when gender, religiosity, and urban/rural are introduced into the mix.

I tested these possibilities by running multivariate regression analyses that allow explanatory variables to compete with each other to explain variance. In this way, we can determine which if any of the concepts matter when the effects of the others are controlled. Since regression tables can be off-putting, I relegated them to an appendix at the end of the chapter (see Tables 6.1A to 6.4A) and merely summarize the results here. I selected four models that I thought would be of most interest. Since current understanding of the differences between the political left and right are fairly well developed and since teasing apart Trump venerators from non-Trump-venerating conservatives is the real challenge, the dependent variable in all the models is whether the respondent is a Trump venerator or a non-Trump-venerating conservative. Liberal and moderate respondents are not included in the regressions.[33]

The first model (Table 6.1A) starts with the core demographics—age, race, education, income, sex, urban/rural, and church attendance—and then adds two variables: two-item indices on a submissive personality (for example, "I like it when others make decisions and shape my life") and on a securitarian personality (for example, "Projecting weakness is about the worst thing a person could do"). The interesting finding here is that, with all these variables included, only two demonstrate any ability to distinguish Trump venerators from non-Trump-venerating conservatives: age and a securitarian personality. Even when other demographic variables are taken into consideration, compared to non-Trump-venerating conservatives, Trump venerators are older and they are more likely to value personal strength and to worry about evil people. This means that if one individual is fifty-two years old and has securitarian personality traits and another is also fifty-two years old but does not have securitarian traits, the securitarian is significantly more likely to be a Trump venerator. A securitarian personality is not merely a stand-in for age or any other demographic variable. Submissiveness, on the other hand—the central element of an authoritarian personality—is not statistically significant when other variables are controlled.[34]

The next three tables shift the focus from personality to worldview. In the first, the six-item securitarian societal (not personality) index introduced earlier in this chapter (see Table 6.8) was included along with the more established measures of authoritarianism to see whether securitarianism offers explanatory power beyond existing measures. If it does, it will be statistically significant even when the established measures are entered alongside it. In Table 6.2A, the securitarian battery is included along with a sixteen-item right-wing authoritarianism (RWA) index. The key finding here is that when they are both included in the same model, the securitarian battery is significant ($p < .05$) whereas the RWA battery is not, even at the .10 level (none of the demographic variables, even age, achieve significance in this model).

Even if in head-to-head tests the RWA battery had performed better at identifying Trump venerators, it includes so many diverse concepts and double-barreled items that it is difficult to know the reason for the high correlations. Writing survey questions that correlate with the liberal-conservative spectrum—or even with Trump supporters and Trump opponents—is not difficult. Item references to concepts such as communism and atheism will do the trick. As political psychologist Stanley Feldman notes, the crucial challenge is to draft items that reveal the psychological processes generating the relationship and on this front the RWA battery comes up short.[35]

The four-item child-rearing battery does not achieve significance when the securitarian political battery is included alongside it (see Table 6.4A) but Social Dominance Orientation (SDO) does (see Table 6.3A). Though its influence is smaller than that for the securitarian battery (beta of .15 as opposed to .25), SDO performs the best of the older measures in distinguishing between Trump venerators and non-Trump-venerating conservatives. This fact fits nicely with my theoretical argument in that SDO stresses groups and hierarchy in a fashion that meshes well with my vision of insiders and outsiders.

The key point is that the securitarian index does not wither away when included in the same models as older, established measures. In fact, the older measures are the ones that wane when entered with the securitarian battery. To the extent that the established authoritarian batteries distinguish between Trump venerators and non-Trump-venerating conservatives, it is partially because they are related to the securitarian battery.[36]

Conclusion

Consider the following four survey items:

1. I sometimes like it when others shape my life and make decisions for me.
2. I think a good deal about the security of my family.
3. What this country needs is a mighty, forceful leader.
4. Our country will be destroyed if we don't put the security of our own people first.

The first two are personal, with references to "I" and the last two are societal, with references to "country"; items 1 and 3 deal with authority and items 2 and 4 deal with security. As valuable and creative as previous work has been, the measurement strategies they employed often mix the personal and the societal as well as the desires for authority and for security. In this chapter, I kept these four types of items separate, thereby making it possible to identify the pivotal motivation of avid Trump supporters.[37]

That motivation turns out to be security, both at the societal level and, to a surprising degree, at the personal level. Trump's core supporters believe that their country's central goal should be strength but they also believe that being prepared for threats is the best motto for living their own life and that personal weakness is about the worst thing imaginable for an individual. The reason they revered Donald Trump was his deep concern for outsider threats; he fought to preserve the cultural and physical integrity of insiders; he put America first and did not apologize for doing so; he knew the value of strength; and he recognized that the world abounds with dangers requiring vigilant deterrence lest outsiders get the upper hand. The last thing many Trump venerators want is to be forced to "obey authority at the expense of personal freedom";[38] the first thing they want is to be secure from outsider threats.[39]

Confusion on this point is understandable because authoritarianism and securitarianism have often overlapped. For much of our time as homo sapiens and even before, authorities were our primary source of security. In a dangerous world where protection was paramount, troop members looked to the alpha male, serfs looked to the vassal, tribal members looked to the chief, and subjects looked to the king or queen. For much of human history, authority and protection were inseparable. Eventually, however, protection from outsiders came at too steep a price for some and a distinctive phenotype developed that was as averse to centralized, insider power as securitarians are to outsider threats.

Moreover, times change and, much to the chagrin of securitarians, the primary purpose of authority figures is no longer solely the preservation of the dominant insider culture. In fact, from a securitarian perspective, modern authorities are disturbingly prone to sympathizing with outsiders, to tolerating untoward levels of in-migration; to allowing supra-national entities to supplant local control; to ignoring the needs of the military and police; and to giving so many rights and privileges to outsiders that members of the core cultural group feel as though they no longer belong in their own country. From a securitarian perspective, authorities in the United Kingdom stood by and watched as Brussels diminished British sovereignty, paving the way for hordes of outsiders to swarm their country and irreversibly weaken

British culture. From a securitarian perspective, decades of authorities in the United States pursued globalism, multiculturalism, foreign aid, immigration, and multinational trade agreements without giving a fig for how vulnerable these tactics made traditional white America. To securitarians, most modern leaders care more about outsiders than insiders, which is why securitarians so venerate the rare leader who unflinchingly does not.

Appendix

TABLE 6.1A Regression with Submissive and Securitarian Personality Indices

Variable	"B"	S.E.	Beta	t	significance
constant	1.970	.211		9.331	.001
age	.005	.002	.159	2.81	.005
white	-.010	.063	-.009	-.165	.869
education	-.019	.018	-.054	-1.006	.315
income	-.001	.001	-.058	-1.095	.274
female	-.047	.054	-.047	-.877	.381
rural	-.006	.056	-.006	-.104	.918
church attendance	-.036	.054	-.036	-.663	.508
submissive personality (2 items)	.020	.019	.060	1.038	.300
securitarian personality (2 items)	.041	.019	.120	2.122	.035

$N = 350; R^2 = .07; F = 3.03 (p<.01)$

TABLE 6.2A Regression with RWA and Securitarian (Societal) Indices

Variable	"B"	S.E.	Beta	t	significance
constant	1.764	.297		5.938	.001
age	.001	.002	.021	.256	.798
white	.016	.091	.013	.171	.865
education	-.040	.025	-.117	-1.608	.110
income	-.002	.001	-.108	-1.515	.132
female	-.049	.071	-.049	-.689	.492
rural	.032	.075	.031	.431	.667
church attendance	-.147	.073	-.148	-.2.018	.045
RWA (16 items)	.008	.005	.128	1.581	.116
securitarian society (6 items)	.023	.012	.181	2.007	.046

$N = 187; R^2 = .14; F = 3.20 (p<.01)$

TABLE 6.3A Regression with SDO and Securitarian (Societal) Indices

Variable	"B"	S.E.	Beta	t	significance
constant	1.241	.335		3.704	.001
age	.004	.003	.152	1.712	.089
white	−.052	.086	−.047	−.604	.547
education	.011	.027	.030	.394	.694
income	.001	.001	−.032	−.426	.671
female	−.094	.077	−.094	−1.234	.219
rural	−.070	.078	−.069	−.898	.371
church attendance	.073	.075	.073	.075	.331
SDO (12 items)	.013	.007	.150	1.955	.052
securitarian society (6 items)	.032	.012	.251	2.767	.006

$N = 161; R^2 = .16; F = 3.27 (p<.01)$

TABLE 6.4A Regression with the Child-Rearing and Securitarian (Societal) Indices

Variable	"B"	S.E.	Beta	t	significance
constant	2.043	.319		6.405	.001
age	.001	.002	.024	.290	.772
white	.001	.094	.001	.007	.994
education	−.043	.025	−.127	−1.739	.084
income	−.002	.001	−.108	−1.503	.134
female	−.050	.072	−.051	−.705	.482
rural	.023	.075	.022	.301	.764
church attendance	−.127	.072	−.128	−1.758	.080
Child-rearing (4 items)	−.006	.033	−.012	−.170	.865
securitarian society (6 items)	.032	.010	.249	3.106	.002

$N = 187; R^2 = .13; F = 2.28 (p<.01)$

| The Many Faces
of Trump Veneration

I MAGINE A LARGE number of Trump venerators in an arena, eagerly awaiting
a rally headlined by Trump himself. They had to arrive early to ensure
getting a seat so to pass the time they decide to distribute themselves around
the facility according to the political issues important to them. Those most
concerned with abortion go to one part of the hall; those most concerned with
gun rights to another, and so on. What would the arena look like?[1]

Securitarians, Social Warriors, the Economically Concerned, and Tea Partiers

The April 2019 survey makes it possible to answer this question because,
in addition to a representative sample, it contained an oversample of
Trump supporters. Given that most Americans are not fervent supporters
of Donald Trump, nationally representative samples typically contain too
few Trump venerators to divide meaningfully into subcategories. Combining
the oversample with the representative sample leaves 669 individuals who
strongly agreed that Donald Trump was "one of the very best presidents in
the entire history of our country"—a number that is sufficient to identify the
different types of Trump venerators. Another feature of the survey was that
it presented respondents with nineteen issues and asked them to identify the
one that was the most important to them. I used this "most important issue"

response to place Trump venerators into various categories and, figuratively, into various parts of the arena.

As the left side of Table 7.1 indicates, when this strategy is adopted, the largest group by a comfortable margin is those who identify immigration as the most important issue: 28% of all Trump venerators. Those mentioning national defense/security as the most important issue constitute the only other group of reasonable size at 19.4%. Groups prioritizing religious rights, guns, abortion, economic health, and health care each compose between 5% and 10% of all attendees, and groups mentioning the federal deficit, lack of patriotism, and trade constitute less than 2%. Trump venerators citing racial justice, income inequality, women's rights, and homosexuality as the most important issue facing the country are even smaller at less than 1%.[2]

The number of groups resulting from this approach seems unwieldy so somebody suggests combining groups that prioritize similar types of issues. Discussion ensues since there are countless ways of clustering issues. The ultimate solution is that those attaching most importance to immigration, national security, guns, law and order, or a lack of patriotism will go to one corner of the hall. They bond and quickly start referring to each other as securitarians. Those seeing religious rights, abortion, or homosexuality as the most important group of issues facing the country decamp to another corner where they call themselves social warriors.[3] Those mentioning economic health, health care, or trade as the most important go to a third corner where they quickly realize that they are united by their abiding economic concerns and a general perception that the economy and their own situation in it are fragile. Finally, those citing government spending, taxes, government regulations, welfare spending, or the federal deficit move to the fourth corner and proudly call themselves "tea partiers."

This fourfold categorization excludes only a few wayward Trump venerators who insist that the most important issue facing the country is either racial justice, income inequality, or women's rights. Though legitimate responses, those on the political left will no doubt find it baffling that anyone according supreme importance to racial justice, economic equality, or women's rights could also claim that Donald Trump was one of the very best presidents in the entire history of the country; nonetheless, seventeen individuals did just that. Given their small numbers and novel politics, these "enigmas" do not form a caucus of their own.

This fourfold categorization scheme seems logical. Immigration, national security, guns, law and order, and patriotism are at the core of securitarianism

TABLE 7.1 Most Important Issue to Trump Venerators

From Top to Bottom		Grouped	
Issue	% Identifying	Issue	% Identifying
Immigration	28.0	**Securitarians**	
National defense/security	19.4	Immigration	28.0
Religious rights	8.8	National defense/security	19.4
Guns	8.0	Guns	8.0
Abortion	6.0	Law and order	2.7
Economic health	5.7	Lack of patriotism	1.2
Healthcare	5.1	(total	59.3)
Government spending	3.5		
Taxes	3.0	**Social Warriors**	
Law and order	2.7	Religious rights	8.8
Government regulations	1.7	Abortion	6.0
Welfare spending	1.5	Homosexuality	.1
Federal deficit	1.4	(total	14.9)
Lack of patriotism	1.2		
Trade with other nations	1.2	**Economically Concerned**	
Racial justice	.9	Economic health	5.7
Income inequality	.9	Health care	5.1
Women's rights	.8	Trade with other nations	1.2
Homosexuality	.1	(total	12.0)
(total	99.9)		
		Tea Partiers	
		Government spending	3.5
		Taxes	3.0
		Government regulations	1.7
		Welfare spending	1.5
		Federal deficit	1.4
		(total	11.1)
		Enigmas	
		Racial justice	.9
		Income inequality	.9
		Women's rights	.8
		(total	2.6)

N = 661

as I have been using the term; religious rights, abortion, and gay marriage are hot button social issues; those who mention the economy, health care, or trade likely have general anxieties about the economy; and those who cite government spending, taxes, regulations, welfare, and the deficit have a more focused, tea-party-like interest in the economy that is not driven by economic anxiety but rather by a desire for small government and the adoption of somewhat libertarian ideals.

Given these procedures, how populated are each of the corners of the arena? The numbers on the right side of Table 7.1, presented graphically in Figure 7.1, indicate that the securitarian corner is the most crowded. Consistent with my claims, a clear majority of Trump's most earnest supporters—nearly 60%—are in the securitarian corner. More often than not, the issue they mentioned was either immigration or national defense but some cited other issues having to do with personal, familial, and group security.

Still, 40% of Trump venerators are in one of the other corners of the arena. Though most Trump venerators accord the highest importance to a security issue, not all of them do. About 15% are social warriors in the sense that they identify religious or social issues as most important, 12% mention generic economic concerns, and another 11% cite tea-party-type issues

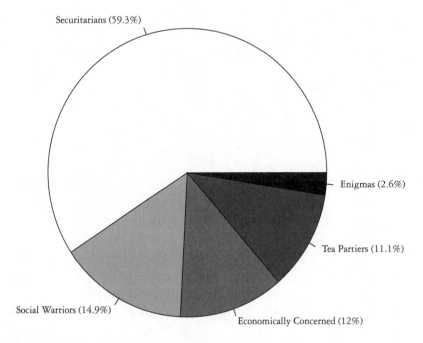

FIGURE 7.1 Types of Trump Venerators

centering primarily on an aversion to big government and an attraction to free market economics.

In the two previous chapters, I compared the average Trump venerator to the average liberal, the average moderate, and the average non-Trump-venerating conservative. This approach brought Trump venerators into focus as it showed that compared to those with other political orientations, they focus heavily on securing protection from outsiders. Comparing group averages leaves the inaccurate impression that all members of each group are functionally the same, making it impossible to identify variations within each group. In this chapter, I set aside liberals, moderates, and non-Trump-venerating conservatives to investigate the four types of Trump venerators. I ascertain the demographic, psychological, personality, and attitudinal correlates of each type because it is unlikely that all Trump venerators are demographically identical and share the same concerns.

In order to communicate the degree to which securitarians, social warriors, the economically concerned, and tea partiers are different from each other, I present each group's means (averages) on a wide range of variables (see Tables 7.1A to 7.4A in the appendix to this chapter). I also calculate the degree to which each subgroup of Trump venerators is different from all Trump venerators not in that particular group. To do this, I use bivariate correlations, which essentially become a difference in means test, to determine whether each group is significantly different from all other Trump venerators.[4] For example, for each variable, such as percentage white, I compute the difference between securitarian Trump venerators and all other Trump venerators and check to see whether that difference is statistically significant. I then compute the difference between social warrior Trump venerators and all other Trump venerators and check to see if that difference is statistically significant. Then I do the same for those Trump venerators best classified as "economically concerned" and finally for the tea party group of Trump venerators. In this way, these analyses parallel those in earlier chapters except that the groups are no longer liberals, moderates, non-Trump-venerating conservatives, and Trump venerators but rather securitarian Trump venerators, social warrior Trump venerators, economically concerned Trump venerators, and tea-party Trump venerators.

So as not to swamp readers in a sea of numbers, rather than include all the findings in the main text, for each variable I present summary tables indicating whether differences for each group are significant and if so whether that particular group is higher or lower than all other Trump venerators. Then, as some readers will want to know the exact percentages in each category, the actual correlation coefficients, and the level of statistical significance, I provide this information in four tables in the appendix—Tables 7.1A to 7.4A.

To illustrate, consider the first rows of Table 7.2. The row for percentage white is blank, meaning that those Trump venerators who are securitarians, social warriors, economically concerned, and tea partiers do not differ much in their racial composition. The mean for one type is never significantly higher or lower than the mean for all Trump venerators not of that type. Income, found in the second row, generates a different pattern. Compared to all other Trump venerators, securitarians are doing better financially. Conversely and not surprisingly, compared to all other Trump venerators, those who are economically concerned are doing significantly less well financially. The incomes of social warriors and of tea partiers are not significantly different from that of other Trump venerators.

If the summary of patterns provided in Table 7.2 is insufficient, Table 7.1A in the appendix indicates that the percentage white varies from 81 for economically concerned to 87 for social warriors and that the percent making more than $50,000/year varies from 39% for the economically concerned group to 60% for securitarians.[5] It also indicates that when it comes to race, no group of Trump venerators is significantly different from the others (so all are labeled "NS"). In terms of income, securitarians are only modestly higher than other Trump venerators (r = .07; p < .10), but the economically concerned group is solidly lower than other Trump venerators (r = -.10; p < .05).[6]

Demographics, Personality, Emotionality, and the Types of Trump Venerators

With these explanatory comments and illustrations out of the way, we turn to the results themselves. First, what do they say about the largest type of Trump venerator, the securitarians? Given their focus on security, logic might expect them to be particularly vulnerable—financially precarious, uneducated, older, rural, and perhaps seeking comfort in religion. Is this true?

Mostly not. Some of the most notable results pertain to the areas where securitarians are *not* any different from other Trump venerators. For example, they are not significantly different in terms of racial composition, education,

TABLE 7.2 Demographic, Personality, and Emotionality Correlates of Trump Venerators

Traits	Securitarians/ Other Trump Venerators	Social Warriors/ Other Trump Venerators	Economically Concerned/ Other Trump Venerators	Tea Partiers/ Other Trump Venerators
Demographics				
% white				
income	higher		lower	
education				
% rural or small town		higher		
church attendance	lower	higher		
% born again	lower	higher		lower
% female				
mean age	higher		lower	lower
Political involvement				
political knowledge (0–4)	higher		lower	lower
% interested in politics	higher		lower	
% registered to vote	higher			lower
Personality				
extraverted			higher	
quarrelsome	lower	higher		
dependable	higher			
anxious	lower		higher	
open				
set in ways		higher		
frustrated	lower		higher	
pessimistic	lower		higher	
Emotions				
bitter about treatment		higher		
angry about status	lower		higher	
resent wealthy	lower		higher	higher
resent educated	lower		higher	
socially unfulfilled	lower		higher	higher
bothered by flyswatter				
bothered by glass eye	lower		higher	

blank = not significantly different
lower = significantly lower
higher = significantly higher

percentage female, and percentage living in rural areas. To be sure, they are different on a few demographic variables—though often in surprising ways. Relative to other Trump venerators, securitarians are doing well financially (60% report income levels of more than $50,000/year) and they are less religious (only 37% claim to go to church even a couple of times a month). They are older, however, with a mean age of fifty-seven.[7]

The other three types of Trump venerators follow more predictable patterns. Social warriors are significantly more likely to live in rural areas, to go to church regularly, and to consider themselves born again (78%). The "economically concerned" are significantly more likely to be young and not well off (only 39% make $50,000/year). Tea partiers are young and not religious. Remember that for all these results, the comparison group is other Trump venerators. Securitarians and tea partiers may be less religious than other Trump venerators are but they are still more religious than liberals and moderates.

Though not demographic, I include in Table 7.2 three variables tapping involvement in politics. The first is a measure of political knowledge. In the survey, I asked respondents to take a quiz consisting of four multiple choice items: the name of the (then) vice president (Mike Pence), the level of congressional support needed to override a presidential veto (two-thirds), the party that held majority control in the US House of Representatives at the time of the survey (the Democrats), and the institution whose responsibility it is to determine constitutionality (the Supreme Court). These civics-style questions have been subject to appropriate challenge as of late but they still offer a rough indication of people's level of basic political knowledge.[8] I measure interest in politics by agreement with a single item asking whether respondents are interested in politics "most of the time"; I measure involvement by whether respondents report that they are registered to vote.[9]

In terms of political knowledge, the pattern across types of Trump venerators is interesting. Securitarian Trump venerators are significantly more knowledgeable than all other Trump venerators—getting three of the four items correct on average.[10] Securitarian Trump venerators are also significantly more likely to report being interested in politics and to be registered to vote.[11] The types at the other end tend to be the economically concerned (lower than all other Trump venerators in political interest and involvement) and tea partiers (lower in knowledge and involvement). Between being the largest component group of the Republican Party and being the most informed, active, and interested, it may be difficult to dislodge or to work around securitarians (more on this in the next chapter).

What about personality traits? In Chapter 5, we found that compared to conservatives who do not venerate Donald Trump, those who do, are significantly more extraverted, conscientious, and open to new experiences—and they are significantly less neurotic. When the analysis is limited only to Trump venerators, how do the various types compare to each other? The answer is in the middle portion of Table 7.2.

Personality differences across the four types of Trump venerators are modest but worth noting. The two most distinctive types are the securitarians and the "economically concerned." Tea partiers and social warriors, on the other hand, differ from all other Trump venerators on only one trait and that is that social warriors are significantly more "set in their ways" (58%). Compared to other Trump venerators, those with economic concerns are more quarrelsome, more anxious, more frustrated, and, not surprisingly, more pessimistic. Securitarians are just the opposite, reporting that they are significantly less likely to be quarrelsome, anxious, frustrated, and pessimistic. (They also claim to be significantly more dependable.) Compared to securitarians, economically concerned Trump venerators are twice as likely to be anxious (34% to 17%) and nearly three times as likely to be frustrated (34% to 12%)

These patterns continue when attention shifts to negative emotions. Relative to other Trump venerators, those who are economically concerned are socially unfulfilled, disgust-sensitive, angry about their "status in the world," and resentful of those who are wealthy but do not have to do "physical labor" as well as of those who have lots of education and live on the coasts. Securitarians are the Trump venerator type that is the least angry, resentful, unfulfilled, and disgust-sensitive. Only 11% of securitarians say they are socially unfulfilled and in need of a better support network. By way of a broader comparison, 42% of liberals—nearly four times the figure for securitarians—report being socially unfulfilled.[12]

In sum, economic concerns appear to exact a psychological toll and push some individuals toward ardent support of politicians such as Donald Trump. At the same time, bear in mind that those individuals in the "economically concerned" category—some of whom at one time may also have been attracted to candidates such as Bernie Sanders—constitute only 12% of all fervent Trump supporters. Those Trump venerators who prioritize security from outsiders constitute the clear majority and, compared to all other Trump venerators, report themselves to be fulfilled and emotionally positive. Even compared to other Trump venerators, securitarians are a happy bunch. Given that all Trump venerators are likely to be more upbeat because he was president at the time of the survey, something else is going on with securitarians to make them so much more emotionally positive than their fellow Trump venerators. The most likely explanation is that the very process of pursuing vigilance, security, and preparedness makes securitarians feel satisfied and even ennobled.

Threats, Race, Sex, and the Types of Trump Venerators

We discovered in Chapter 5 that Trump venerators are significantly more likely than liberals, moderates, and even non-Trump-venerating conservatives to feel threatened by terrorist attacks, criminals, immigrants, liberals, and the might of other countries such as China. The question now shifts to variation in felt threat across the four main types of Trump venerators and the results are in Table 7.3.

The first finding of note is that securitarians, even though by definition they listed immigration, national defense, gun rights, patriotism, or law and order as the most important issue to them, are not more threatened than other Trump venerators by immigrants, criminals, terrorist attacks, and the might of foreign countries. If fear is the sole motivator, the first six threat sources listed in Table 7.3 should all be especially bothersome to securitarian Trump venerators, but they are not. The level of threat felt by securitarians on these six is never significantly higher than it is for other Trump venerators. Threat does not seem to drive their focus on security.

Securitarians instead are separated from other Trump venerators by the entities they find *less* threatening—the last five threat items in the table: the growing income gap, people without health care, racists, conservatives, and natural disasters. Only 20% of securitarian Trump venerators agree that they feel threatened by "the large number of people without health care" whereas 50% of tea-party Trump venerators do. It is almost as if securitarians do not want anything distracting from a focus on outsider threats. If this supposition is true, it could help to explain the complete lack of urgency—and even hostility—that many securitarians feel regarding climate change and environmental threats. Such issues have the potential to divert attention from what securitarians see as life's central mission: deterring outsiders from infiltrating and weakening insiders, thereby diminishing insider preparedness and security.

TABLE 7.3 Felt Threat, Race, Sex and the Types of Trump Venerators

	Securitarians/ Other Trump Venerators	Social Warriors/ Other Trump Venerators	Economically Concerned/ Other Trump Venerators	Tea Partiers/ Other Trump Venerators
I feel threatened by				
countries like China.				
criminals.				lower
immigrants.				
terrorist attacks.			lower	
federal government.				
liberals.				lower
growing income gap.	lower		higher	higher
people lacking health care.	lower		higher	higher
racists.	lower			lower
conservatives.	lower			higher
natural disaster.	lower		higher	
Two-item race indices				
Blacks just need to try harder.	higher			lower
Blacks get what they deserve.	higher			lower
Blacks are not as talented.	lower			higher
Two-item sex indices				
Women's rights gone too far.				
Benevolent sexism.		higher		lower
Women are not as talented.				

blank = not significantly different
lower = significantly lower
higher = significantly higher

When it comes to perceptions of threat, social warriors are the prototypical Trump venerators, never differing significantly from the other three types taken together. The economically concerned and tea partier types differ on their perception of a few potential threats: compared to other Trump venerators they are more likely to feel threatened by the growing income gap and by the lack of health care. The economically concerned are naturally worried about the income gap and health care but it is more surprising that tea partiers are as well. Perhaps they are concerned but do not support government-led efforts to address income inequality and health care. Those with economic concerns but who venerate Donald Trump are likely to feel that traditional approaches to these problems have not been solved by either Democrats or cookie-cutter Republicans so they turn to Trump as a radical alternative, reasoning "what have we got to lose."[13]

Table 7.3 also contains the results for six survey items pertaining to attitudes toward blacks and six items pertaining to attitudes toward women (the same 12 items used in Chapter 5). These items come in pairs, with two addressing perceptions of the reasons for racial disparities (blacks are not trying hard enough or, alternatively, are the victims of continuing discrimination), two addressing whether blacks are getting what they deserve, and two addressing whether blacks are inferior to whites in terms of talent and capabilities. Moving to the gender items, two address whether the movement to grant women equal rights has gone too far or not far enough, two address benevolent sexism (for example, in a disaster, women should be saved before men), and two address whether women are less talented and capable than men. Possible answers ranged from 0 (strongly disagree) to 4 (strongly agree) and I combined the pairs of items so that higher numbers on the resultant 0–8 index indicate a less charitable view.

Of all the Trump venerators, securitarians are the harshest on blacks when it comes to the reasons for racial disparities—in other words, securitarians are the most likely to say that disparities are the result of blacks not making sufficient effort—and they are also the most likely to say that blacks are indeed getting at least as much as they deserve. On the other hand, they are actually the least likely of all types of Trump venerators to assert that blacks are inherently less "talented and capable" than whites (mean score on the 0–8 index of only 2.01). Remember, however, that these comparisons are only to other Trump venerators. The overt racism scores for other political orientations are 1.80 for non-Trump-venerating conservatives, 2.00 for moderates, and just 1.20 for liberals. Securitarian Trump venerators are less overtly racist than other Trump venerators but they are significantly more overtly racist than liberals and even non-Trump-venerating conservatives.

In terms of racial attitudes, tea partiers are the opposite of securitarians: they are less likely than other Trump venerators to believe blacks just need to try harder and that blacks are currently getting all that they deserve but they are *more* likely to believe that blacks are not as capable and talented as whites. To the extent that securitarians have negative attitudes toward blacks, these attitudes seem to derive primarily from hypervigilant concerns that everyone (and especially those who give hints of being outsiders) makes an effort so that they do not require assistance that will then weaken insiders.[14] This is why the prospect of immigrants receiving benefits and being in the "public charge" is so concerning to them.[15] At the same time, it is rare for securitarian Trump venerators to express overtly racist beliefs regarding differences in talents and abilities across races.

Turning to perceived sex differences, variations across the four types of Trump venerators are infrequent. Of the twelve relationships, only two are statistically significant and both involve benevolent sexism. Those Trump venerators who are social warriors (prioritizing abortion, homosexuality, and religious rights) are the most likely to engage in benevolent sexism (that is, to say that women should be rescued first and that they should be "protected" by men) whereas tea-party Trump venerators are the least likely. Securitarians do not stand out from other Trump venerators when it comes to attitudes toward women.

In sum, securitarians differ from their fellow Trump venerators on the three racial indices but not on any of the sex indices, raising the possibility that as the decades go by securitarians will accept women more quickly than minorities as full-fledged insiders who can be trusted to help to fight off outsiders.

Personal Behaviors and the Types of Trump Venerators

Attitudes are one thing but behaviors are another. In trying to sort out the underlying differences across the various types of Trump venerators, it is useful to look not just at what they think but what they do. I employed this strategy in grappling with the differences between Trump venerators, liberals, moderates, and conservatives who did not venerate Trump (see Table 5.6) and was surprised to find only very modest differences in terms of "naughty" behaviors such as smoking, drinking, gambling, and telling inappropriate jokes. Perhaps these kinds of behaviors are equally ineffective in distinguishing the different types of Trump venerators. I test this possibility by way of the analysis reported in Table 7.4.

One group of Trump venerators does turn out to be behaviorally distinct from the others and it is those Trump venerators who emphasize tea-party-type issues. Tea-party Trump venerators, bless them, are significantly more

TABLE 7.4 Personal Behaviors and the Types of Trump Venerators

	Securitarians/Other Trump Venerators	Social Warriors/Other Trump Venerators	Economically Concerned/Other Trump Venerators	Tea Partiers/Other Trump Venerators
Personal behavior				
smoke/use tobacco/nicotine	lower			higher
watch pornography				higher
receive traffic tickets				higher
drink alcohol	lower			higher
play the lottery				higher
gamble for higher stakes	lower			higher
tell off-color jokes		lower		higher
family owns a firearm				
travel overseas		lower		
hunt/fish				
How far would you go to stop a politician you opposed?				
not serve in your restaurant	lower		higher	higher
spread possibly false rumor	lower		higher	higher
attend potentially violent rally				
heckle the politician's speech				higher
curse the politician in private		lower		higher
attend sit-in protest	lower			
send highly critical message				
assist in minor property damage	lower			higher
avoid restaurant of the politician				
remove neighbor's yard sign	lower			higher
purposely misplace ballots	lower			higher
contribute beyond limit	lower			higher

blank = not significantly different

lower = significantly lower

bigger = significantly bigger

likely than all other Trump venerators to smoke cigarettes, watch pornography, drive too fast, drink alcohol, play the lottery, gamble for high stakes, and tell off-color jokes. They go seven for seven on these kinds of behaviors and sometimes the differences between them and other Trump venerators is sizable. For example, 42% of tea-party Trump venerators acknowledge that they enjoy watching pornography. To put this in context, only 27% of moderates, 22% of non-Trump-venerating conservatives, 21% of Trump venerating securitarians, and 12% of social warriors do the same. When it comes to watching porn, the only group that comes close to tea-partiers is liberals (37%).

The six other behaviors follow similar though slightly less extreme patterns. In terms of drinking, 36% of tea-party Trump venerators consume at least four alcoholic drinks a week. The comparable figures for securitarians is 16%, for social warriors 14%, for liberals 21%, and for non-Trump-venerating conservatives 23%. Over half of tea-party Trump venerators say they "tell jokes that might be considered off-color or inappropriate." All this would seem to fit with the libertarian ethos frequently characterizing a tea-party-like approach to politics and life.

The other types of Trump venerators do not have as clear a behavioral identity. I would have expected social warriors to be particularly low in these kinds of behaviors but, except for a reluctance to tell off-color jokes, this is not the case. Of all the types of Trump venerators, securitarians appear to be the most likely to be on the straight and narrow: they are the least likely to smoke, drink, and gamble. To the extent that Trump venerators in general project a freewheeling, devil-may-care, proper-society-be-damned, biker image, it does not come from securitarians but rather from the tea-partiers.[16] Securitarians' pursuit of protection for insiders may be too serious for hedonistic behaviors.

In the survey, I asked respondents about three other behaviors: owning a firearm, traveling overseas, and hunting or fishing but with only one exception (social warriors are less likely to travel overseas), the types of Trump venerators are not significantly different from each other on these. Having a family member who owns at least one firearm is quite common among Trump venerators—more than two-thirds do; it is just that all four types are about the same (tea-partiers are the highest; economically concerned the lowest). Actively hunting or fishing in the previous five years is surprisingly low among Trump venerators, regardless of type.

The other battery of items analyzed for Table 7.4 taps hypothetical rather than actual behaviors that respondents believe they would engage in if they wanted to stop a politician they believed with all their heart to be enacting policies that are "deeply wrong and harmful to the country." Recall that in Chapter 6, we found that liberals were actually significantly more likely than those on the political right to agree that they would engage in many of these behaviors—a result likely attributable to the fact that they gave their answers in the middle of Donald Trump's presidency. Whatever the explanation, 80% of liberals but only about 63% of conservatives say they would curse the politician in private; 62% of liberals but only about 40% of conservatives say they would send a highly critical message to the politician; and 47% of liberals but only 19% of conservatives say that if they owned a restaurant they would refuse to serve the politician. Though liberals are certainly not prone to engage in more serious and problematic acts, such as spreading possibly untrue rumors about the politician, going on to a neighbor's yard to remove a sign, assisting in minor property damage during a riot, contributing financially over the legal limit, and purposely misplacing a box of ballots that would have helped the politician win, conservatives on the whole seem less politically assertive than liberals and moderates—at least in 2019.

Now the question becomes whether, among only Trump venerators, certain types are more likely than others to engage in these politically charged behaviors. The results indicate that one type stands out. Continuing the pattern established in the top part of Table 7.4, Trump venerators identifying tea-party type issues as the most important are the most likely to assert that they would engage in these acts. They are more likely to refuse to serve the politician if they owned a restaurant, to spread rumors even if they might be false, to heckle the politician while he or she was giving a speech, to curse the politician, to assist in inflicting minor property damage in the midst of a riot, to remove a neighbor's sign supporting the problematic politician, to purposely misplace a box of ballots that could affect the election outcome, and to contribute financially beyond the legal limit if doing so would assist in defeating the politician.[17] The type of Trump venerator serving as a counterpoint to the tea party Trump venerators is securitarians. Of the twelve hypothetical behaviors, securitarians are never significantly higher than other Trump venerators but are significantly lower on seven of them, including removing the yard sign, misplacing the box of ballots, and contributing beyond the legal limit. Relative to all other Trump venerators, securitarians behave themselves and tea partiers do not.

Authoritarianism, Securitarianism, and the Types of Trump Venerators

Behaviors are interesting but our core concern is the relationship across types of Trump venerators in the degree to which they hold securitarian as opposed to authoritarian attitudes. Despite numerous claims that Trump's base is authoritarian and eager to submit to all authority figures, Trump venerators actually are slightly more likely than those with other political orientations (e.g., liberals) to resist being controlled by a powerful authority figure (see the top portion of Table 6.1). They may be slightly more conventional and slightly more aggressive (two features of the modern conceptualization of authoritarianism), but the evidence for these claims wilts when the focus is on personality rather than worldview. Perhaps variation within the types of Trump venerators obscures the connection between Trump venerators and measures of authoritarianism. Maybe certain types of Trump venerators like to be told what to do—for example, it seems likely that social warriors might—whereas other types are more resistant to authority. To take one example, my suspicion is that securitarians are not particularly willing to follow authority.

As is apparent in the top portion of Table 7.5, securitarians are indeed the least submissive of all the Trump venerator types. In other words, those Trump venerators who prioritize a security-against-outsiders issue (e.g., immigration or national defense) actually are significantly more likely than other Trump venerators to want to be independent of others and are significantly less likely to want others to make decisions for them. At least among Trump venerators, securitarians' desire for security does not lead to authoritarianism—and sometimes discourages it.

At the personality level, conventionalism and aggression do not correlate with the various types of Trump venerators. Neither two-item index (see Table 7.4A for the items) correlates with any type except that those rascally tea partiers are more likely than the other types of Trump venerators to say that they have been in a physical fight (47% compared to only 26% of social warriors) and to lose their temper frequently (42% compared to only 27% of securitarians). To sum up, securitarians are less submissive and tea partiers more aggressive but beyond those two relationships, authoritarian personality traits are not particularly useful in teasing apart the various types of Trump venerators.

The commonly used measures of authoritarianism move well beyond personality traits and frequently incorporate worldview items. How do they

TABLE 7.5 Authoritarianism, Securitarianism, and the Types of Trump Venerators

	Securitarians/Other Trump Venerators	Social Warriors/Other Trump Venerators	Economically Concerned/Other Trump Venerators	Tea Partiers/Other Trump Venerators
two-item index on submissive personality traits	lower	higher	higher	higher
two-item index on conventional personality traits				
two-item index on aggressive personality traits				higher
16-item right-wing authoritarianism index		higher		lower
12-item social dominance orientation index	higher	higher		lower
4-item index on authoritarian child-rearing		higher		
Securitarian personality items				
The worst thing is for a person to be weak.	higher	lower		lower
I think a good deal about security.	higher			
I let others worry about keeping me secure.	lower	higher	higher	higher
Accidents are a bigger threat than evil people.	lower	higher		higher
I would rather be seen as nice than strong.	lower	higher	higher	
Being prepared for threats is the best life motto.				
6-item index on securitarian personality traits (see above)	higher	lower	lower	lower

blank = not significantly different
lower = significantly lower
higher = significantly higher

fare in distinguishing the different types of Trump venerators? Table 7.5 holds the answer. The best-known measure is Right-Wing Authoritarianism (RWA) and the April 2019 survey included 16 RWA items, making it possible to see whether an index created from them correlates with type of Trump venerator.

It does, though interestingly, securitarians—60% of all Trump venerators—are neither more nor less likely than other Trump venerators to score high on RWA. The group scoring significantly higher than the others is the social warriors and this makes sense given the number of RWA items referencing abortion, school prayer, atheists, homosexuality, immorality, and women's rights. Tea partiers score significantly lower on RWA than the other Trump venerator types, another finding that makes sense in light of the thrust of the RWA items and tea partiers' libertarian inclinations.

A second descendant of authoritarianism is Social Dominance Orientation (SDO), a valuable battery tapping views on groups and group hierarchy. The items in it are cleaner and less politically loaded than RWA but still mention issues such as income and social inequality. My survey contained twelve SDO items that combine to create a useful additive index. Compared to other types of Trump venerators, securitarians tend to be significantly higher on SDO and tea partiers tend to be significantly lower. As mentioned in Chapter 6, the group-based SDO items seem to map nicely onto desires for insider security.

The final measure of authoritarianism percolating in the existing literature is the four-item child-rearing index. Two of the individual child-rearing items achieve significance for some of the types (see Table 7.4A in the appendix). Social warriors are more likely and tea partiers less likely to say that parents should raise their children to respect elders rather than be independent and social warriors are more likely and securitarians less likely to say that parents should raise their children to be obedient rather than self-reliant. The differences are sometimes big: 65% of social warriors agree that children should be raised to be obedient rather than self-reliant but only 36% of securitarians agree. If any group buys into a traditionalist way of rearing children, it is social warriors and not securitarians. When the four child-rearing items are combined, however, the four types of Trump venerators are basically the same.

In previous chapters, I presented an index of six items that, in contrast to RWA, exclusively addresses personality rather than worldview and pertained specifically to security matters. I found that this six-item battery performed well in explaining the variation that exists from liberals to moderates to non-Trump-venerating conservatives to Trump venerators (see Table 6.3). Now it is time to apply that index to variations in the different types of Trump venerators (see the bottom part of Table 7.5).

Given that they form by far the largest group of Trump venerators, a key goal is to learn what distinguishes securitarians. As pointed out above, the RWA battery, even though it includes sixteen items, is not significantly related to being a securitarian as opposed to the other types of Trump venerators—and neither is the four-item child-rearing battery. The SDO battery does correlate with securitarian Trump venerators, though rather modestly at .14. The securitarian personality battery, on the other hand, even though it has only six items, correlates with securitarian Trump venerators at a solidly significant .26.

Compared to other Trump venerators, securitarians are not more likely to be right-wing authoritarians and they are not more likely to want children to be raised to be obedient and well-behaved but they are more likely to think a good deal about security and they are significantly less likely to value niceness over perceived strength and to say that "accidents are a bigger threat than evil people." In short, they are more likely to have the personality predispositions that at the political level lead them to say immigration, national defense, law and order, guns, and patriotism are the most important issues.

Types and Archetypes

To return to the arena filled with Trump venerators, we now know that the people in the four corners differ not only in the issues they think are most important but also in a notable range of not-overtly-political traits. I will summarize the findings in this chapter by describing four fictional archetypes.

SOCIAL WARRIOR

Daniella Brunson is a straight white female who attended just a couple of community college classes before deciding additional schooling was not for her. She goes to church regularly and views herself as born again. She just turned fifty-six and lives where she grew up in a town of 1,200 people. She is married and her family is comfortable but not wealthy. She cares deeply about selected political issues, primarily abortion which she views as murder, pure and simple. Trump was not her initial choice in the

2016 Republican primaries: most of the people at her church favored Ted Cruz so she did too but with time she grew to adore Trump. His judicial appointments and encouragement of tougher state laws regulating what she views as the abortion industry pleased her greatly. She acknowledges that she is set in her ways and somewhat bitter about the rest of society's views of religious people like her. She thinks women are the fairer sex and does not mind the idea of a man taking care of her. In fact, that is her preference. She appreciates people whose speech is direct and despises political correctness which she believes merely excuses all kinds of behaviors and people. She does not like cursing and crude jokes; thus, as much as she venerates Trump, she disapproves of the language he uses, especially in his tweets. She has little time for atheists, newfangled ways, homosexuals, protesters (except for her anti-abortion colleagues who take to the streets every year on march-for-life day), and those who attack the rights of God-fearing Christians. As a religious person, she would rather be seen as nice than strong but she does worry a good deal about evil in the world and she thinks it is important and necessary that society prepare for the dark days ahead. We would be foolish not to do so.

ECONOMICALLY CONCERNED

Bill Schendts has not caught any breaks. He is forty years old, works two jobs, and still struggles to clear $35,000 in annual income. This is hardly enough because the city in which he lives has a relatively high cost of living. He started college but could not afford the tuition payments so dropped out. He had intended to go back but never got around to it. He is white and has lived with the same partner—who also holds down two jobs—for nearly ten years. He is not particularly attuned to politics but became fascinated by Trump's candidacy. He thought that a straight-talking businessman would be able to fix the economy and help hard-working real Americans like him. His life experiences have left him frustrated, pessimistic, relatively quarrelsome, and lacking a good social support network of family and friends. He is understandably angry about his status in the world and resentful of the wealthy and educated. He worries about the growing income gap and the large number of people who do not have health care. In fact, he is afraid he might soon join them because his main employer is on the verge of declaring bankruptcy. If he loses that job, he will also lose his health coverage. He does not have enough money to go to bars, travel, or generally enjoy himself. Compared to some of the other

Trump supporters he knows at work, he is not hung up on race, immigrants, liberals, criminals, and security. He has more immediate problems. He still has hopes that a unique leader and successful businessman like Trump will be able to make a difference in his life.

TEA PARTIER

Britt Kittleston is a forty-two-year-old white male. He is divorced, doing well financially, lives in a suburb, has a college degree, and never goes to church. He is registered to vote but did not pay a great deal of attention to politics until he became completely smitten with Donald Trump, largely because of his devil-may-care, stick-a-thumb-in-their-eye approach. Here was a politician who did what he wanted and let the chips fall where they may. If society disapproves, tough. Britt does not have a great circle of friends and sort of resents those who do not need to work hard but still seem to have loads of money. Compared to other enthusiastic Trump supporters, he is concerned about health care and the growing income gap. These situations need to change but he does not think the government can or should be the source of the change. It wastes enough money and bungles enough programs as is. On race, he believes that if black people tried harder most of the disparity in incomes would go away but he certainly does not believe blacks are inherently inferior to whites. He also believes that women are doing fine in American society and do not deserve special treatment. He believes he has the right to behave as he wishes. If sometimes he sneaks a smoke, watches porn, has a few drinks, plays the lottery, bets on his favorite sports teams, gets in a fight at the bar, or tells sexist jokes to his friends, it is his business. He does not like people who make him feel guilty for the way he behaves. He is something of a novice to the political scene but he would not think twice about doing whatever it took to help Trump, even if this involved spreading false rumors, heckling, assisting in a riot, tearing down his neighbor's yard sign, making illegal campaign contributions, and misplacing a box of ballots that would have resulted in Trump losing. He thinks children should be independent (like he is) and not unduly obedient. He does not agree with religious people's disapproval of issues such as birth control and gay marriage but he does not mind the fact that some groups seem to be doing better than others. After all, that is just the way life is. He also doesn't get why some Trump supporters are so worried about immigrants and criminals.

Ralph Reburg never thought he would live to see the day that somebody like Donald Trump became president. Here was a politician who got it—who recognized that the world is dangerous and that we need to do whatever is necessary to protect real Americans from a range of threats. Ralph is seventy years old and, even though he never set foot on a college campus, has made quite a good living for himself and his wife of thirty-five years. They rarely go to church, but they believe the old-fashioned way of doing things is best and safest. He liked the days when America could act on its own and did not have to rely on other countries. He liked the days when it was clear who was an authentic American and who was not. He has always followed politics but his interest kicked into overdrive with the arrival of Trump. On a personal level, he is quite content with his life and is neither anxious, frustrated, angry, resentful, pessimistic, nor unfulfilled. He does not understand the fixation of some people on health care, income disparities, racists, and natural disasters. He does, however, think society pays way too much attention to noisy minority groups and he is deeply bothered by what he sees as an unending influx of immigrants into his town.

He still thinks we can handle things if people just behave dependably and stay on their toes and if he continues to keep his supply of guns at the ready. We need to recognize that people and groups are different and that certain types of people need to be kept out. That is just the way the world is. If we focus on security, strength, and preparedness, everything will be fine. Ralph does not want anybody controlling his life and telling him what to do, especially outside forces such as the United Nations and powerful countries with their own interests, such as China; he wants everybody in society to contribute so that real Americans survive and prosper despite all the craziness going on in the world. He lives life largely on the straight and narrow but not because he is a do-gooder. Being able to take care of himself and his family makes him feel satisfied and he is worried that, after Trump, politicians will go back to an overly intrusive government that can interfere with his ability to self-protect.

Conclusion

Trump venerators are certainly not all the same. Some, like Daniella, are attracted to him because they are socially and religiously conservative; some, like Bill, because they are financially insecure and searching; and some, like Britt, because they are free-spirited, straight-talking, hard-living, keep-the-government-away-from-me non-conformists. The thing is, those who venerate Trump for these reasons are in the minority. The lion's share of fervent, unbending supporters of Donald Trump—60%—are in the same corner of the arena as Ralph. They do not necessarily disagree with the social warriors, the economically concerned, and the tea-partiers—after all, any friend of Trump is a friend of theirs. Still, the problem they see as the most important facing the country—namely, outsiders—is different. What does this heavily securitarian nature of Trump veneration mean for the future of American politics when there is no Trump? I address that question in the next chapter.

Appendix

TABLE 7.1A Demographic, Personality, and Emotionality Correlates of Trump Venerators

	Securitar.	Social Warrior	Econom. Concerned	Tea Partier	Securitar./ Other Corr.	Social Warrior/ Other Corr.	Econom. Concerned/ Other Corr.	Tea Partier/ Other Corr.
Demographics								
% white	86	87	81	85	NS	NS	NS	NS
% above $50,000 income	60	50	39	56	.07*	NS	-.10**	NS
% with some college	59	49	54	56	NS	NS	NS	NS
% rural or small town	45	51	37	28	NS	.07**	NS	-.11**
% attend church twice/ mo.	37	72	43	50	-.18**	.23**	NS	NS
% born again	48	78	55	40	-.12**	.21**	NS	-.09**
% female	48	55	43	48	NS	NS	NS	NS
Mean age in years	57.0	56.4	51.4	50.1	.13**	NS	-.09**	-.11**
Political involvement								
political knowledge (0–4)	3.42	3.10	3.04	2.94	.22**	NS	-.08**	-.11**
% interested in politics	78	68	56	60	.19**	NS	-.17**	NS
% registered to vote	95	94	89	89	.09**	NS	NS	-.07*

I see myself as

extraverted	47	38	54	38	NS	NS	.10*	NS
quarrelsome	15	24	34	22	-.17**	NS	.16**	NS
dependable	91	92	83	84	.10*	NS	NS	NS
anxious	17	28	34	27	-.17**	NS	.19**	NS
open to new experiences	68	66	63	65	NS	NS	NS	NS
set in my ways	42	58	54	41	NS	.11**	NS	NS
frustrated	12	16	34	16	-.20**	NS	.20**	NS
pessimistic	17	18	31	27	-.15**	NS	.16**	NS

Emotions items

I feel bitter about treatment.	42	54	43	38	NS	.10*	NS	NS
I am angry about my status.	26	30	46	32	-.12**	NS	.12**	NS
I resent wealthy who don't work.	16	20	34	41	-.20**	NS	.12**	.18**
I resent educated who live on the coasts.	11	20	23	22	-.16**	NS	.10*	NS
I see myself as socially unfulfilled.	11	18	34	32	-.25**	NS	.21**	.14**
It would bother me to drink flyswatter soup.	76	82	66	50	NS	NS	NS	NS
It would bother me to see a glass eye removed.	47	58	60	51	-.12**	NS	.12**	NS

* = significant ($p<.10$); ** = significant ($p<.05$); N = 661 for demographics and political involvement; 328 for personality and emotions

TABLE 7.2A Felt Threat, Race, Sex and the Types of Trump Venerators

	Securitar.	Social Warrior	Econom. Concerned	Tea Partier	Securitar./ Other Corr.	Social Warrior/ Other Corr.	Econom. Concerned/Other Corr.	Tea Partier/ Other Corr.
I feel threatened by								
countries like China.	69	65	69	67	NS	NS	NS	NS
criminals.	83	86	89	69	NS	NS	NS	-.13**
immigrants.	70	70	69	75	NS	NS	NS	NS
terrorist attacks.	82	84	73	83	NS	NS	-.11**	NS
the federal government.	70	67	78	67	NS	NS	NS	NS
liberals.	82	80	87	72	NS	NS	NS	-.13**
the growing income gap.	24	39	42	44	-.20**	NS	.11**	.10*
people w/o health care.	20	27	36	50	-.24**	NS	.12**	.16**
racists.	41	59	60	39	-.11**	NS	NS	NS
conservatives.	8	12	16	25	-.22**	NS	NS	.22**
natural disasters.	41	55	69	47	-.19**	NS	.19**	NS
Two-item race indices								
Blacks just need to try harder (2 items).	5.83	5.41	5.31	5.11	.16**	NS	NS	-.11**
Blacks get what they deserve (2 items).	5.17	4.73	4.73	4.58	.14**	NS	NS	-.09*

Blacks are not as talented as whites (2 items).	2.01	2.04	2.56	2.97	-.11**	NS	NS	.15**
Two-item sex indices								
Women's rights have gone too far (2 items).	4.40	4.37	4.11	4.22	NS	NS	NS	NS
Benevolent sexism (2 items).	5.21	5.90	5.47	4.36	NS	.16**	NS	-.19**
Women are not as talented as men (2 items).	2.74	3.02	2.56	3.19	NS	NS	NS	NS

* = significant (p<.10); ** = significant (p<.05); N = 341

TABLE 7.3A Personal Behaviors and the Types of Trump Venerators

	Securitar.	Social Warrior	Econom. Concerned	Tea Partier	Securitar./Other Corr.	Social Warrior/Other Corr.	Econom. Concerned/Other Corr.	Tea Partier/Other Corr.
Personal behavior								
Smoke	21	24	31	42	-.17**	NS	NS	.17**
Watch Porn	21	12	22	42	NS	NS	NS	.14***
Many Traffic Tickets	22	20	24	36	NS	NS	NS	.14***
Drinks/Week	16	14	24	36	-.12**	NS	NS	.20**
Play the Lottery	23	16	24	50	NS	NS	NS	.21**
Gamble	27	25	40	47	-.11**	NS	NS	.19**
Tell Off-Color Jokes	40	25	42	53	NS	-.14**	NS	.11**
Own a Firearm	67	67	64	75	NS	NS	NS	NS
Travel Outside the United States	37	20	34	30	NS	-.12**	NS	NS
Hunt or Fish	38	40	43	32	NS	NS	NS	NS
How Far Would You Go to Stop a Politician?								
Not Serve the Politician	10	22	22	28	-.19**	NS	.11**	.11**
Spread False Rumors	12	16	22	31	-.16**	NS	.11**	.13**
Attend Rally	21	27	27	25	NS	NS	NS	NS
Heckle the Politician	19	18	24	31	NS	NS	NS	.10**
Curse the Politician	65	43	67	56	NS	-.17**	NS	.21**

Engage in a Sit-In	17	27	22	28	-.13	NS	NS	NS
Send Critical Message	42	37	38	42	NS	NS	NS	NS
Assist in Riot	4	18	16	31	-.27**	NS	NS	.23**
Avoid Eating	54	45	51	58	NS	NS	NS	NS
Remove Sign	6	16	20	28	-.25**	NS	NS	.19**
Lose Ballots	5	18	9	31	-.25**	NS	NS	.24**
Contribute over Limit	8	16	16	31	-.18**	NS	NS	.19**

*= significant (p<.10); ** = significant (p<.05); N = 341

TABLE 7.4A Authoritarianism, Securitarianism and the Types of Trump Venerators

Item	Securitar.	Social Warrior	Econom. Concerned	Tea Partier	Securitar./ Other Corr.	Social Warrior/ Other Corr.	Econom. Concerned/ Other Corr.	Tea Partier/ Other Corr.
Item								
I like others to make decisions for me.	7	18	23	25	-.25**	.07*	.15**	.12**
I prefer to be independent of others.	88	77	80	78	.15**	NS	NS	NS
two item submissiveness index.					-.28**	.11**	.14**	.12**
I enjoy ruffling society's feathers.	43	46	40	54	NS	NS	NS	NS
I live life by the book.	58	58	54	54	NS	NS	NS	NS
two-item conventionalism index.					NS	NS	NS	NS
I have been in a physical fight as an adult.	35	26	42	47	NS	NS	NS	.11**
I frequently lose my temper.	27	39	40	42	-.17**	NS	NS	NS
two item aggression index.					NS	NS	NS	.11**
Standard indices								
index of 16 Right-Wing Authoritarianism items					NS	.18**	NS	-.14**
index of 12 Social Dominance Orientation items					.14**	NS	NS	-.11**
Child rearing items								
respect elders more than be independent	80	88	76	58	NS	.09**	NS	-.17**

be obedient more than self-reliant	36	65	42	31	-.12**	.21**	NS	NS
have good manners more than be curious	68	69	69	72	NS	NS	NS	NS
be well-behaved more than considerate	41	37	38	44	NS	NS	NS	NS
4-item child-rearing index (see above items)					NS	.10*	NS	NS
Securitarian personality								
The worst thing is for a person to be weak.	66	55	62	60	NS	-.07*	NS	NS
I think a good deal about security.	91	83	85	78	.12**	NS	NS	-.10**
I let others worry about keeping me secure.	7	20	19	27	-.26**	.10**	.11**	.16**
Accidents are a bigger threat than evil people.	19	23	25	42	-.12**	NS	NS	.15**
I would rather be seen as nice than strong.	24	45	38	40	-.22**	.13**	.08*	NS
Being prepared for threats is the best life motto.	82	79	75	78	NS	NS	NS	NS
6-item securitarian personality index					.26**	-.11**	-.11**	-.15**

* = significant (*p*<.10); ** = significant (*p*<.05); N=661 for authoritarian and securitarian personality items; 341 for child rearing, RWA, and SDO items

CHAPTER 8 | Politics and Life after Trump

RUMP HAPPENED; HE served as president of the United States. How will this fact affect the sweep of history? Will we view his presidency as an inconsequential blip or a sea change? Will "before Trump" and "after Trump" come to denote the major pivot point in America's modern political evolution? How do Trump venerators behave when there is no Trump? My focus in this chapter is not on predicting the parties and candidates likely to win specific elections—a fool's errand—but rather on changes in the general contours of political conflict, debate, and mood.

Trump's base was dominated by securitarians, an ancient political phenotype that is instinctively suspicious of outsiders and relentlessly eager to pursue protections for insiders generally and for themselves personally. Their universal presence around the world and throughout history might encourage the conclusion that events and occurrences are irrelevant, that politics does not matter, and that debate is a waste of time. None of this is true.

The battle between securitarians and unitarians is timeless, rendering incorrect those who claim that "history will end" with the universal acceptance of Western-style, democratic capitalism.[1] Even if free market, non-totalitarian systems should come to dominate—an eventuality that seems increasingly unlikely—history will continue because the conflict between securitarians and unitarians will continue. Disagreements over the definition and treatment of outsiders is the evolutionarily central dividing point of social life. Disagreements over economics can be intense but largely because their contours often follow the securitarian-unitarian division, with pro-business policies pleasing insider-friendly securitarians and socialistic redistributive policies pleasing the help-those-who-are-struggling unitarians.[2]

The ubiquity of the securitarian-unitarian divide does not damn us to unending trench warfare, however.[3] Politics will continue to matter and to change. At any given time, the arguments made by securitarians and unitarians can be rendered more or less effective by the events of the day or the talents of particular leaders. Moreover, those people in society who are neither dyed-in-the-wool securitarians nor unreconstructed unitarians can be moved one way or the other by occurrences and persuasive rhetoric.[4]

Events and the passage of the years will modify visions of who is and who is not an outsider in the eyes of securitarians. Women, gays, the disabled, and atheists are in the process of moving from outsiders to insiders just as Roman Catholics and several ethnic groups did generations ago. Racial minorities may eventually follow the same path though, as mentioned earlier, skin color is a primary indicator of outsider status, so this is likely to be a much longer and more difficult process. Still, change is possible. In 1968, 73% of the American public disapproved of interracial marriage; by 2013, just 11% did.[5] Americans, including most securitarians, have come to accept interracial marriage. This acceptance does not mean securitarians now view blacks as full-fledged insiders, but it is an indication that movement is possible, even on issues relating to racial groups and skin color.

Securitarianism, along with everything else, takes place in a context. If a realistic option is to keep insiders pure and integral by banning interracial marriage, securitarians will be the first to sign on. If a realistic option is to get tough on crime by imposing the death penalty, securitarians will be the first to sign on. Should those options not be available (public support for capital punishment is also declining year by year), securitarians will merely shift to anthem protesters and the threat of Sharia Law. Securitarians cannot control the specific issues that are salient at any given time, but they can take pro-vigilant, pro-security, pro-insider stances on whatever issues are at play. To put it differently, I could not predict what issues will be salient in ten years, but whatever those issues happen to be I could tell you which side securitarians will be on. With this proviso in mind, we turn to the long-term political consequences of Donald Trump and the forces that elevated him—a topic on which scholars are far from agreement.

Ephemeral Backlash or Permanent Presence?

Based on his analysis of copious over-time data, political scientist Ronald Inglehart has documented rising support for "post-material" politics across Europe, North America, Australia, and New Zealand, among other countries.[6]

Post-materialists are concerned with the environment, equality, and human rights. Over the last seventy-five years, across much of the West, support has blossomed for non-traditional sexual identifiers, ethnic and racial minorities, globalization, criminal rights, carbon taxes, those with disabilities, diverse religions, and gender equality.[7] Inglehart notes that these post-materialist views are consistently more prevalent among younger than older people and that, occasional bouts of conservative governments notwithstanding, they are bound to become ascendant.[8]

How then to explain Brexit, Trump, and the explosion of anti-immigrant "people's parties" in the West and beyond—events that seem at odds with an inexorable shift toward post-materialism. Inglehart's answer, expressed most clearly in his book with Pippa Norris, is that we are living through an inevitable but ephemeral backlash against post-materialism.[9] Their argument is that many people—especially those of relatively advanced years—feel threatened by globalization and the pace of change. The last-gasp, rear-guard action of these individuals found its voice in Marine Le Pen, Geert Wilders, Nigel Farage, Boris Johnson, Viktor Orban, and of course Donald Trump. Not to worry; in the long-term this backlash will be no match for mortality tables. Wave upon wave of post-materialists will replace doddering materialists. As Norris and Inglehart put it, in the long term, demographic trends will produce a population "more open to the values of multiculturalism, cosmopolitanism, and social liberalism."[10] All that remains is to withstand what they refer to as a "tipping point era," when the indignant final hurrah of materialists temporarily "disrupts politics and society."[11]

The backlash thesis is at odds with the argument that neither of the two groups cleaving societies is going away—that, though there may be some variance across age cohorts, the opposition to post-materialism, is robust and enduring. Two British writers cogently express this view: David Goodhart and Eric Kaufmann.

Goodhart groups people into those who are from "somewhere" and those who are from "anywhere." To those from somewhere, place matters. They may live in the same small town or ethnic urban neighborhood as their ancestors but even if they do not, the culture of the place where they do live will always be important to them. In contrast, those from anywhere tend to congregate in cities but they move around a good deal without ever setting down meaningful connections to any geographical place. Anywheres tend to be highly educated and as a result exert disproportionate influence on societal norms. This they do to such a degree that somewheres feel excluded and even demeaned. The somewheres eventually decide they have had quite enough and become more assertive with the intent of restoring a proper balance.

The forces of what Goodhart calls "decent populism" make the anywheres accept "boundaries," "good discrimination," and "Brexit," and more of this will happen in the future. In Goodhart's view, far from being a dying breed, "the somewheres are not going anywhere."[12]

Eric Kaufmann's *Whiteshift* contains similar sentiments. As the title implies, Kaufmann sees politics in racial terms. He reads the data as indicating that 63% to 80% of whites in a whole range of countries believe white self-interest on issues such as immigration is perfectly legitimate, leaving only 20% to 37% believing that white self-interest is automatically racist.[13] Kaufmann asserts that by defining racism too broadly, "left modernists" (his label for Goodhart's "anywheres") make it virtually impossible to hold a reasoned discussion of immigration reform.[14] Like Goodhart but unlike Ingelhart, Kaufmann does not see the left-modern, post-materialist, anywheres as destined to dominate the political scene in the near future or ever. He notes that the ultra-Orthodox movement currently dominating Jerusalem will soon do the same across all of Israel and that the rising birth rates of fundamentalists in the United States and elsewhere will pose a continuing challenge to the left-modern agenda.[15] With regard to the rapidly increasing numbers of mixed race individuals, he hypothesizes that most "will connect to their ancestors' portraits and statues via the white archetype."[16] Maybe; maybe not; but the evidence he presents raises serious questions about the assertion that those eager to protect their society's dominant race and culture will soon fade away.

So what about it? Whether they are called materialists, somewheres, decent populists, or securitarians, how long are they likely to be around? Is nationalistic nativism on its last gasp or in perfect health and ready to go the distance? Was Brexit a death knell or the report of a starter's gun? Was Donald Trump an aberration or a harbinger?

Age and Securitarianism

A single survey does not allow elaborate cohort analyses but it can provide a start in answering these sorts of questions. Most of the existing literature suggests that from about age twenty-five on, an individual's political beliefs are surprisingly stable across the life span.[17] The drift to the right that is alleged in so much conventional wisdom on aging does occur—if people change at all politically, they are more likely to move right than left—but by far the most common pattern is remarkable stability.[18] Thus, an adult's views at a given time, though certainly not a perfect predictor of views at a later life stage, are usually a reasonably accurate indicator. How does Trump veneration and securitarianism vary from young to old?

The first two rows of Table 8.1 give hope to those wanting to believe that generational replacement will move American politics away from Trumpism. As of April 2019, only 3% of Americans under the age of thirty, compared to 31% of those seventy-and-over, strongly agreed that Donald Trump is one of the very best presidents in the entire history of the country. Moreover, just 13% of under-thirty Americans, compared to 44% of seventy-and-over Americans, agreed that they would wear a "Make America Great Again" hat.

TABLE 8.1 Age, Trump Support, and Securitarianism

Variable	Less than 30	30–39	40–49	50–59	60–69	Over 69	All ages
Trump venerator	3	13	15	22	21	31	
Would wear a MAGA hat	13	33	26	39	39	44	32
Trump supporter	20	35	30	46	45	53	38
support reducing immigration	22	39	36	51	48	58	41
feel threatened by immigrants	21	25	26	40	33	38	30
feel threatened by criminals	56	48	45	69	73	63	58
feel threatened by China	43	39	42	58	58	63	50
feel threatened by terror attacks	57	49	47	58	58	60	54
If we are not vigilant, we will be victimized.	24	42	45	56	52	58	46
The worst thing for a country is to be perceived as weak.	38	46	47	62	63	77	55
In choice between democracy and security, take security.	28	37	32	33	32	32	32

N = 997

To a certain extent, however, the paucity of young people agreeing that Trump is one of "the very best ever" may reflect their aversion to hyperbole of any kind just as their reluctance to don a "MAGA" hat may be the product of simple sartorial preference. Subsequent items tapping attitudes toward first Trump and then securitarianism reveal more meaningful response patterns. Of Americans under thirty, 20% supported Donald Trump, 22% supported reducing current levels of immigration, 21% agreed that they feel threatened by immigrants, 24% believed national vigilance is vital, 38% said just about the worst thing for a country is to be weak, and 28% would take security over democracy if given a choice (see Figure 8.1). With one or two exceptions, support for these items among young people is substantially lower than the support apparent in the other age brackets and the differences are often dramatic. Support for Trump rose from 20% for the under-thirty cohort to 53% for the seventy-and-over group and just 38% of those under

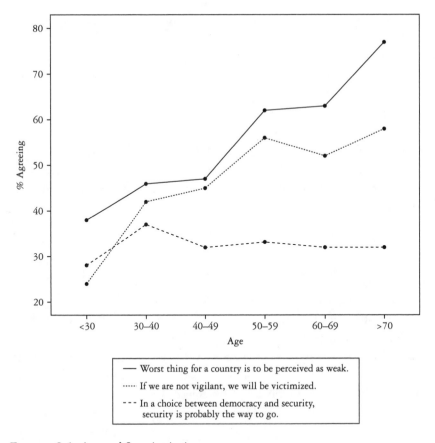

FIGURE 8.1 Age and Securitarianism

thirty compared to 77% of those seventy-and-over believed the worst thing for a country is to be weak.[19]

Exceptions to this general pattern are worth noting. One important survey item that did not increase with age is "if a country had the choice between being secure and being democratic, being secure is probably the way to go": 28% of those under age thirty agreed and 32% of those seventy-and-over agreed so there is very little change across the life cycle. Regardless of age, just under one-third of Americans were at best casually committed to democracy.[20] Two of the "feel threatened" items also did not increase with age. Compared to those individuals seventy-and-over, those under thirty were about as likely to feel threatened by criminals as by terrorist attacks. Feeling threatened by "the military and by economic might of other countries such as China" went up with age but started from a surprisingly high base: 43% of those under thirty agreed that they feel threatened by foreign countries. Also notice that, compared to other items, feeling threatened by immigrants did not increase as sharply with age, primarily because the elderly are not as threatened by immigrants as they are by criminals, terrorist attacks, and the might of countries like China.

In sum, though securitarianism is less common among younger than older people, a solid 20% of Americans under the age of thirty are securitarians with attendant sympathies for Trump, and this number almost certainly would be higher with a more relatable and more social media savvy spokesperson than the septuagenarian Donald Trump. For the foreseeable future, somewhere between 20% and 30% of the overall population will continue to have clear securitarian tendencies. In fact, for a somewhat surprising reason the percentage of practicing securitarians may very well increase.

Race and Securitarianism

Blacks vote overwhelmingly Democratic, especially when the party's presidential candidate is black (2008 and 2012) or the racial sensitivities of the Republican presidential candidate are in serious question (2016), but blacks' voting proclivities obfuscate a worldview that is often decidedly securitarian.[21] As it turns out, black Democrats and white Democrats have markedly different orientations and preferences.

Nearly twice as many black Democrats as white Democrats (39% to 21%; see Table 8.2 and Figure 8.2) agree that vigilance is essential to avoid victimization, 62% of black Democrats but only 36% of white Democrats agree

TABLE 8.2 Whites, Blacks, Hispanics, and Securitarianism (Democrats Only)

	Whites	Hispanics	Blacks	Total
Securitarian items				
If we are not vigilant, we will be victimized.	21	26	39	26
The worst thing for a country is to be perceived as weak.	36	44	62	42
In choice between democracy and security, take security.	14	30	42	22
A country's central goal should be becoming strong.	31	39	55	37
It is probably best to assume outsiders intend to do us harm.	12	20	26	16
Biggest threat is not outsiders but concentration of power.	83	69	48	74
Selected issue stances				
Abortion rights	83	64	64	76
Gay marriage	83	61	42	71
School prayer	25	36	56	32
Ready availability of birth control	91	75	66	84
Lower taxes on all	34	56	68	44
Higher taxes on the rich	89	52	60	78
Racial affirmative action in hiring	58	59	61	59
Black lives matter	76	64	79	74
Securitarian issue stances				
Death penalty	28	31	36	30
Reduce immigration	19	18	24	20
Protect gun rights	23	28	45	28
Increase defense spending	16	26	39	22
English as the national language	45	38	69	47
Athlete anthem protests	66	62	60	64

N = 414

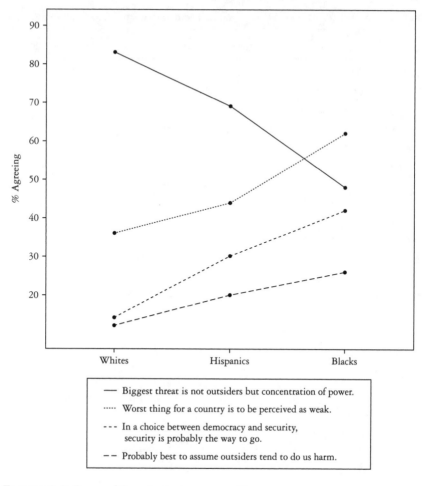

FIGURE 8.2 Race and Securitarianism among Democrats

that being weak is just about the worst thing possible for a country, three times as many black Democrats as white Democrats opt for security over democracy (42% to 14%), and more than twice as many black Democrats as white Democrats believe "it is probably best to assume outsiders intend to do us harm (26% to 12%).[22] The last item in this group is worded such that agreement indicates the opposite of securitarianism (that is, it references threats from insiders rather than outsiders), so the pattern should be and is reversed: 83% of white Democrats but only 48% of black Democrats believe the biggest threat to our country is not criminals and other countries but the concentration of power in our own country. Hispanic Democrats' response patterns on these items are quite diverse but on average they land between black and white Democrats.

The pattern is similar when we turn to issue preferences. Previous research documents that relative to white Democrats, black conservatism is highest on social issues.[23] In my April 2019 survey, support for both abortion rights and gay marriage runs at 83% among white Democrats but only 64% and 42%, respectively, among black Democrats (64% and 61% among Hispanic Democrats). More than twice as many black Democrats as white Democrats (56% to 25%) agree with the concept of school prayer. Note, however, that differences extend to economic and other issues as well: 68% of black Democrats but only 34% of white Democrats support lower taxes on all, and blacks are also significantly less supportive of increasing taxes on the rich.

Black Democrats' more conservative views on policy matters extend to securitarian issues as well. Compared to white Democrats, they are more likely to favor the death penalty, immigration reductions, gun rights, higher defense spending, and English as the designated national language. Black Democrats are even slightly less likely than white Democrats (60% to 66%) to endorse anthem protests by athletes, which is surprising given that these protests are being spearheaded by black athletes and are designed to call attention to continuing racial discrimination. Hispanics, again, on average, are in the middle except for reducing immigration and establishing English as a national language and even here the differences are modest.

Pulling these findings together, blacks' overwhelming support for Democratic candidates is not due to a rejection of the securitarian worldview or to left-leaning stances on issues but instead is driven by their status as outsiders. As the decades go by and blacks increasingly perceive themselves as insiders rather than outsiders, the securitarian impulses held by a significant portion of the black community, rather than being suppressed, increasingly will be reflected in their political choices, to the detriment of Democratic candidates. Members of the LGBTQ community are likely to show similar voting shifts as societal acceptance grows. More gays will display their securitarian colors by joining with existing Log Cabin Republicans, to the benefit of Republican candidates, or at least those Republican candidates who are not fervent social warriors.[24]

My best guess is that in the coming decades, marginal but important increases in the number of black, Hispanic, Asian, and GLBTQ individuals manifesting their securitarian inclinations will at least counterbalance diminished generational replacement of white securitarians, leaving securitarians at around 25% of the adult population, only modestly changed from current levels. The vision of the future offered by Goodhart and Kaufmann is likely to be more accurate than Norris and Inglehart's. That said, does the fact that securitarianism will continue to be the orientation of only one-fourth of the population mean that as the memory of Trump fades securitarians will not play an influential role in American politics? The answer depends on party coalitions.

Who Wants to Play with Securitarians?

With Trump's departure from the political scene, will the Republican Party split into a securitarian and a non-securitarian wing or will the party continue as it long has with securitarians and non-securitarians participating in a workable, if sometimes uneasy, coalition? Having had control of the levers of power in the form of the most unapologetically securitarian president ever, how will securitarians respond to the candidacies of less-securitarian Republicans?

No one can know the answers to these questions, but we can glean hints by paying close attention to the issue priorities of securitarians and their fellow Republicans. In the representative portion of the 2019 survey (N = 1,000), there were 341 individuals who identified with the Republican Party— some strongly, some just leaning. Of those, 160 (47%) identified one of the securitarian issues (immigration, defense, law and order, patriotism, or gun rights) as the most important to them; 60 (18%) identified a "social warrior" issue (abortion, homosexuality, or religious rights) as the most important issue; 66 (19%) identified general economic concerns (healthcare, the health of the economy, and trade); 45 (13%) identified a tea party issue (taxes, the deficit, excessive spending, welfare, or government regulations); and 10 (3%) identified racial justice, income inequality, or women's rights. Securitarians, defined in this fashion, constitute nearly half of the Republican Party.

Still, this means that slightly over half of all Republicans did not mention a securitarian issue as most important to them. Were these individuals likely to have chafed under the Trump presidency and its persistent emphasis on immigration, defense, crime, and guns? Boring down to the issues each respondent identified as second most important can be useful in answering this question and this is the analysis I report in Figure 8.3.

The first bar of each of the four pairs presents the percentage of the respondents in each category who mentioned an issue from that same category as the second most important issue. In other words, it indicates the percentage of the cases in which someone who mentioned either abortion, homosexuality, or religious rights as the most important issue listed one of the other issues in the social warrior category as the second most important.

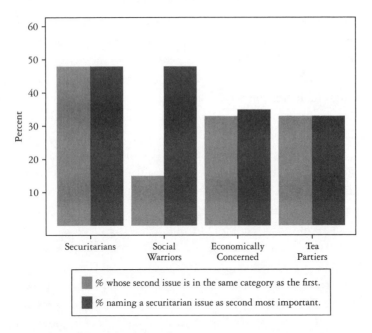

Legend:
- % whose second issue is in the same category as the first.
- % naming a securitarian issue as second most important.

FIGURE 8.3 Second Most Important Issue

Likewise, the lighter bar for tea partiers reflects those who also mentioned a tea party issue as second most important to them. To provide a comparison, the shaded bar in each pair shows the percentage in each category shifting to a securitarian issue as second most important.

The take-away from this exercise is that securitarian issues are remarkably popular as Republicans' choices for second most important issues even when their first choice is a social or economic issue. Republicans who mention a social issue as most important are more likely to mention a securitarian issue as second most important than one of the other social issues. The economically concerned and the tea partiers are about as likely to mention a securitarian issue as to stay within category. In sum, even non-securitarian Republicans are quite sympathetic to securitarian concerns. They may have listed another type of issue as most important to them but securitarian concerns are not far behind.

The four groups of Republicans I have identified are not much at odds with each other. Priorities may vary a bit but the overall package preferred is quite similar. Republicans who are social warriors or tea partiers are not opposed to the securitarian agenda that so motivates some Trump venerators. Part of the reason for the overlap is likely that conservative stances on almost all issues relate to security in one way or another. Social issues prop up ways of preserving the established order, which in turn connects to insider stability and security; economic health obviously promotes insider security; and tea partiers' goal of reducing the size of the government keeps precious resources from benefiting and encouraging outsiders such as welfare recipients and foreign countries. Supporters of all categories (though this is least true of the economically concerned) seek to build up insiders in the face of outsider threats.

The simplest way to summarize the situation is to note that 22% of Republicans listed a tea party issue as either the first or second most important issue to them; 26% listed a more general economic concern as either the first or second most important; 33% listed a "social warrior" issue as either the first or second most important; but 85% listed a securitarian issue as either the first or second most important, with immigration and national defense being the runaway top picks. These numbers may be somewhat inflated by the fact that at the time of the survey, Trump was keeping these kinds of issues in the news, but however you cut it, securitarian concerns are important to most Republicans. As a result, it is unlikely that Trump's securitarian priorities have been deeply off-putting to them.

When it comes to policy substance, most Republicans did not have to swallow hard to ingest Trump's agenda. Many grumbled about his tweets and coarseness, just as many seriously regretted that his cavalier attitude toward the law created electoral problems for Republicans and for conservatism generally—and the lack of total agreement within the party become apparent on issues such as Trump's abrupt decision in 2019 to pull US troops from Syria, opening the door for Turkey to attack the Kurds—but most Republicans supported the great majority of his policy positions.[25] The broad Republican buy-in to Trump's policies surprised observers but the numbers in Figure 8.3 help to explain it. Many tea partiers, many economically concerned, and many social warriors have definite securitarian tendencies. Add to this the fact that Trump gave social warriors Justices Gorsuch and Kavanaugh, the economically concerned an extended period of (pre-coronavirus) economic prosperity, and tea partiers a big tax break and regulatory relief, and it is not surprising that Republicans rallied around him.

Given that securitarians' issue demands fit comfortably within the Republican orbit, the Republican Party did not grow weary of those demands, but growing weary of Trump himself is another matter, and this is the situation that holds potential danger for the Republican Party going forward. As Trump became an electoral liability (seen first in the 2018 midterms), some Republicans moved away from him while true believers stuck with him until the bitter end and even beyond. The real question is how Trump's hard-core base will respond to the perceived apostasy of those Republicans who have the temerity to put the party's electoral concerns ahead of fealty to Trump's legacy. Will Trump venerators turn on a party that can never be as unsullied as they demand—a party they may come to see as complicit in the failure to sustain Trumpism? Will Trump venerators deprived of Trump opt for purity even if doing so relegates them to a wilderness of lopsided electoral defeats, laughable conspiracy theories, and bitter recriminations? If so, Trump will turn out to be the worst thing that ever happened to Republicans—and to securitarians.

In 2019, 47% of Republicans listed a securitarian issue as most important to them and 48% of that 47% also mentioned a securitarian issue as second most important. This 22.5% of Republican identifiers is firmly locked into the securitarian agenda. These are the individuals to watch as the years go by. Will they recognize that they can best promulgate their agenda by going along with those Republicans who are something other than unalloyed securitarians or, having had one of their own in power, will they reject all non-securitarians? Economists are correct that demands are inflexible downward. In light of this feature of the human condition, how much mischief will former President Trump and his most ardent followers make? He tends not to behave well when someone else is the center of attention. As Dallas Mavericks owner and occasional political commentator Mark Cuban once put it, "With Trump, it's him . . . there is no one else . . . and this makes [his time in power] a countdown rather than a systemic change."[26]

To what degree will the larger Republican Party accede to the purists' demands? Will non-Trumpist Republicans tire of giving veto power to one wing of their party? What will happen if the Republican Party goes back to nominating candidates such as Mitt Romney and John McCain who then proceed to question some of Trump's more outlandish statements and actions?[27] Having had their moment in the sun, Trump venerators may be unwilling to go gently into that good night. If the Republican Party comes under serious strain, it will be because of Trump the person and not the issues he championed.[28]

To those in Trump's thrall—that is, to those convinced he was insiders' best hope for their preservation and security—anyone who questions Trump is automatically an outsider or worse.[29] In their eyes, casual criticism, let alone whistleblower complaints and impeachment proceedings, can only be endorsed by traitors.[30] In their eyes, Republicans who recognized the need for congressional oversight, rule of law, and attention to the Constitution were sacrificing the nation's vital security for nothing more than pedantry— and this was inexcusable.[31]

Will Trump venerators be able to reside in the same party as those with priorities they perceive to be out of whack? Compromising on policies and subjugating themselves to a political movement is always difficult for securitarians; in the post-Trump era it will be even more of a challenge, and this situation could pose serious problems for Republican strategists. Trump venerators may need to decide whether they want to fend off gun control, continuing immigration, criminal rights, and multilateralism or promote a cult of personality based on the memory of Trump's presidency. Of course, this is likely to be an individual rather than group decision. Trump venerators do not like being told what to do and will decide on their own how enthusiastically to respond to the candidacies of Republicans who are not Donald Trump.[32]

The Real Enemy Is Not Outsiders but the People Who Support Them

Quite apart from the future electoral successes or failures of the Republican Party, the Trump phenomenon accelerated a fascinating and potentially worrisome ongoing shift. The fundamental political distinction in the world increasingly is no longer insiders and outsiders but people who support insiders and people who support outsiders. To be sure, clashes will long continue between Sunnis and Shiites, Hutus and Tutsis, Pashtuns and Hazara, and Yooks and Zooks;[33] still, the focal point of more and more conflicts will not be differences in the degree to which individuals are outsiders but rather differences in the degree to which individuals promote the cause of outsiders. For a securitarian, the only thing worse than outsider threats are ostensible insiders who refuse to embrace insiders unreservedly. Increasingly, the divisions that matter are not demographic but ideological. In time, the concept of demographic outsiders may be little more than a useful prop in the central drama playing out between securitarians and unitarians. Lines dividing ethnicities, religions, genders, sexual orientations, and even races are becoming murkier; lines dividing those predisposed to pull in outsiders and those predisposed to wall them off—that is, lines dividing unitarians and securitarians—are becoming ever more vivid and meaningful.[34]

The data in Chapter 5 indicate that 75% of Trump venerators feel threatened by immigrants. This is a high number, but note that a virtually identical share—74% of Trump venerators—feel threatened by liberals. The reverse is equally true: 68% of liberals feel threatened by the number of people without health care and 69% of liberals feel threatened by conservatives.[35] The remarkable hostility between the two ideologies has been well documented; for example, political scientists Shanto Iyengar and Sean Westwood find that more people nowadays would rather their child marry across racial than ideological lines.[36] What explains this antipathy?

Look at it this way: Both securitarians and unitarians have jobs to do, and in each instance those jobs are made more difficult by the very existence of the opposing ideology. Securitarians are intolerable to unitarians because they make it more challenging for unitarians to embrace and support vulnerable outsiders. Unitarians are intolerable to securitarians because they make it more challenging for securitarians to protect against the infiltration of threatening outsiders. Denizens of each side need the concept of outsiders.[37] They do not need (and cannot understand) individuals who prevent them from doing their job and so they reserve a special form of vilification for them.[38]

Imagine presenting a securitarian Trump venerator with two options. The first is living in an extremely diverse, multiethnic, multi-racial neighborhood but one in which everyone strongly supports gun rights, increased defense spending, border walls, lower taxes, patriotism, small government, and law and order. The second is living in a neighborhood that is composed entirely of white Christian straight, employed, law abiding, fourth-generation Americans, but all of whom are strong advocates for open borders, increased spending on foreign aid and social welfare, criminal rights, the United Nations, strict gun control, and higher taxes on the wealthy. In which of these two neighborhoods do you think securitarians would prefer to live? I believe an overwhelming majority would select the multi-ethnic, securitarian option and that the percentage who do will only increase as time goes by. Securitarians are built to work toward insider security and homogeneity, not to achieve it. Besides, insiders who thwart efforts to preserve and protect insiders are not really insiders.

I also suspect the reverse is true of unitarians; that is, if forced to choose, most of them would opt to live in a lily-white but fervently unitarian neighborhood rather than one in which they were surrounded by intransigent securitarians even if those securitarians were racially and ethnically diverse.[39]

Exactly what is it that securitarians and unitarians are after for their country: a desired demographic profile or a desired ideological profile? As the years go by, people with strong political beliefs are spending less and less time addressing what to do about insiders and outsiders and more and more time attacking those whose ideologies regarding insiders and outsiders differ from their own. The Trump experience has clarified and hastened this transition and we need to consider its implications. Down deep, whites and blacks are the same; down deep securitarians and unitarians are not.

James Madison craved a polity in which numerous cross-cutting cleavages led to constantly evolving coalitions.[40] In this fashion, given individuals might be in opposition to each other on one issue but be in agreement with each other on the next, making it more difficult for them to be rigid, permanent foes. As politics is ever more frequently and overtly fought between securitarians and unitarians rather than a multiplicity of racial, ethnic, religious, and economic groups, cleavages will become less diverse and more consistently rigid; as a result, political conflict will become less forgiving and more ferocious. So much for Madisonian democracy. Danielle Allen astutely points out that the world has never built a multi-ethnic democracy—that is, a democracy in which no particular group is in the majority.[41] We may or may not figure out how to do that, but the real, long-term challenge is creating a bi-ideological democracy—that is, a democracy in which the forces of unitarianism and the forces of securitarianism, both clearly articulated and thoroughly emboldened, can live and govern together.

Democracy in the Post-Trump Era

Imagine a package of laws that made it possible to deport "foreigners" living in the United States, prevented many naturalized citizens from voting, and prohibited all public opposition to the government. Imagine further that these laws led to the imprisonment of a person who described the president as "having an unbounded thirst for ridiculous pomp, foolish adulation, and self-avarice." Donald Trump's distaste for foreigners, aversion to immigrants, fondness of pomp, desire for adulation, and familiarity with avarice might lead to the conclusion that if any president pushed such an agenda, it would be Trump. A related conclusion might be that even if a president were successful in passing this legislative package, the courts would strike it down with alacrity.

Students of history know the punchline. At the president's urging, Congress did indeed pass such legislation, the courts affirmed it, and the individual who uttered the quote above was imprisoned as a result, but all this happened during the administration of John Adams, not Donald Trump. In 1798, the notoriously thin-skinned Adams convinced Congress that if the fledgling country was to survive, the Federalist Party must retain power at all costs and that the best strategy for doing so was to squelch all opposition and criticism. Apparently, he did not like being referred to as "His Rotundity." Congress dutifully passed the Alien and Sedition Acts, but Adams may have underestimated the fallout. Several states refused to enforce the acts within their borders and, in a direct challenge to the fledgling federal Constitution, declared the acts null and void. The legislation ended up being so unpopular that it played a role in Adams's defeat in the bitter election of 1800, after which Congress allowed the acts to expire.

This episode was not a fluke. Free speech and other democratic rights were severely curtailed during World War I, when opposition to the war and to capitalism landed many in jail. Thousands of innocent Japanese were interned during World War II. The McCarthy Scare of the 1950s drew attention to the fragility of democratic rights as did the tumult and civil rights movement of the 1960s. For much of our country's history, large chunks of society, including women and blacks, were denied basic human rights.

The point of reciting this painful litany is not that "we survived previous assaults on democratic values so we will survive this one as well." The point instead is that democracy is always under threat so constant nurturing, not to mention bravery, is required to protect it. We need to bear this point in mind now more than ever because democracy will be under duress in the post-Trump era. Trump's ego makes it impossible for him to accept the possibility that he could lose legitimately, leading to realistic fears of a constitutional crisis.[42] Even without this worst-case scenario coming to fruition, the basic elements of a functional democracy will be difficult to restore in the wake of Trump.

Steven Levitsky and Daniel Ziblatt cite four key threats to democracy: weak commitment to democratic rules of the game; denial of the political opponents' legitimacy; tolerance or encouragement of violence; and—echoes of the Alien and Sedition Acts—readiness to curtail the civil liberties of opponents and the media.[43] These inclinations are foreign neither to Trump venerators nor to Trump. His venerators have convinced themselves that Trumpism is essential if insiders are to be secure—their non-negotiable objective. If non-democratic action is required to protect securitarian values, so be it: 59% of Trump venerators agree that if the choice is between democracy and security, "security is probably the way to go."[44] Securitarians were fine when in the 1980s Ronald Reagan and Oliver North disobeyed a democratically passed law (signed by Reagan himself) because they believed illegal actions were necessary in order to keep Nicaragua from becoming a first-order outsider threat. Trump venerators are not obedient to norms and laws; they are obedient to insiders' need for preservation and security.

Though it is possible that democratic values will bounce back to the status quo ante Trump, it is more likely that some lasting damage has been done. Democracy does not come naturally to humans and will always lack "solid guardrails."[45] The "mutual tolerance" and "institutional forbearance" necessary for democracies to function is usually in short supply.[46] Democrats wonder why they should play by democratic rules when the Trump administration did not. Much will depend on the willingness of subsequent presidents to be transparent, cooperative, trusting, and open to necessary oversight by both the media and Congress. The bar has been lowered; more than ever, we will need our leaders to raise it. Have gracious concession speeches gone the way of the passenger pigeon? What about a legitimate and responsible opposition or, perhaps more important, an opposition that is perceived to be responsible and legitimate? Is compromise a relic? These concerns were building before Donald Trump became our 45th president; they have now acquired additional urgency.

Political scientists Marc Hetherington and Jonathan Weiler are correct when they point out that political disputes do not always parallel distinctions in fundamental worldview but that when they do, the political climate will be hostile, tense, and polarized.[47] That is exactly what has happened now. Current political disputes perfectly mirror the most central of evolutionary cut points: how to treat outsiders. In the past, when political battles of the day mapped onto this division (such as during the Civil War and in the 1960s), politics was bitter and bloody; reconciliation difficult and draining. The modern era will be no different.

Recognizing that Trump venerators focus on security is a start, but on its own this recognition does little to obviate the danger resulting from a willingness to trade in democracy to achieve their true goal. Democracy needs people who are committed to it even when they are not getting the policies and outcomes they want.[48] Securitarians now and in the future are in no mood to offer that commitment because, from their perspective, safeguarding insiders is far too important to leave to the vicissitudes of democracy.

Are unitarians any more committed to democracy? Would unitarians trade in democracy if doing so made it possible to save the planet and, for good measure, to redistribute wealth and influence in a humane and equitable fashion?[49] Unitarians see this as a trick question: what good is democracy if life on the planet is impossible? Quite so, but the most important lesson about Trump's core supporters that I can offer is this: For Trump's base, life without personal security and the preservation of worthy insiders in the face of teeming outsiders is the equivalent of total planetary collapse. This position, of course, seems completely absurd to those of us who are not securitarians, but there you have it.[50] Realize this and you will have taken a giant step toward understanding Trump venerators.[51]

Is there any hope? We can begin by recognizing what divides us. Securitarians need to realize and accept that they will not get all the security they want.[52] Though it runs against their grain, they need to fight against their instinct to strive for individual and insider security anywhere and always. Unitarians need to realize that it will not be possible to wipe away all distinctions between insiders and outsiders in one fell swoop. The philosophies that divide securitarians and unitarians are directly at odds but virtually all of the specific issues separating them, including immigration, have middle-ground policy options. The political climate will only begin to improve when people stop viewing their positions as nonnegotiable and sacred.[53] The necessary changes are more psychological than political.[54]

In the late winter of 2020, the novel coronavirus rapidly spread across the world, leaving in its wake bronchial problems, shaken psyches, and often death. The United States was not immune. Just as decision-makers in Washington were reaching a cross-ideological consensus on the proper governmental response—including massive stimulus spending—President Trump began pointedly referring to the affliction as the "Chinese virus," in light of the source of the original outbreak. Many of his supporters quickly embraced this rhetoric. For example, at one point Senator John Cornyn (R-Texas), asserted that "China is to blame because [it is a] culture where people eat bats and snakes and dogs and things like that." Blowback was swift, with many calling that type of language "racist" and the equivalent of a "dog whistle."

This controversy, at the very time cooperation was most needed, perfectly illustrates the securitarian-unitarian divide—a divide that itself is a virus of sorts. Securitarians viewed the situation in "us versus not-us terms." They believed it to be a perfect illustration of why we would all be better off if the "not-us's" of the world would be kept well away. After all, outsiders only bring disease, disunity, and danger to the table. From a unitarian perspective, in contrast, the source of the outbreak is irrelevant and what is really needed is for the world to share information, strategies, ideas, testing kits, reagents, resources, research, vaccines, person power, and moral support. We are all in this together, they point out, and inter-group recriminations are wildly counterproductive. Why foster divisions when doing so will only hinder our ability to get past a grave crisis?

And so it goes. The issues, problems, and challenges change; the two lenses through which the issues, problems, and challenges are viewed stay the same.

Conclusion

At root, Donald Trump's fervent supporters do not crave generic authority; they do not even crave generic security; they crave a very specific kind of security and that is security from outsiders. These outsiders can physically reside outside the country but they can also be individuals who reside in the country but who, in the minds of Trump supporters, have not given firm evidence that they are first and foremost committed to the safety and prosperity of the historical core of the country: its insiders. From securitarians' perspective, immigrants, racial minorities, and unitarians pose the clearest threats to insider strength, cultural unity, and national pride. Consider Trump's remarks to the United Nations General Assembly on September 25, 2019: "The true goal of a nation can only be pursued by those who love it; by citizens who are rooted in its history, who are nourished by its culture, committed to its values, attached to its people."

These attitudes sometimes spill over into hatred of outsiders, even violence. This should never be minimized but also should not obscure the fact that even those many Trump supporters who are not hateful would rather that non-insiders stay away. They think that is the way the world should work—separate nations and where possible separate races and separate cultures each doing their own thing and each in competition with the other. It is Adam Smith's invisible hand elevated from individuals to nation-states. Trump again in the same speech: "So to all leaders here today . . . lift up your nations, cherish your culture, honor your histories, treasure your citizens, make your countries strong." The message is not "We are better than you so we will take you over"; the message is "You do your thing and we do ours; separate is best." Fascist, interventionist leaders would never exhort their competitors to make their countries strong but securitarian isolationist leaders do.

As long as securitarians are a key constituency of the Republican coalition, efforts like Marco Rubio's post-2012 attempt to remake that party into one more welcoming to Hispanics and other minorities will be unlikely to succeed. If an influential portion of the party is instinctively reticent with regard to minority groups, that party is going to be hard pressed to attract racial minorities. True to form, despite a certain degree of ideological congruence between Republicans, Hispanics, and blacks, the GOP's diversifying effort went nowhere fast. Trump's persistent bragging about low minority unemployment rates under his watch did not make much of a dent either. What does all this mean for Trump's base and the country moving forward?[55]

In the short term, Trump venerators are likely in for tough times. Trump's narcissism makes it challenging for securitarians to identify new leaders. Those with a securitarian mindset are difficult to lead in the best of times (contrary to being authoritarian, they are leery of authority) and especially difficult if they are pining for the good old days when one of their own was in the White House.[56] A countdown that reaches zero without a clear sense of what comes next is a problem.

In the post-Trump era, ardent Trump supporters likely will have difficulty securing major policy change in the direction of securitarianism, but this does not mean they cannot play havoc. Their need to strive to defend insiders from outsider threats will lead them to be perennially disgruntled with a political system that sometimes has other priorities. In fact, if the account of Trump venerators provided here is accurate, the most likely post-Trump eventuality is not a unified and successful authoritarian takeover of government but rather it is that nearly one-fourth of the US population will drift away from the system, seduced by whatever bizarre alternative narrative fits their need to believe they are under siege from outsiders and their enablers. Securitarians' instinct is to attack government, not join it. If the rest of society generally and those holding power specifically lack the common sense and determination to keep outsiders at a safe distance, securitarians will have to do so themselves at the micro-level by retreating to increasingly isolated enclaves. In the wake of the Trump presidency, the imminent danger posed by those who were his most loyal followers is not authoritarianism but anarchy; it is not omnipotent leaders but anemic ones. A belief that Trump supporters are authoritarians is not just a semantic error; it leads those who are worried about the health and stability of our democracy to look over the wrong shoulder.[57]

In April of 2020, after most states had responded to the coronavirus by instituting closures, lockdowns, and social distancing mandates, demonstrations sprang up around the country. The protesters carried signs demanding that the governors end these restrictions. A few waved Confederate flags, some held "Trump/Pence" signs; many wore "Make America Great Again" hats. Though the protests themselves were small and though over 60% of the American public disapproved of them, a solid 22% approved. This 22% is Trump's base and this book has been about them. They do not seek more authority but less. They bristle at governmental restrictions that they are convinced could weaken the American way of life and limit their own ability to defend themselves and their country not from a pathogen but from human outsiders.

Trump's core supporters do not need politics; they need people who see the world as they do. The disposition of Trump's intense base cannot be shamed away by name-calling; it cannot be driven away by censure; it cannot be wiped away by expunging One America News Network; it cannot be reasoned away with facts; it cannot be imagined away by hope; and it cannot be bludgeoned away by force. As challenging as it may be, if we are to improve politics in the post-Trump era the first step is that each of us must realize that many of our fellow citizens have a fundamentally different orientation toward outsiders than we do.

Humans have figured out how to tame the atom, defeat pathogens, manipulate DNA, harness the wind, ply the ocean, and walk on the moon, but we have not figured out how to structure societies in a fashion that is simultaneously acceptable to securitarians, unitarians, and everybody in between. More than ever, we are at each other's throats. Social media is a cesspool, family reunions are minefields, and our institutions are imperiled. Recent leaders and modern technology allow us to indulge our predispositions, bringing into bold relief a difference that has lurked for millennia and that is not going to leave: the difference between those who live to embrace outsiders and those whose solemn duty is to keep outsiders at bay. As distasteful as we find those who have a view of social life wholly different from our own, the answer is not to attack them; it is to learn to live with them.

NOTES

Chapter 1

1. Lakoff (1996).
2. Steven Pinker (2002) aptly refers to the part of our brain responsible for constructing this narrative as the "baloney generator."
3. Haidt (2016).
4. Skocpol and Williamson (2012, p. 12).
5. Journalist Leonard Pitts, however, asserts that we should not make any effort to understand those who formed Trump's base (2018).
6. A point made nicely by Katz (1960); see also Stenner (2005, p. 330).
7. See Martin (2001), Will (2003), and Jost (2006).
8. Though there is an interesting debate about whether liberals and conservatives are equally biased by motivated reasoning. Crawford (2012), Kahan (2013), Brandt et al. (2014), and Ditto et al. (2019) mostly say that they are; Baron and Jost (2019) are not so sure.
9. As Dionne, Ornstein, and Mann (2017) point out, many people, especially "liberals and pro-Trump conservatives each have characteristic blind spots in analyzing the Trump upsurge" (p.150).
10. Adkisson and Peach (2017).
11. Abramowitz (2018).
12. Sides, Tesler, and Vavreck (2018).
13. For example, Norris and Inglehart (2019).
14. Zito and Todd (2018).
15. Cramer (2016), Wuthnow (2018), and Duina (2018).
16. For example, Adorno et al. (1950); also see Jost et al. (2003).
17. The international polling firm YouGov conducted the survey.

18. The topic of polarization justifiably has received a good deal of attention. Particularly insightful treatments of it include Theriault (2008), Arceneaux and Johnson (2013), Campbell (2016), McCarty (2019), and Klein (2020). Campbell's emphasis on the bottom up rather than top down forces driving polarization is perfectly consistent with my thesis as is Arceneaux and Johnson's evidence that viewers are polarized long before they tune in to their favorite news outlet.

19. Among the best work on this long-running strain of politicians and thought is Mudde (2007) and Mudde and Kaltwasser (2017).

20. Hitler is not on this list for reasons I will explain shortly.

21. In fact, the major reason for the recent prevalence of nativist sentiment is that so many outsiders are now inside. This situation is very bothersome to the people who support Donald Trump and other leaders like him.

22. This account can be seen as somewhat consistent with the influential work of Jonathan Haidt (2012b) on moral foundations. Haidt identifies five (later six) moral foundations: harm avoidance, fairness, purity, authority, and in-group/out-group orientations. These then aggregate into two mega-foundations: the individualizing ones (harm avoidance and fairness) and the binding ones (purity, authority, and in-groups/out-groups). Five or six is a little busy for my tastes but Haidt's larger distinction between people who favor binding foundations (seemingly reminiscent of securitarians) and those who give more emphasis to individualizing orientations (similar to unitarians) is dead on target. Parallels can also be glimpsed in Gelfand's (2018) distinction between tight and loose societies and Hetherington and Weiler's (2018) distinction between fixed and flexible people. For more on the advantages of the mega-foundations, see Smith et al. (2017).

23. Bergh et al. (2016) adopt a similar perspective. They present evidence that marginalized groups within the country are often treated as unfavorably as groups that are more traditionally viewed as outgroups. This is why they also eschew the term outgroups in favor of "marginalized groups"—similar to what I am calling outsiders. See also Dunwoody and McFarland (2018).

24. Brandt et al. (2014) support this claim empirically. They find that among white conservatives, prejudice against blacks disappears when blacks are portrayed as having conservative political orientations.

25. Kurzban, Tooby, and Cosmides (2001).

26. In this sense, I do not completely agree with those claiming that Trump supporters "find community by rejoicing in the suffering of those they hate and fear" (Serwer 2018). Some undoubtedly do but most find community in their shared eagerness to be vigilant in the face of outsider threats. For them, fear and hatred are less of a factor than Serwer suggests.

27. Federico and Malka (2018) also emphasize security, along with a desire for certainty. Ardent Trump supporters focus like lasers on concepts such as "invasion" and "cultural replacement." See Peters et al. (2019).

28. In this sense, ardent Trump supporters tend to have a strong sense of national identity and the literature on that topic is very useful. See, for example, Kosterman and Feshbach (1989); Huddy and Khatib (2007); Pehrson, Vignoles, and Brown (2009); Ariely (2011); Carter and Pérez (2015); Osborne, Milojev, and Sibley (2017); and Kessler and Elad-Strenger (2019). Of particular relevance is Theiss-Morse's (2009) account emphasizing the distinction between prototypical and marginalized Americans. Some people may live in the country but, as she notes, they are not always recognized as "fully belonging" (p. 4). She goes on to demonstrate that strong national identifiers are more likely to minimize those who are not prototypical members of the national group. Strong identifiers perceive the group to be homogeneous (examples she provides include Christian, capitalist, English speakers, native born) and those who do not fit the stereotype tend to be mistrusted (pp. 75, 93). This thinking is related closely to the valuable work of Marques, Abrams, and Serôdio (2001) on the "black sheep effect." Other excellent work on the topic includes Schildkraut (2011) and Masuoka and Junn (2013).

29. Chait (2019); Cockburn (2019).

30. Skocpol and Williamson find some similar patterns among the Tea Party supporters they analyzed (2012).

31. Johnston, Lavine, and Federico (2017).

32. Even so, many commentators continued to insist it is all about the economy. See, for example, Reich (2018).

33. Sides, Tesler, and Vavreck (2018) recognize this, as do others. Cramer (2016) and Sides, Tesler, and Vavreck (2018) see attitudes toward welfare and redistribution as essentially group based and social. This may be why Johnston, Lavine, and Federico (2017) find that economics can sometimes constitute a central dimension of politics.

34. Mendelberg (2001); Alesina and Glaeser (2004); Petersen et al. (2010); Cramer (2016, pp. 24, 88); Mutz (2018); Hetherington and Weiler (2018), among others.

35. Frank (2004); Zeitz (2017); Taub (2017); Metzl (2019).

36. Du Bois (1935).

37. Long and Clement (2018).

38. Goodwin and Milazzo (2017). In a similar vein, polling conducted by Stanley Greenberg indicates that the best predictor of a "leave" vote was opposition to immigration [see Hetherington and Weiler (2018, p. 204)].

39. Despite its pre-existing connection to religion, the word nicely captures a worldview in which there are no insiders and outsiders; in which everyone is equally worthy of dignity, assistance, and care. Having known several Unitarians, I am comfortable using the lower-case phrase as a more general descriptor of those who are the opposite of securitarians.

40. Hill et al. (2011).

41. Pinker (2011).
42. More amorphous and novel threats such as those posed by man-made climate change, as important as they might be, are not evolutionarily primal.
43. Hill et al. (2011).
44. Woodburn (1982).
45. Lee (1988).
46. Boehm (1999; 2014).
47. Hobbes (2010).
48. See Kinder and Kam (2010).
49. Those who are eager to defend against outsiders tend to set high standards for qualifying as an insider; those who want to embrace outsiders do not.
50. For interesting discussions of the universality of left and right, see Bobbio (1996) and Jost (2006).
51. Matthew Continetti on *Talk of the Nation* (2008).
52. Medved (2011).
53. This distinction is evident in differing attitudes toward scientific evidence. On climate change and other topics, the consensus of scientists means little to conservatives but a great deal to liberals. Objective scientific truth exists for liberals in a way that it does not for most strong Trump supporters [for a related point, see Mooney (2005)].

Chapter 2

1. As one example, see Cole (2019). Also see, Reich (2018).
2. Lazarsfeld, Berelson, and Gaudet (1948).
3. However, some academics have relied on their own surveys. Fortunato, Hibbing, and Mondak (2018); Rapoport, Abramowitz, and Stone (2016); Ludeke, Klitgaard, and Vitriol (2018); Smith and Hanley (2018); Womick et al. (2018); and Parker et al. (2018) have conducted valuable surveys that are distinct from exit polls.
4. Another point to bear in mind is that exit polls are biased toward college-educated voters who, it turns out, are more likely to cooperate with inquisitive pollsters; see Edsall (2018). Parker et al.'s (2018) work with validated voters serves as a partial corrective to exit polls.
5. For example, Reich (2018).
6. Sarlin (2016) and Hochschild (2018).
7. Quoted in Sides, Tesler, and Vavreck (2018).
8. Rothwell and Diego-Rosell (2016).
9. Manza and Crowley (2017).
10. Smith and Hanley (2018).
11. For example, Elliott (2016); Casselman (2017).
12. See Sides, Tesler, and Vavreck (2018, p. 216), Inglehart (2018), and Norris and Inglehart (2019).

13. Bartels (2017); see also Kaufmann (2019); Sides, Tesler, and Vavreck (2018); Abramowitz (2018); and Bricker and Ibbitson (2019). Dionne, Ornstein, and Mann (2017) accurately note that supporters of the "economic" explanation usually analyze county data rather than survey data. As Sides, Tesler, and Vavreck (2018) note, however, "Counties don't vote," and many of the counties with marginal economies contain populations with other relevant traits and psychological dispositions such as concerns about immigration and preservation of the dominant culture. Economics is not irrelevant but more often than not it is spurious, with the core concerns being security and culture. This is not to say no one is driven to national populism by economic concerns; see Wuthnow (2018); Duina (2018); Zito and Todd (2018). Also on this issue, see Reich (2018) and Green and McElwee (2019).
14. For more on this point, see Sides, Tesler, and Vavreck (2018).
15. Parker et al. (2018).
16. Burton (2018).
17. Summarized in Ekins (2018).
18. For a different view, see Djupe and Burge (2017).
19. Parker et al.'s (2018) numbers based on validated voters in their long-term tracking poll are close to the same.
20. Also, gender differences varied from race to race.
21. Smith and Hanley (2018).
22. Manza and Crowley (2017).
23. See Abramowitz (2018) and Sides, Tesler, and Vavreck (2018).
24. Bishop (2009).
25. Smith and Hanley (2018, p. 197). For additional support of these patterns in a non-American context, see Maxwell (2019), who concludes that "geographic polarization is a second-order manifestation of deeper divides" (p. 456).
26. Jost et al. (2003).
27. Inbar, Pizarro, and Bloom (2009).
28. Cramer (2016).
29. Vance (2016).
30. Kimmel (2018).
31. Griffith (2017).
32. Schwartz, Caprara, and Vecchione (2010).
33. Graham, Haidt, and Nosek (2009); also see Haidt (2012b).
34. Jost et al. (2003).
35. Carney et al. (2008).
36. Hirsh et al. (2010).
37. Mondak (2010).
38. Costa and McCrae (1993), McCrae and Costa (2003), and Gerber et al. (2010).
39. Fortunato, Hibbing, and Mondak (2018).

40. Smith et al. (2011).
41. Inbar, Pizarro, and Bloom (2009).
42. Graham, Haidt, and Nosek (2009).
43. See Haidt (2012a; 2012b).
44. Billingsley, Lieberman, and Tybur (2018).
45. Liuzza et al. (2018).
46. Baragona (2019).
47. Schwartz (1992). In studying values, Schwartz follows a long line of scholars. See especially Rokeach (1973).
48. Schwartz, Caprara, and Vecchione (2010).
49. Vance (2016); Lamont, Park, and Ayala-Hurtado (2017); and Hochschild (2018).
50. Cramer (2016).
51. Cramer (2016).
52. Vance (2016).
53. Current divisions between Republicans and Democrats capture the unitarian and securitarian divide in a way that partisanship previously did not. Not that long ago, Democrats were more likely to oppose immigration and Republicans, especially the business community, valued immigration.
54. For example, Brader (2006), Valentino et al. (2008), Valentino et al. (2009), and Albertson and Gadarian (2015).
55. The authors of these stories, in order, are Kosur (2018), Schreindl (2013), Keim (2008), Jacobs (2017), Young (2018), Azarian (2016), and Ball (2016).
56. Norris and Inglehart (2019, p. 7); see also Hetherington and Weiler (2018, pp. ix–xxii).
57. Hofstadter (1964).
58. Burns and Herndon (2018).
59. Of course, asking people to self-report has its downsides as well since people have the desire to be socially acceptable and at other times are simply unaware of what is going on inside them—why they do the things they do and how they feel.
60. Chapman University (2019).
61. Feldman and Stenner (1997) wisely observe that authoritarians are not generally more fearful of personal threats like snakes but may be more fearful of threats to the social order. See also MacWilliams (2016b).
62. Howard Lavine and his colleagues (2002) have it right when they reference an "acute sensitivity to threat." MacWilliams (2016b) mentions "hypervigilance" but then adds "always threatened" (p. 19). He is half right. We need to get used to the idea that people can behave in a hyper-vigilant fashion without being threatened.
63. Huddy et al. (2005); see also Marcus, MacKuen, and Neuman (2000) and Albertson and Gadarian (2015).
64. Green (2017).

65. Grier (2016), Kimmel (2018), Milligan (2018), and Edsall (2019a). Zito and Todd's (2018) interviews include numerous references to anger, frustration, and anxiety, leading them to refer to the "revenge of the working class whites," to emotional impulsiveness, and to "rage" and hostility toward government, corporations—anything big (pp. 19–20). In addition, the interviews conducted by Robert Wuthnow (2018) report substantial levels of outrage, fear, and anger (p. 6).
66. See several of the references in note 65.
67. Sides (2017); see also, Sides, Tesler, and Vavreck (2018, pp. 6, 31).
68. Brandt et al. (2014).

Chapter 3

1. See citations in note 47.
2. For good discussions of projection, see Berelson, Lazarsfeld, and McPhee (1954), Jung (2006), and Lewis-Beck et al. (2008).
3. On Adorno's life, see especially Müller-Doohm (2005), but also see Wiggershaus (1995), Hammer (2006), Claussen (2008), and Gordon (2016a).
4. Müller-Doohm (2005, p. 178).
5. Sanford (1986).
6. Adorno (1983, p. 34).
7. Ross (2014).
8. Wiggershaus (1995).
9. Adorno (1987).
10. Adorno et al. (1950, p. vii).
11. Adorno et al. (1950, p. ix).
12. Adorno et al. (1950, p. 1).
13. Adorno et al. (1950, p. 1).
14. Adorno et al. (1950, p. 546).
15. Adorno et al. (1950, p. 223).
16. Adorno et al. (1950, p. 9).
17. Adorno et al. (1950, p. 223).
18. Adorno et al. (1950, pp. 226–227).
19. Hyman and Sheatsley (1954).
20. E.g., Hyman and Sheatsley (1954) and Ray (1983).
21. Though in this case it gets tricky because acquiescent tendencies arguably are part of being a submissive authoritarian.
22. Yet another methodological problem is the tendency to include "double-barreled" items; that is items that reference two separate concepts, making it difficult to know which referent influenced the respondent's response.
23. Adorno et al. (1950, p. 628).
24. Adorno et al. (1950, pp. 613–614).
25. Adorno et al. (1950, p. 632).

26. Brown (1965, p. 504).

27. Adorno et al. (1950, p. 975).

28. Fromm (1941).

29. Adorno et al. (1950, p. ix).

30. Adorno (1983).

31. Adorno et al. (1950, p. 287).

32. Adorno et al. (1950, p. 904).

33. Adorno et al. (1950, p. ix).

34. Adorno et al. (1950, p. 971). In this, they are in line with other work on fascism: Fromm (1941) says those with fascist tendencies are "isolated, powerless, and insecure people." Rokeach (1973) says they have had adverse experiences, possibly enduring, that create anxiety and cause dogmatism and intolerance.

35. Adorno et al. (1950, p. 971).

36. Adorno et al. (1950, p. 971).

37. Altemeyer (1981; 1988; 1996).

38. He also insisted that these three components actually constitute a single dimension. Later work, however, makes a convincing case that aggression, conventionalism, and submission are distinct dimensions [see, for example, Duckitt et al. (2010)].

39. Sidanius and Pratto (1999). This collection of items shows that some people believe there is a natural hierarchy of groups and that society will unavoidably reflect that basic fact while others believe all groups are equal and that any societal inequity is a mistake that needs to be rectified through appropriate public policies. SDO includes items such as "we should do what we can to equalize conditions for different groups" and "we should strive to make incomes as equal as possible." As pointed out by Duckitt and Sibley (2009), the emphasis on group hierarchies within society is different from that found in RWA even as the mixture of societal structure items and policy preferences is the same.

40. This is a point made forcefully by Duckitt et al. (2002) and by Duckitt and Fisher (2003); see also Sibley and Duckitt (2013).

41. Indeed, this is likely why RWA correlates so highly with ideology; the focus is often directly on outsiders.

42. For more on this fascinating debate, see Eysenck (1954), Shils (1954), Rokeach (1960), Eysenck and Coulter (1972), Ray (1983), Feldman (2003a), Jost et al. (2003), and Conway et al. (2017).

43. The list includes Martin (1964), Feldman (2003a), Stenner (2005), and Hetherington and Weiler (2009).

44. Hetherington and Weiler (2009, p. 48).

45. Feldman (2003a), Stenner (2005), and Hetherington and Weiler (2009, ch. 5).

46. MacWilliams (2016a and 2016b) also makes excellent use of the child-rearing items. To be clear, unlike AFLS, these more recent authors do not think child-rearing is a cause of political attitudes but rather an indicator.

47. The authors of these articles, in order, are Illing (2016), Ross (2016), Bernstein (2017), Gordon (2016b), MacWilliams (2016a; 2016b), Womick et al. (2018), Linden (2017), Gray (2017), and Taub (2016).

48. Dean (2017).

49. Altemeyer (2016).

50. Walsh (2019).

51. Altemeyer (1988, p. 4). This line of thinking is also apparent in work on system justification. See, for example, Jost, Banaji, and Nosek (2004) and Jost (2020).

52. On support for anti-democratic policies, see Hetherington and Suhay (2011).

53. A similar argument could be made regarding their orientation to the military. Securitarians are much more likely to revere the military than to serve in it.

54. O'Reilly and Dugard (2013).

55. The poem was written by Emma Lazarus.

56. Altemeyer (1988, p. 4).

57. Altemeyer (1988, p. 5).

58. A common approach, found in the RWA battery, is to measure aggression by recording people's responses to items that include aggressive words such as "destroy," "smash," and "crush" in items. The thinking is that if respondents agree with such items, they must be aggressive but this logic is likely flawed. Asking respondents, for example, whether they agree that "godless people should be put out of action" is not an item tapping generic aggressive tendencies so much as an item tapping feelings toward atheists. Dunwoody and Funke (2016) make this point very nicely.

59. Ludeke, Klitgaard, and Vitriol (2018, p. 8). For related work stressing variations in cognitive ability, see Choma and Hanoch (2017).

60. Womick et al. (2018). Stanley Feldman astutely notes that common measures of aggression are really only measures of opposition to "nonconformists" (2003b, p. 67).

61. Adorno et al. (1950, p. 234).

62. Martin (2001, p. 2).

63. Gordon (2016b).

64. Quoted in Gordon (2016b).

65. Sears and Funk (1999), Peterson, Smith, and Hibbing (forthcoming).

66. See, for example, Martin et al. (1986); Alford, Funk, and Hibbing (2005); Jost (2006); Hatemi et al. (2007); Settle et al. (2010); Haidt (2012b); and Hibbing, Smith, and Alford (2014).

Chapter 4

1. Inconsistently, he believed that plants could pass along these traits to the next generation. How this transmission could occur without genetics is a mystery.
2. Becker (1998).
3. Dugatkin and Trut (2017).
4. Goldman (2010).
5. Dugatkin and Trut (2017).
6. Wade (2006).
7. See, for example, Albert et al. (2009).
8. For readers unfamiliar with the term, a phenotype is a set of observable individual characteristics resulting from the interaction of genotype and the environment.
9. This tendency can be seen in many of the other securitarian leaders around the world as well as their followers. They are not known for their internationalism.
10. Weber, Peterson, and Hoekstra (2013).
11. Personal communication with Nicole Bedford of the Hoekstra Lab (March 19, 2019).
12. See Martin et al. (1986); Alford, Funk, and Hibbing (2005).
13. Pinker (2002).
14. Huddy et al. (2005), Mueller and Stewart (2018), and Crisanti and Merolla (2019).
15. However, those who do not look like or act like insiders clearly lose more points. Race obviously matters a great deal to securitarians.
16. Dodd et al. (2012).
17. Mills et al. (2014).
18. Carraro, Castelli, and Macchiella (2011).
19. Mills et al. (2016).
20. Shook and Fazio (2009).
21. Oxley et al. (2008).
22. Amodio et al. (2007).
23. Schreiber et al. (2013).
24. Ahn et al. (2014).
25. For example, see Azarian (2016).
26. Ahn et al. (2014).
27. Bradley (2000).
28. See, for example, Knoll, O'Daniel, and Cusato (2015), Osmundsen et al. (2019), and Bakker et al. (2019). Conservatives have embraced the interpretation that they are not fearful [see, for example, Gilson (2018)] and their eagerness to do so makes sense. Posturing and projecting strength are key securitarian strategies, so being fearful would be counterproductive. From

a securitarian perspective, one of the most insulting labels imaginable is snowflake.

29. A shift from biases in negativity to biases in threats was urged on me by Lilienfeld and Lazman (2014). I think they are correct.

30. Carver and White (1994).

31. This argument is consistent with Hart's findings that much of Trump's appeal has to do with how he makes his followers feel (2020).

32. Norris and Inglehart (2019, p. 445).

33. This is not to deny that sometimes these security concerns for insiders cross the line into cruelty against outsiders. See Serwer (2018). The scholarly literature contains fascinating treatments of the role of the various negative emotions (see, for example, Huddy et al. [2005] and Albertson and Gadarian [2015]), with one influential account (Marcus, MacKuen, and Neuman [2000]) holding that anxiety should not be viewed as a negative emotion because it stimulates attention, awareness, and involvement. However anxiety is viewed, it is important to recognize that attention can lead individuals to feel good about themselves in the form of duties fulfilled, obligations met, and responsibilities accepted.

34. Taylor, Funk, and Craighill (2006).

35. Napier and Jost (2008); Brooks (2012); Jetten, Haslam, and Barlow (2012); and Burton, Plaks, and Peterson (2015). One group of scholars, however, after documenting that liberals smile more than conservatives [see Wojcik et al. 2015)], wondered if conservatives were merely claiming to be higher in well-being, though another explanation for the smile differential could be that, compared to liberals, conservatives and especially conservative males have been found to be less facially expressive regardless of emotion [see Peterson et al. 2018)].

36. This explanation is consistent with some claims in previous research regarding the psychological benefits of an ego defense system. See Jost and Hunyadi (2003), Stenner (2005), and Henry (2011).

37. Onraet et al. (2016).

38. Unfortunately, providing conclusive tests of this hypothesis will have to wait. Given that fervid Trump supporters almost certainly felt better about themselves during the Trump presidency, to be convincing, data would need to be collected under at least two ideologically different administrations.

39. Scholarly research suggests that Clinton was right to combine attitudes toward many diverse groups. Kinder and Kam refer to "the generality and consistency of out-group rejection" (2010, p. 16) and their evidence, echoing the conclusions of Adorno et al. (1950), demonstrates that people who are prejudiced against one group tend to be prejudiced against all groups.

40. Dionne, Ornstein, and Mann (2017); Sides, Tesler, and Vavreck (2018); Mutz (2018); and Norris and Inglehart (2019).

41. Lopez (2017).

42. In light of the 2017 white supremacist march in Charlottesville, social media comments, and the positions and statements of key players in the Trump orbit such as Stephen Miller, Sebastian Gorka, and Steve Bannon, it seems clear that a subset of impassioned Trump supporters are racist by any definition.

43. Goodhart (2017, p. 32).

44. Dionne, Ornstein, and Mann (2017), put it well: "Understanding the legitimate worries of those troubled by immigration is better than dismissing a large share of our fellow citizens as bigots" (p. 216).

45. Luttig, Federico, and Lavine (2017).

46. Political scientist Ashley Jardina makes a similar argument when she writes that "whites' racialized attitudes and behaviors are not always out-group oriented" in that they are also "motivated by their desire to protect their in-group" (2019, p. 267).

47. Malkin (2019).

48. Dionne, Ornstein, and Mann (2017) accurately point out that it is a mistake to view Trump supporters as "a solid phalanx of racists" (p. 151) before going on to say that "being honest about the role of prejudice in the rise of Trump is not the same as accusing all or most of his voters of racism" (pp. 160–161). See also Hetherington and Weiler (2018, p. 44).

49. Kinder and Kam (2010).

50. Theiss-Morse (2009, p. 94); see also Picket and Brewer (2005).

51. Kinder and Kam (2010, p. 8).

52. Kirby (2019). This is a perfect description of how securitarians see the international arena.

53. Plott (2019).

54. Jason DeParle asserts that migration is the defining issue of the twenty-first century and I think he is correct (2019).

55. Hetherington and Weiler (2018, pp. 51–55).

56. Zito and Todd (2018, p. 139; see also pp. 109–110). Relatedly, one rust belt voter interviewed by Zito and Todd (2018) said, "A lot of people probably think, 'Oh you're a woman with a gun. You're probably a bitch.' That's probably what they think [but] . . . it doesn't make me a bad person. It makes me a protected person" (p. 85). Another female gun owner they interviewed said, "[Carrying] does make you feel better" (p. 139).

57. Setzler and Yanus (2017).

58. Inglehart (2018).

59. Kaufmann (2019, p. 221).

60. Norris and Inglehart (2019, p. 69).

61. Norris and Inglehart (2019, p. 7).

62. Norris and Inglehart (2019, p. 72).

63. To offer a few examples, see Taylor (2018), Beinart (2018), Jacobs (2018), and Stanley (2018).

64. Libertarian Party (2018).

65. Somin (2018).

66. Iyer et al. (2012, p. 17).

67. Abramowitz (2018, pp. 135–160); also see Sides, Tesler, and Vavreck (2018).

68. Krugman (2019).

69. Chait (2018).

70. Douthat (2018).

71. French (2014).

72. Feuer (2013). An NPR *Weekend Edition* story [Simon and Bowman (2018)] pointed out that black gun ownership has surged in recent years, in part because of Trump but also for other reasons. Many of those interviewed tended to not trust anybody, including Trump.

73. Feuer (2013).

74. French (2014).

75. Malkin (2019).

76. Ostrom (1990).

77. Oliver and Wood (2018).

78. Duina (2018, pp. 116–117).

79. Duina (2018, p. 116).

80. Wuthnow (2018, p. 40).

81. Brooks (2019).

82. Wuthnow (2018, p. 27).

83. Wuthnow (2018, p. 38).

84. Wuthnow (2018, p. 15).

85. See, for example, Kymlicka (1988).

86. Clinton (1996).

87. Norris and Inglehart (2019, p. 65). For a good discussion of the varied meanings of populism, see Dionne, Ornstein, and Mann (2017, pp. 34–37). For a good application of the concept of populism to Trump's win in 2016, see Oliver and Rahn (2016).

88. Collin (2019).

89. Hibbing et al. (2018); see also Hibbing and Theiss-Morse (2002).

90. Norris and Inglehart (2019); Lind (2016).

91. Grossman and Hopkins (2016).

92. Grossman and Hopkins (2016, p. 324).

93. Converse (1964); see also Kinder and Kalmoe (2017).

94. Jost (2006).

95. Important research by Mark Brandt, Jarett Crawford, and others [see, for example, Brandt et al. (2014)] presents liberals and conservatives as virtual mirror images of each other, with one side just happening to dislike fundamentalist Christians and corporate tycoons and the other just happening to dislike immigrants and lawbreakers. Identical orientations; just different target groups. Jonathan Rauch (2019), among others, does an excellent job of

explaining the forces that exacerbate political tribalism once it is established. Missing in most of these accounts is a persuasive explanation of how people initially end up in the tribes that they do. My assertion is that many liberals have a unitarian mindset that leads them to dislike powerful insiders and entities perceived to be hostile to outsiders while many conservatives harbor a securitarian mindset that leads them to dislike outsiders and those who defend them. As Grossman and Hopkins (2016) ably demonstrate, these very distinct orientations then lead to important differences between Democrats and Republicans in terms of policy preferences, coalitional possibilities, and organizational structures.

96. Of course, Republicans draw some support from blacks, Latinxs, and other minorities, but the numbers are usually amazingly small with the exception of those Latinxs for whom the anti-abortion platform of the Republican Party is a major draw.

97. One of Bob Altemeyer's (1988) many astute observations about authoritarians is that they "do not typically realize they are unusually submissive to authority, unusually hostile, and unusually conventional" (p. 319). This is true but applicable to all of us. Humans, whether they be authoritarian, unitarian, or securitarian, lack a good sense of themselves and why they are the way they are.

Chapter 5

1. Respondents had the following options: strongly agree, agree, neither agree nor disagree, disagree, or strongly disagree.

2. Levendusky (2009).

3. There is no perfect way to isolate Trump venerators. The approach adopted here seems reasonable to me. Future scholars may want to try another one, though the results are likely to be quite similar.

4. I also eliminated from the analyses three individuals who said they believed Donald Trump was one of the best presidents in the history of our country but then went on to say that they strongly opposed him. It appears these individuals missed the spirit of the "best ever" item. They were probably acknowledging what they saw as Trump's political skills even as they strongly opposed the objectives he was using his skills to achieve. Since there are only three of them out of 1,000, their presence or absence does not affect the results and, given their likely misinterpretation, leaving them out seems cleaner.

5. As examples, see Cole (2019) and Reich (2018).

6. One asterisk means the relationship is marginally significant. For more information, see note 12 below.

7. Especially since the number of cases is smaller than for the overall correlations.

8. Though they might with a larger data set.
9. McCrae and Costa (1987; 2003). For a good account of the history of the Big 5, see Mondak (2010). Having two items per trait rather than one heightens accuracy of measurement.
10. Gerber et al. (2010) and Mondak et al. (2010).
11. Recall that Fortunato, Hibbing, and Mondak (2018) looked at the difference between Republicans who supported Trump in the 2016 primaries and those Republicans who did not.
12. The standard level of statistical significance is a p value of .05 or less, indicating that there are, at most, five chances in 100 (or 1 in 20) that the results are occurring by chance. However, in this table and several to follow I also indicate whether a significance level of .10 is achieved. This is a very permissive standard and I only use it here because, due to the number of items I wanted to include in the survey, I was forced to divide the sample in half, giving some items to one half and other items to the other half. Since significance levels are sensitive to the number of cases (see note 14 below), the sizes of many of these coefficients suggest they would have been significant at the .05 level if the relevant items had been asked to the full sample.
13. For readers who like to see the exact item wordings, they follow. Extraverted: "I see myself as someone who is extraverted and enthusiastic" and "I see myself as someone who is reserved and quiet." Agreeable: "I see myself as someone who is critical and quarrelsome" and "I see myself as someone who is sympathetic and caring." Conscientious: "I see myself as someone who is dependable and self-disciplined" and "I see myself as someone who is disorganized." Neurotic: "I see myself as someone who is anxious and easily upset" and "I see myself as someone who is calm and emotionally stable." Openness: "I see myself as someone who is complex and open to new experiences" and "I see myself as someone who is conventional and uncreative." Fortunato, Hibbing, and Mondak's study of the 2016 primaries (2018) found Trump supporters to be significantly less neurotic and this was when few people believed he would actually become president. It appears something beyond their enjoyment of having Trump as president makes Trump supporters less neurotic.
14. Perspicacious readers may note that larger correlations in column 5 sometimes achieve lower significance levels than smaller coefficients in column 4. This is because the number of cases is substantially lower in column 5 which is limited to only those participants who are conservative. Statistical significance is affected by the number of cases. Since it is an indication of how confident we can be in the results, this only makes sense. Also bear in mind that the means in the first four columns indicate the percentage agreeing, whether the agreement is strong or not strong. The correlations, on the other hand, reflect the full, five-point range of the variables from strongly disagree all the way to strongly agree. Thus, differences in the percentage

agreeing will not perfectly predict when the correlations are statistically significant.

15. The exact item wordings for these eight traits follows. Dogmatism: "I see myself as someone who is set in my ways and convinced my views are correct" and "I see myself as someone who is impartial and open to others' views." Preferring closure: "I like problems that have many possible correct answers" and "I dislike novels and movies that end without making it clear exactly what happened to the characters." Preferring agreement: "I have to admit I prefer to be around people who have the same beliefs I do" and "I like being in a group with lots of different types of people." Being social fulfilled: "I see myself as someone who is socially content and has lots of friends" and "I see myself as someone who is unfulfilled and in need of a better support system." Anger: "I see myself as someone who is angry and frustrated" and "I see myself as someone who is carefree and cheerful." Conformity/conventionalism: "Sometimes I enjoy ruffling the feathers of 'proper' society" and "I see myself as someone who mostly lives life 'by the book.'" Submissiveness: "I sometimes like it when others shape my life and make decisions for me" and "I prefer to be independent of others and largely self-sufficient."

16. These three items tap extraversion, openness, and neuroticism, respectively. Examples of items tapping the other two personality traits follow. Agreeableness: "I see myself as someone who is sympathetic and warm." Conscientiousness: "I see myself as someone who is dependable and self-disciplined."

17. These items are designed to tap rural resentment so do not address racial resentment. Though it does not pertain to resentment directly, a related item that might be of interest asked whether respondents agreed that they "sometimes wish they had more education." Just under 50% of the entire sample agreed with this statement and that was the case with Trump venerators as well (49% agreed). There were no significant differences across groups. Trump venerators do not spend their days pining about going to college. They may not always "get" those with college degrees, but they do not resent them and they give little indication that they would like to join their ranks.

18. Unlike most of the other items in Table 5.4, there was a counterbalancing, negatively worded item on social fulfillment in the survey ("I see myself as someone who is socially content and has lots of friends"). When this item is reverse coded and added to the other, the group reporting the most social fulfillment by far is Trump venerators. In fact, they are significantly more socially fulfilled than non-Trump-venerating conservatives ($r = -.18$).

19. Though this could be because their demands are lower on this factor.

20. Haidt (2012a).

21. The clearer patterns for disgust-sensitivity appear not for overall ideology but for positions on selected issues. For example, individuals who are generically

disgust-sensitive are consistently more likely to take traditional positions on sexually related matters such as opposing gay marriage. See Inbar, Pizarro, and Bloom (2009) and Smith et al. (2011).

22. Dahl (1963).

23. See Smith, Hibbing, and Hibbing (2019).

24. The numbers in parentheses right after the behaviors indicate the percentage of the overall sample reporting that they engage in that particular behavior.

25. The survey did not include an item on environmental concerns as a threat but it seems likely that securitarians would have been less likely to feel threatened by climate change and environmental degradation in part because they are not convinced that addressing these threats can be done without harming insiders and without helping outsiders. If these perceptions change (for example, if environmental changes are shown to hinder national defense), securitarians may well become more supportive of doing something about the environment.

26. Oh (2019). Many right-wing parties around the world support expansive social welfare systems; what these parties do not support is extending that social welfare system to immigrants and other outsiders. The real left-right ideological division in the US and around the world is based not on economics, but view of groups. For more on this point, see Klein (2020, pp. 121–122). As Robison and Moskowitz (2019) point out, the same could also be said for partisan divisions.

27. The first two are part of a standard Belief in a Dangerous World (BDW) battery (Altemeyer 1988) and are nicely balanced with a "pro-trait" wording and a "con-trait" wording so could be combined. The third item is not part of the standard BDW battery but captures the sentiment.

28. Other BDW items that were not included in my survey focus even more on outsider threats. For example, "Our society is [not] full of immoral and degenerate people who prey on decent people" (Altemeyer 1988, p. 196).

29. These findings are consistent with Gibson's important point that perceptions of threat do not need to be based on prejudice (2011). They are also consistent with Dunwoody and McFarland's otherwise puzzling empirical result that "perceptions of threat increased support for anti-Muslim policies more for low than high authoritarians" (2018, p. 102).

30. This interpretation is consistent with the results of a fascinating set of experiments by Hopkins, Sides, and Citrin. People tend to overestimate the percentage of immigrants in the United States but these researchers found that correcting misconceptions does nothing to improve people's attitudes toward immigrants. The authors speculate, accurately in my opinion, that misinformation "may be a consequence, rather than a cause, of attitudes" (2018, p. 315).

31. Baker and Haberman (2019).

32. Adorno et al. (1950) and especially see Kinder and Kam (2010).

33. Of course, desires for social acceptability may mean more Trump venerators are overt racists than appears to be the case based on self-report survey items. On the other hand, a surprising number of people have been found to be eager to express prejudice (Forscher et al. 2015).

Chapter 6

1. The quote is from Altemeyer (1988, p. 259).
2. Note also that these items are double- and triple-barreled in that they include multiple, distinct referents, making it more difficult to know what responses actually mean.
3. Several have criticized RWA as just another measure of conservativism. See, for example, Ray (1985). For a discussion, see Altemeyer (1988, pp. 7–8). This is why Feldman and others are attracted to child-rearing items. See Feldman (2003a).
4. Though the expectation that Trump supporters are not authoritarian goes against a great deal of conventional wisdom, to date, no empirical evidence finds that Trump supporters are more submissive to authorities. See Ludeke, Klitgaard, and Vitriol (2018) and Womick et al. (2018).
5. Another relevant survey item goes against this pattern. It reads "I like to be influenced by powerful people." Few respondents agree with this statement but there is a slight increase from liberals (just 7%) to Trump venerators (22%). The difference across all four groups is significant but from non-Trump-venerating conservatives to Trump venerators is not (though it comes close and would be with a larger sample). It may be that this item is at odds with the other "submissiveness" items because, with Trump as president, the "powerful person" most had in mind was Donald Trump.
6. As pointed out in Chapter 4, defense hawks are not typically securitarians' first choice.
7. Jost et al. (2003).
8. Ludeke, Klitgaard, and Vitriol (2018) and Womick et al. (2018).
9. Burke (1790); also see Jost et al. (2003).
10. Altemeyer (1988, p. 318).
11. Altemeyer (1988, p. 107).
12. There is a healthy and helpful literature on left-wing authoritarianism [see, for example, Van Hiel, Duriez, and Kossowska (2006); Conway et al. (2017)]. My goal is to stay away from the debate over whether authoritarians can be on the left as well as the right and instead to determine whether what might appear to be authoritarian motivations are actually driven by the desire for security—security from outsiders in the case of securitarians and security from powerful insiders in the case of unitarians.
13. Altemeyer (1988, p. 109).

14. Besides, merely agreeing with items that include action words such as "destroy" or "attack" does not automatically make someone aggressive. Feldman has made the same point I am making here on the flaws of previous measures of aggression (2003b, p. 67).
15. Note that, unlike most of the indices presented here, the item pair for this one is not counterbalanced with a "con" trait item and a "pro" trait item and so is subject to acquiescence bias. Another survey item that is relevant to this discussion of aggression reads: "In getting what you want, it is sometimes necessary to use force against other groups." Only 20% of people agree with this statement but there is a slight increase in agreement as we move from liberals (15%) to Trump venerators (28%). The difference between Trump venerators and non-Trump-venerating conservatives is not significant but comes close, so would be significant with a larger sample.
16. This difference just misses statistical significance.
17. The "work-quietly-behind-the-scenes as opposed to work-aggressively-for-needed-change" item could be interpreted either way. Working behind the scenes seems to suggest going along with societal conventions but working aggressively could be consistent with the "aggression" leg of modern authoritarianism. If the item is seen as a measure of aggression, it is consistent with authoritarian expectations; if it is seen as a measure of conventionalism, it is inconsistent with authoritarian expectations (since working aggressively would seem to go against conventionalism and conformity).
18. From a scholarly standpoint, if the concept of securitarianism is thought to have any merit, this short securitarian personality battery obviously will need to be tested, modified, extended, factor analyzed, validated, and improved. I have started such a process. In the meantime, these rough-and ready items should provide a general sense of the theoretical direction in which I believe we need to go, should others wish to join in item drafting, testing, and refining.
19. The issues were immigration, taxes, health care, the federal deficit, national defense/security, law and order, racial justice, excess government spending, income inequality, economic health, abortion, homosexuality, religious rights, women's rights, trade with other countries, lack of patriotism, welfare spending, gun rights/gun control, and government regulations on business.
20. I should note that agreement among moderates on the top four was much lower than for liberals. In other words, though many of the same issues were at the top, designation of these issues as most important was done by far fewer moderates than liberals because moderates are decidedly heterogeneous in their issue priorities.
21. For similar efforts, though not in the context of Trump supporter, see Schwartz (1992); Graham, Haidt, and Nosek (2009); and Haidt (2012b). The goal is to get underneath the issues to larger approaches, motivations, and objectives that specific policies may serve.

22. I should note that the survey did have an item stating simply, "Our country desperately needs a forceful, mighty leader," and respondents on the right were more likely to agree with this statement, with Trump venerators were marginally more likely ($p < .10$) to agree with the statement than non-Trump-venerating conservatives. It may be that conservatives and especially Trump venerators are more desirous of political authority regardless of the ideological tinge to that authority. Then again, it may be that these generic responses are reflective of the political context at the time of the survey. Repeating the item when a liberal controls the levers of government would go a long way toward determining whether particular ideologies are really more or less eager for authoritarian leadership.

23. The argument usually made is that authoritarian aggression is different from aggression and must be directed at those individuals that the authorities have singled out for attack. Altemeyer (1988) explicitly states that "the targets of authoritarian aggression could be anyone" (p. 5). I disagree. Securitarians could not be made to turn on entities they believed vital to preserving the security of insiders.

24. Ludeke, Klitgaard, and Vitriol (2018); Womick et al. (2018).

25. Given people's documented desire to give socially acceptable responses, the real number is likely to be higher.

26. Still, my hunch is that activities such as sit-ins, boycotting establishments owned by political foes, and declining to serve those foes are more likely to be engaged in by liberals regardless of the occupant of the White House. Some actions are simply more quintessentially liberal than others.

27. Somit and Peterson (1997).

28. It would be interesting to see how committed to democracy liberals are if the alternative was protecting the environment, redistributing income, or lessening the suffering of outsiders. Throughout history, it has not been unusual for people on the left to be willing to sacrifice democratic principles to enact change. Unfortunately, no such items are in this survey. For example, a useful item would have been, "If a country had to choose between being more compassionate to the suffering poor or else being democratic, being more compassionate would probably be the way to go." Alas, the focus here is on Trump supporters, so assessing others' commitment to democracy in such a fashion will have to wait.

29. See Graham and Svolik (2019) and Svolik (2019).

30. Altemeyer (1988) claims that those at the opposite end of the spectrum from authoritarians are "fair-minded, evenhanded, tolerant, nonaggressive. . . . [T]hey do not maintain the double standards we find among the highs." He also claims that "they do not feel superior to persons with opposing opinions. They are not mean-spirited" (p. 262). I am not certain that the evidence supports these assertions.

31. I wish we could do parallel analyses for authoritarianism. Unfortunately, not all of the personal authoritarian items were asked of the same portion of the sample, so I can't compile them into a single index that could then be correlated with the societal authoritarian index.

32. Readers should avoid the inclination to assume that societal preferences flow out of personal preferences and therefore lack primacy. The social aspect of human life is ancient, deep, and powerful as is apparent in the fact that certain parts of the brain are largely dedicated to social life: facial recognition, to offer one example (Parvizi et al. 2012). People get more worked up by differences in societal preference (witness all the fraught conversations at family reunions) than by differences in personality traits (Smith, Hibbing, and Hibbing 2019), and they are significantly more likely to choose mates and friends on the basis of shared sociopolitical preferences than shared personality traits (Alford et al. 2011). There is very little evidence that personalities are more central to our beings than sociopolitical preferences and a case can be made that to the extent there is a causal direction, it runs from political preferences to personality (Verhulst, Eaves, and Hatemi 2012).

33. I used ordinary least squares (OLS) to estimate these initial models since it is more intuitive; but since the dependent variable is dichotomous, future work may want to use more suitable techniques. I can tell you that, when this is done, interpretations change very little.

34. In the bivariate analysis, submissiveness was actually significant in the direction of Trump venerators being *less* submissive.

35. He writes, "the more important issue should not be which scale predicts better, but which perspective provides greater theoretical guidance" (2003b, p. 69).

36. I also ran multivariate models that included racism and sexism (not shown). Compared to non-Trump-venerating conservatives and with demographics controlled, Trump venerators scored significantly higher on the racism index but not significantly higher on the sexism index. Finally, I ran models with the familiar demographics as well as the three indices of policy stances (the Wilson Patterson measures of social, economic, and securitarian stances). When this was done, preferences on social items drop out, but both securitarian issue positions and economic issue positions are useful in identifying Trump venerators even with other factors controlled. In sum, compared to non-Trump-venerating conservatives, Trump venerators are distinguished by their conservative stances on economic and security issues but not on social issues.

37. For those interested in bivariate correlations, a sixteen-item version of RWA correlates with political views generally and even helps to distinguish between Trump venerators and non-Trump-venerating conservatives ($r = .19$). A twelve-item Social Dominance Orientation (SDO) battery does slightly

worse. The securitarian battery (Table 6.8) distinguishes between Trump venerators and non-Trump-venerating conservatives at .30, a 58% improvement over RWA but, as noted in the text, the real value of the securitarian items is not a marginal improvement in explanatory power but a substantial improvement in theoretical value. Authoritarianism should be measured with items on authority; securitarianism should be measured with items on security.

38. Azarian (2018).

39. A popular belief is that Trump is merely playing a role in that he adopts positions not because he believes them but because he knows they will resonate with a certain segment of the population. I disagree. Trump's aversion to outsiders has been a central part of his outlook for his entire adult life. Witness his early and outspoken opposition to the "Central Park 5," a group of African American youth wrongly accused of raping a woman in New York's Central Park in 1989. Trump spent $85,000 of his own money to take out newspaper ads asserting the guilt of the five boys. Even after DNA evidence cleared them, and even after another person admitted to the crime, Trump refused to accept their innocence [for details, see Rupar (2019)]. When it comes to an aversion to outsiders, Donald Trump does not have to play the part.

Chapter 7

1. As Pettigrew points out, it is unlikely that only one factor explains all Trump supporters (2017).

2. Interestingly, of all nineteen political issues included in the survey, Trump venerators mentioned homosexuality least often—less than 1/10th of 1 percent.

3. Homosexuality is a tricky label for an issue as it could indicate a desire for more rights for LGBTQ individuals, though it seems likely that those very few Trump venerators who prioritize this issue were not applying that interpretation, so they probably belong with the social warriors. Regardless, only a few individuals fell into this category.

4. When calculating these comparisons, the "others" to whom each type is compared always includes the "enigmas"—those whose numbers were too few to give them a category of their own. There are more sophisticated and accurate ways of doing this but they produce results that are quite similar and this procedure is the most intuitive for a generalist audience.

5. Attentive readers may have noted that the percentage white suggested for Trump venerators in Table 7.2 (around 84% to 85%) is higher than that in Table 5.2 (78%). This is because Table 5.2 reports the results for the representative sample only while Table 7.2 also includes the oversample of Trump supporters. Diagnostics indicate that Trump supporters in the oversample

approximate those in the representative sample on most variables but not on race, where the oversample is slightly whiter.

6. Sometimes, the significance levels look off, given the differences in percentages but this can always be explained by the difference in number of cases across the categories and especially the much larger number in the securitarian category. For example, social warriors are slightly more dependable (a measure of conscientiousness), 92 to 91, than securitarians and higher than the other two types (83 and 84, respectively); social warriors are not significantly different from other Trump venerators, but securitarians are. The reason is that there are so many more securitarians than social warriors (about 4 to 1).

   As with the results in chapters 5 and 6, I calculated the correlations with the full range of the variable available and not the dichotomized form (for example, the correlations are based on the sixteen income categories rather than merely whether income was above or below $50,000). In this way, information is not being discarded and the correlations reported are more accurate.

7. The big split in age is between securitarians and social warriors on the one side and the economically concerned and tea partiers on the other. The latter two groups are six or seven years younger than the first two.

8. Delli Carpini and Keeter (1997), Boudreau and Lupia (2011), Barabas et al. (2014), and Lupia (2015).

9. As is well known, self-reports on items such as these should be taken with a grain of salt.

10. For those interested, the average number correct for liberals was 3.3 and for moderates was 3.2, just a little worse than securitarian Trump venerators and somewhat better than other Trump venerators.

11. Self-reported voter registration does not vary much; well over 90% say they are registered.

12. For those interested, multivariate results for this chapter are available from the author.

13. I also conducted an experiment (results not shown). Half of the sample was selected at random to report the degree to which they felt threatened by the eleven entities in Table 7.3 (these are the results that we have been discussing), but the other half instead reported the degree to which they believed that "more should be done to protect people from" each of the eleven. For the most part, people were more likely to say "more should be done to protect people" than to say they "felt threatened" but there was some interesting variation in this difference across the different types of Trump venerators. For example, when it comes to immigrants, economically concerned and tea party Trump venerators were actually more likely to say they felt threatened than to say more should be done to protect people (by 15 points and 11 points, respectively) whereas securitarians were more likely to say "more should be done to protect people" than to say they felt threatened (by 8 points).

Health care provides another contrast. If the comparison is between tea partiers and securitarians, the pattern is similar to that for immigration: tea partiers are 17 points more likely to say they feel threatened than to say more should be done but securitarians are eight points more likely to say more should be done than to say they feel threatened (more evidence that felt threat is not necessary for securitarians to want to neutralize outsiders). The economically concerned Trump venerators provide an interesting twist with regard to health care, however. Though they were more likely to say that immigrants threatened them than to say more should be done, on health care it was the opposite: they were nineteen points more likely to say more should be done than to say they felt threatened.

14. Petersen et al. (2010) and Jensen and Petersen (2016).

15. In 2019, Acting Director of the United States Citizenship and Immigration Services Ken Cuccinelli issued a regulation making it easier for the Trump administration to reject low-income green card and visa applicants because of the increased risk they would be in the public charge (that is, receiving government benefits). The courts blocked the regulation in October of 2019 but it is the perfect embodiment of securitarian attitudes toward immigration.

16. This may be why securitarians don't get as much media attention as their numbers suggest they should.

17. These results are perfectly consistent with Skocpol and Williamson's findings on Tea Party supporters (2012, p. 34). Similar to some of my findings on securitarians, they conclude that Tea Party supporters' use of aggressive language is often for show (2012, p. 34).

Chapter 8

1. Fukuyama (1992). Fukuyama's mistake was to think the fundamental human conflict is between liberal, democratic, capitalistic values and the alternatives. In truth, disputes over neither mass-scale economic nor political systems are evolutionarily central. Disputes over appropriate attitudes toward outsiders are evolutionarily central and thus will continue to be the driving force of human history.

2. As I have noted repeatedly, numerous scholarly works on modern politics stress the importance of groups and identity. Among the most recent and insightful to do so, is Klein (2020, see especially ch. 3).

3. In some respects, history is a strong force and the underlying distinction between securitarians and unitarians is a weak force—but a weak force that provides the backdrop for all manner of historical change.

4. And this is where political science research can continue to make a contribution.

5. Bowman (2017).

6. See, for example, Inglehart (2016) and Inglehart (2018).

7. Inglehart (2018).
8. Inglehart (2016; 2018).
9. Norris and Inglehart (2019).
10. Norris and Inglehart (2019, p. 17).
11. Norris and Inglehart (2019, p. 17). Yuval Harari agrees, noting that "as the twenty-first century unfolds, nationalism is fast losing ground" (2015, p. 207). Highlighted by Brexit and the election of Donald Trump, things looked a little different a few years after he wrote those words.
12. Goodhart (2017, p. 221).
13. Kaufmann (2019, p. 372).
14. For more on the controversy surrounding the definition of racism, see Kendi (2019).
15. Kaufmann (2019, pp. 500–501).
16. Kaufmann (2019, p. 534).
17. Sears and Funk (1999) and Peterson, Smith, and Hibbing (forthcoming).
18. Thus, despite stability being the norm, the data provide a kernel of support for aphorisms such as "If you are not liberal when you are 20 you don't have a heart and if you are not conservative when you are 30 you don't have a brain." See Peterson, Smith, and Hibbing (forthcoming).
19. For early evidence on the importance of generational replacement to aggregate political and social attitudes, with special attention to race, see Greeley and Sheatsley (1971).
20. As mentioned previously, if the survey had included an item asking about willingness to sacrifice democracy in order to save the environment or assist suffering "outsiders," support for democracy among the young likely would drop dramatically.
21. For related points on black conservatism relative to whites, see Welch and Foster (1987); Tate (2010); Philpot (2017); and Engelhardt (2019).
22. Given the level of violence against blacks, their high levels of concern for personal security are understandable. The high percentage of black Democrats saying that "being weak is just about the worst thing for a country to be" is more difficult to explain by reference to historic oppression of blacks.
23. Newport (2008).
24. On "Log Cabin Republicans," see Lampo (2012).
25. If further evidence is necessary, the situation in Syria in 2019 revealed Trump's securitarian instincts. From a securitarian perspective, the central mission of government is not to assist allies but to defend insiders. Isolationism and not foreign interventionism is Trump's instinct and this created rifts between securitarians and those within the Republican Party who were more eager to work with long-time allies to promote a stable world. Isolationist securitarians in the mold of Trump and interventionist securitarians in the mold of, say, Trump's first secretary of state Rex Tillerson, see the world very differently, and this situation could pose policy

challenges for the Republican Party. Of course, the "go it alone" approach does not make sense to unitarians who believe that certain outsiders (our allies) can help with security but securitarians only grudgingly rely on other countries to help with security because to a securitarian no other country can really be trusted to come to our aid.

26. Quoted in Zito and Todd (2018, p. 265).

27. Throughout 2019 and 2020, from his perch in the US Senate, Mitt Romney was ever more openly questioning Trump.

28. For more on partisanship and Trump, see Bartels (2018).

29. Trump would then be in a position to redefine everything. To take perhaps the extreme example of this redefinition, Russia becomes a key to our security rather than a threat to it—all because it seemed to Trump's followers (accurately, as it turns out) that Russia was on his side.

30. For example, Trump called Adam Schiff, chair of the House Judiciary Committee, a "traitor."

31. As Tetlock points out, values (on both sides) quickly become viewed as "sacred," rendering compromise almost impossible (2003). Also see Skitka (2014) on the moralization of politics. Also on this point, see Haidt (2012b).

32. Observers such as Devega (2019) and Hassan (2019) assert that Trump's strongest supporters are best thought of as belonging to a full-fledged cult and speculate as to whether they can be "de-programmed." I contend that Trump has merely been a vehicle for securitarian predispositions, so the concepts of cult and deprogramming do not fit well.

33. At securitarian behest, several libraries in the United States banned Dr. Seuss's *The Butter Battle Book* because it satirized and trivialized the United States' Cold War conflict with the embodiment of outsiders at the time: the Soviet Union.

34. Brandt et al. (2014) make a similar point. In their influential book, Achen and Bartels assert that "group ties and social identity are the most important bases of political commitments" (2016, p. 319) and that therefore scholars are wrong to claim that "ideology trumps identity" (2016, p. 234). In my view, identity is ideology and the real problem with past work is an erroneous conceptualization of ideology as deriving from specific issue positions and usually specific economic issue positions. See Converse (1964) and Kinder and Kalmoe (2017). Psychologists and laypeople often have a more accurate take on ideology as bubbling up from orientations to life that happen to affect preferences for social structure. See, for example, Jost (2006).

35. If the reference had been to Trump venerators, I am convinced the number would have been even higher.

36. Iyengar and Westwood (2014); see also Mason (2012); Hetherington and Rudolph (2015); Mason, Kane, and Wronski (2019); and Spinner-Halev and Theiss-Morse (2020).

37. Before securitarians accuse me of being unfair, I believe the same thing is true of unitarians. In some respects, unitarians need outsiders as much as securitarians do; just for the opposite reason.

38. An interesting and necessary study would compare the amount of time Donald Trump spent tweeting and complaining about outsiders with the amount of time he spent tweeting and complaining about Democrats, the media, the deep state, and other entities that presumably enable outsiders.

39. How much anti-immigrant sentiment among securitarians is fueled by the belief that immigrants will buoy the number of unitarians in the country? It may be that securitarians want to keep immigrants out not because of what they look like but because of what they think like.

40. Madison (1961).

41. Quoted in Levitsky and Ziblatt (2018, p. 227). Also, on this theme, see Klaas (2017) and Mounk (2018).

42. Edsall (2019b).

43. Levitsky and Ziblatt (2018). Also on the threat the Trump phenomenon poses to democracy, see Klaas (2017) and Frum (2018).

44. Levitsky and Ziblatt (2018, p. 192). Consistent with my theme here, Levitsky and Ziblatt are perfectly aware that many of those refusing to support democracy do so because of security concerns.

45. Levitsky and Ziblatt (2018, p. 208). On the match—or lack thereof—between the human condition and democracy, see Somit and Peterson (1997). For a different take, see Boehm (1999).

46. Levitsky and Ziblatt (2018, p. 212).

47. Hetherington and Weiler (2018, p. xvi).

48. This is called diffuse support and it is vital to a democracy (Easton 1975).

49. History's leading advocate of redistribution—Karl Marx—was certainly not a fan of democracy.

50. Just as unitarians are mystified by securitarians' indifference to environmental and planetary health, securitarians are flummoxed by unitarians' indifference to security from outsiders. If securitarians really want to understand unitarians, they need to come to grips with the fact that many of them are perfectly rational people who would nevertheless rather risk being mugged or even shot than carry a weapon on their person. To a dyed-in-the-wool securitarian, such behavior is madness.

51. When it comes to attitudes toward democracy, an important difference between securitarians and unitarians is that democracy is itself a way of potentially empowering outsiders and so therefore is more consistent with unitarian thinking. If unitarians are to have any hope of stopping powerful insiders from dominating society, democracy is essential. This is why unitarians by nature are more concerned than securitarians with preserving democracy.

52. I do not put much faith in the ability of deliberation to bring securitarians and unitarians together philosophically and I am not sure we should force them to. Stenner is correct when she writes that the psychological literature "indicates that exposure to difference, talking about differences, and applauding difference . . . are the surest ways to aggravate those who are innately intolerant" (2005, p. 336).

53. On sacred values, see Tetlock (2003); on moralized politics, see Skitka (2014).

54. Though, as Jonathan Haidt accurately points out, this sort of compromise goes against our nature [quoted in Rauch (2019)].

55. Nothing I have written goes very far in explaining why the flowering of securitarian sentiment—from Brexit to Bolsonaro and from Duterte to Donald—came at the precise time it did. I do not pretend to have the exact answer but I will say this. Securitarian skittishness of outsiders goes to a different level when the outsiders are so very visibly "inside." Securitarians' default strategy of deterrence is ill equipped for such a situation. They advocate building walls when it is far too late for that strategy to produce the outcome they want. Hispanics are in Lexington, Nebraska; Somalis are in Minneapolis, Minnesota; African Americans are no longer confined to the rural South or the hoods of northern cities; Asian Americans are in high-profile Silicon Valley positions; Turks are in Germany; Pakistanis are in the United Kingdom. Securitarians feel squeezed . . . and vote accordingly. For more, see Kaufmann (2019) and Norris and Inglehart (2019).

56. This might be especially true if they perceive that he was forced from office illegitimately—and they will be predisposed to believe that.

57. Levitsky and Ziblatt (2018, pp. 222–224) make a strong pitch for institutional reform but it may well be that changing the way primary elections are organized is overmatched by the elemental division between securitarians and unitarians.

REFERENCES

Abramowitz, Alan I. *The Great Alignment: Race, Party Transformation, and the Rise of Donald Trump.* New Haven, CT: Yale University Press, 2018.

Achen, Christopher H., and Larry M. Bartels. *Democracy for Realists: Why Elections Do Not Produce Responsive Government.* Princeton, NJ: Princeton University Press, 2016.

Adkisson, Richard V., and Jim Peach. "The Determinants of the Vote for Trump: An Analysis of Texas 2016 Primary Results." *Applied Economics Letters* 25, no. 3 (2017): 172–75. https://doi.org/10.1080/13504851.2017.1307927.

Adorno, Theodor W. "Cultural Criticism and Society." In *Prisms*, 17–34. Cambridge, MA: MIT Press, 1983.

Adorno, Theodor W. "Freudian Theory and the Pattern of Fascist Propaganda [1951]." In *The Essential Frankfurt School Reader*, edited by Andrew Arato and Eike Gebhardt, 118–37. New York: Continuum Books, 1987.

Adorno, Theodor W., Else Frenkel-Brunswik, Daniel J. Levinson, and Nevitt R. Sanford. *The Authoritarian Personality.* New York: Harper & Brothers, 1950.

Ahn, Woo-Young, Kenneth T. Kishida, Xiaosi Gu, Terry Lohrenz, Ann Harvey, John R. Alford, Kevin B. Smith, Gideon Yaffe, John R. Hibbing, Peter Dayan, and P. Read Montague. "Nonpolitical Images Evoke Neural Predictors of Political Ideology." *Current Biology* 24, no. 22 (2014): 2693–99. https://doi.org/10.1016/j.cub.2014.09.050.

Albert, Frank W., Örjan Carlborg, Irina Plyusnina, Francois Besnier, Daniela Hedwig, Susann Lautenschläger, Doreen Lorenz, Jenny McIntosh, Christof Neumann, Henning Richter, Claudia Zeising, Rimma Kozhemyakina, Olesya Shchepina, Jürgen Kratzsch, Lyudmila Trut, Daniel Teupser, Joachim Thiery, Torsten Schöneberg, Leif Andersson, and Svante Pääbo. "Genetic Architecture of Tameness in a Rat Model of Animal Domestication." *Genetics* 182, no. 2 (2009): 541–54. https://doi.org/10.1534/genetics.109.102186.

Albertson, Bethany, and Shana Kushner Gadarian. *Anxious Politics: Democratic Citizenship in a Threatening World.* Cambridge: Cambridge University Press, 2015.

Alesina, Alberto, and Edward L. Glaeser. *Fighting Poverty in the US and Europe: A World of Difference.* Oxford: Oxford University Press, 2004.

Alford, John R., Carolyn L. Funk, and John R. Hibbing. "Are Political Orientations Genetically Transmitted?" *American Political Science Review* 99, no. 2 (2005): 153–67. https://doi.org/10.1017/s0003055405051579.

Alford, John R., Peter K. Hatemi, John R. Hibbing, Nicholas G. Martin, and Lindon J. Eaves. "The Politics of Mate Choice." *Journal of Politics* 73, no. 2 (2011): 362–79. https://doi.org/10.1017/s0022381611000016.

Altemeyer, Bob. *Right-Wing Authoritarianism.* Winnipeg: University of Manitoba Press, 1981.

Altemeyer, Bob. *Enemies of Freedom: Understanding Right-Wing Authoritarianism.* San Francisco: Jossey-Bass, 1988.

Altemeyer, Bob. *The Authoritarian Specter.* Cambridge, MA: Harvard University Press, 1996.

Altemeyer, Bob. "Donald Trump and Authoritarian Followers." *The Authoritarians,* July 18, 2016. https://www.theauthoritarians.org/donald-trump-and-authoritarian-followers/.

Amodio, David M., John T. Jost, Sarah L. Master, and Cindy M. Yee. "Neurocognitive Correlates of Liberalism and Conservatism." *Nature Neuroscience* 10, no. 10 (2007): 1246–47. https://doi.org/10.1038/nn1979.

Arceneaux, Kevin, and Martin Johnson. *Changing Minds or Changing Channels? Partisan News in an Age of Choice.* Chicago: University of Chicago Press, 2013.

Ariely, Gal. "Globalization, Immigration and National Identity: How the Level of Globalization Affects the Relations between Nationalism, Constructive Patriotism and Attitudes toward Immigrants?" *Group Processes & Intergroup Relations* 15, no. 4 (2011): 539–57. https://doi.org/10.1177/1368430211430518.

Azarian, Bobby. "Fear and Anxiety Drive Conservatives' Political Attitudes." *Psychology Today,* December 31, 2016. https://www.psychologytoday.com/us/blog/mind-in-the-machine/201612/fear-and-anxiety-drive-conservatives-political-attitudes.

Azarian, Bobby. "A Complete Psychological Analysis of Trump's Support." *Psychology Today,* December 27, 2018. https://www.psychologytoday.com/us/blog/mind-in-the-machine/201812/complete-psychological-analysis-trumps-support?eml.

Baker, Peter, and Maggie Haberman. "Trump Interest in Buying Greenland Seemed Like a Joke." *New York Times,* August 21, 2019. https://www.nytimes.com/2019/08/21/us/politics/trump-greenland-prime-minister.html.

Bakker, Bert, Gijs Schumacher, Claire Gothreau, and Kevin Arceneaux. "Conservatives and Liberals Have Similar Physiological Responses to

Threats: Evidence from Three Replications," 2019. https://doi.org/10.31234/osf.io/vdpyt.

Ball, Molly. "Donald Trump and the Politics of Fear." *The Atlantic*, September 2, 2016.

Barabas, Jason, Jennifer Jerit, William Pollock, and Carlisle Rainey. "The Question(s) of Political Knowledge." *American Political Science Review* 108, no. 4 (2014): 840–55. https://doi.org/10.1017/s0003055414000392.

Baragona, Justin. "Tucker Carlson: Immigrants Have 'Plundered' Our Wealth and Are Coming for More." *Daily Beast*, May 21, 2019. https://www.thedailybeast.com/tucker-carlson-immigrants-have-plundered-our-wealth-and-are-coming-for-more.

Baron, Jonathan, and John T. Jost. "False Equivalence: Are Liberals and Conservatives in the United States Equally Biased?" *Perspectives in Psychological Science* 14, no. 2 (2019). https://journals.sagepub.com/doi/10.1177/1745691618788876.

Bartels, Larry M. "The Wave of Right Wing Populist Sentiment Is a Myth." *Washington Post*, June 21, 2017. https://www.washingtonpost.com/news/monkey-cage/wp/2017/06/21/the-wave-of-right-wing-populist-sentiment-is-a-myth/.

Bartels, Larry M. "Partisanship in the Trump Era." *Journal of Politics* 80, no. 4 (2018): 1483–94. https://www.journals.uchicago.edu/doi/pdfplus/10.1086/699337.

Becker, Jasper. *Hungry Ghosts: Mao's Secret Famine*. New York: Holt, 1998.

Beinart, Peter. "Is Donald Trump a Fascist?" *New York Times*, September 11, 2018. https://www.nytimes.com/2018/09/11/books/review/jason-stanley-how-fascism-works.html.

Berelson, Bernard R., Paul F. Lazarsfeld, and William N. MacPhee. *Voting: A Study of Opinion Formation in a Presidential Campaign*. Chicago: University of Chicago Press, 1954.

Bergh, R., N. Akrami, J. Sidanius, and C. G. Sibley. "Is Group Membership Necessary for Understanding Generalized Prejudice?" *Journal of Personality and Social Psychology* 111 (2016): 367–95. https://dx.doi.org/10.1080/01973530802659638.

Bernstein, Jay M. "Adorno's Uncanny Analysis of Trump's Authoritarian Personality." *Public Seminar*, October 5, 2017. http://www.publicseminar.org/2017/10/adornos-uncanny-analysis-of-trumps-authoritarian-personality/.

Billingsley, Joseph, Debra Lieberman, and Joshua M. Tybur. "Sexual Disgust Trumps Pathogen Disgust in Predicting Voter Behavior during the 2016 US Presidential Election." *Evolutionary Psychology* 16, no. 2 (2018). https://doi.org/10.1177/1474704918764170.

Bishop, Bill. *The Big Sort: Why the Clustering of Like-Minded America Is Tearing Us Apart*. New York: Houghton Mifflin, 2009.

Bobbio, Norberto. *Left and Right: The Significance of a Political Distinction.* Cambridge: Polity Press, 1996.

Boehm, Christopher. *Hierarchy in the Forest: The Evolution of Egalitarian Behavior.* Cambridge, MA: Harvard University Press, 1999.

Boehm, Christopher. "The Moral Consequences of Social Selection." *Behaviour* 151, no. 2–3 (2014): 167–83. https://doi.org/10.1163/1568539x-00003143.

Boudreau, Cheryl, and Arthur Lupia. "Political Knowledge." In *The Cambridge Handbook of Experimental Political Science*, edited by James N. Druckman, Donald P. Green, James H. Kuklinski, and Arthur Lupia, 171–83. New York: Cambridge University Press, 2011.

Bowman, Karlyn. "Interracial Marriage: Changing Laws, Minds and Hearts." *Forbes*, January 13, 2017. https://www.forbes.com/sites/bowmanmarsico/2017/01/13/interracial-marriage-changing-laws-minds-and-hearts/#a494e727c597.

Brader, Ted. *Campaigning for Hearts and Minds: How Emotional Appeals in Political Ads Work.* Chicago: University of Chicago Press, 2006.

Bradley, Margaret M. "Emotion and Motivation." In *Handbook of Psychophysiology*, edited by John T. Cacioppo, Louis G. Tassinary, and Gary G. Berntson, 2nd ed., 602–42. New York: Cambridge University Press, 2000.

Brandt, Mark J., Christine Reyna, John R. Chambers, Jarret T. Crawford, and Geoffrey Wetherell. "The Ideological-Conflict Hypothesis." *Current Directions in Psychological Science* 23, no. 1 (2014): 27–34. https://doi.org/10.1177/0963721413510932.

Bricker, Darrell J., and John Ibbitson. *Empty Planet: The Shock of Global Population Decline.* New York: Crown, 2019.

Brooks, Arthur C. "Why Conservatives Are Happier Than Liberals." *New York Times*, July 7, 2012. https://www.nytimes.com/2012/07/08/opinion/sunday/conservatives-are-happier-and-extremists-are-happiest-of-all.html.

Brooks, David. *The Second Mountain: The Quest for a Moral Life.* New York: Random House, 2019.

Brown, Roger. "The Authoritarian Personality and the Organization of Attitudes." In *Social Psychology*, edited by Roger Brown, 477–546. New York: Free Press, 1965.

Burke, Edmund. *Reflections on the Revolution in France.* London: James Dodsley, 1790.

Burns, Alexander, and Astead W. Herndon. "Trump and G.O.P. Candidates Escalate Race and Fear as Election Ploys." *New York Times*, October 22, 2018. https://www.nytimes.com/2018/10/22/us/politics/republicans-race-divisions-elections-caravan.html.

Burton, Caitlin M., Jason E. Plaks, and Jordan B. Peterson. "Why Do Conservatives Report Being Happier Than Liberals? The Contribution of Neuroticism." *Journal of Social and Political Psychology* 3, no. 1 (2015): 89–102. https://doi.org/10.5964/jspp.v3i1.117.

Burton, Tara I. "Why (White) Evangelicals Still Support Trump." *Vox*, November 5, 2018. https://www.vox.com/2018/11/5/18059454/trump-white-evangelicals-christian-nationalism-john-fea.

Campbell, James E. *Polarized: Making Sense of a Divided America*. Princeton, NJ: Princeton University Press, 2016.

Carney, Dana R., John T. Jost, Samuel D. Gosling, and Jeff Potter. "The Secret Lives of Liberals and Conservatives: Personality Profiles, Interaction Styles, and the Things They Leave Behind." *Political Psychology* 29, no. 6 (2008): 807–40. https://doi.org/10.1111/j.1467-9221.2008.00668.x.

Carraro, Luciana, Luigi Castelli, and Claudia Macchiella. "The Automatic Conservative: Ideology-Based Attentional Asymmetries in the Processing of Valenced Information." *PLoS ONE* 6, no. 11 (2011). https://doi.org/10.1371/journal.pone.0026456.

Carter, Niambi M., and Efrén O. Pérez. "Race and Nation: How Racial Hierarchy Shapes National Attachments." *Political Psychology* 37, no. 4 (2015): 497–513. https://doi.org/10.1111/pops.12270.

Carver, Charles S., and Teri L. White. "Behavioral Inhibition, Behavioral Activation, and Affective Responses to Impending Reward and Punishment: The BIS/BAS Scales." *Journal of Personality and Social Psychology* 67, no. 2 (1994): 319–33. https://doi.org/10.1037/0022-3514.67.2.319.

Casselman, Ben. "Stop Saying Trump's Win Had Nothing to Do with Economics." *FiveThirtyEight*, January 9, 2017. https://fivethirtyeight.com/features/stop-saying-trumps-win-had-nothing-to-do-with-economics/.

Chait, Jonathan. "Donald Trump's Presidency Is the Libertarian Moment." *New York Magazine*, January 29, 2018. http://nymag.com/intelligencer/2018/01/donald-trumps-presidency-is-the-libertarian-moment.html.

Chait, Jonathan. "Trump and the Rhetoric of Fascism." *New York Magazine*, June 20, 2019. http://nymag.com/intelligencer/2019/06/trump-and-the-rhetoric-of-fascism.html.

Chapman University. "The Chapman University Survey on American Fears." Chapman University, 2019. https://www.chapman.edu/wilkinson/research-centers/babbie-center/survey-american-fears.aspx.

Choma, Becky L., and Yaniv Hanoch. "Cognitive Ability and Authoritarianism: Understanding Support for Trump and Clinton." *Personality and Individual Differences* 106 (2017): 287–91. https://doi.org/10.1016/j.paid.2016.10.054.

Claussen, Detlev. *Theodor W. Adorno: One Last Genius*. Cambridge, MA: Harvard University Press, 2008.

Clinton, Hillary R. *It Takes a Village: and Other Lessons Children Teach Us*. New York: Simon & Schuster, 1996.

Cockburn, Patrick. "Is Donald Trump a Fascist? Well, He's Not Mussolini or Hitler Just Yet—but He's Not Far Off." *The Independent*, June 7, 2019. https://www.independent.co.uk/voices/trump-fascism-populism-authoritarianism-hitler-mussolini-a8949496.html.

Cole, Nicki Lisa. "Meet the People behind Donald Trump's Popularity." *ThoughtCo.* June 29, 2019. https://www.thoughtco.com/meet-the-people-behind-donald-trumps-popularity-4068073.

Collin, Katherine. "Populist and Authoritarian Referendums: The Role of Direct Democracy in Democratic Deconsolidation." Brookings Institution, February 26, 2019. https://www.brookings.edu/wp-content/uploads/2019/02/FP_ 20190226_direct_democracy_collin.pdf.

Converse, Philip E. "The Nature of Belief Systems in Mass Publics." In *Ideology and Discontent*, edited by David E. Apter, 206–61. New York: Free Press, 1964.

Conway, Lucian G., Shannon C. Houck, Laura J. Gornick, and Meredith A. Repke. "Finding the Loch Ness Monster: Left-Wing Authoritarianism in the United States." *Political Psychology* 39, no. 5 (2017): 1049–67. https://doi.org/10.1111/ pops.12470.

Costa, Paul T., and Robert R. McCrae. "Bullish on Personality Psychology." *The Psychologist*, no. 6 (1993): 302–3.

Cramer, Katherine J. *The Politics of Resentment: Rural Consciousness in Wisconsin and the Rise of Scott Walker*. Chicago: University of Chicago Press, 2016.

Crawford, Jarret T. "The Ideologically Objectionable Premise Model: Predicting Biased Political Judgments on the Left and Right." *Journal of Experimental Social Psychology* 48, no. 1 (2012): 138–51. https://doi.org/10.1016/ j.jesp.2011.10.004.

Crisanti, Carlin, and Jennifer Merolla. "Bibliography of 'Effects of the 9/ 11 Terrorist Attacks on American Public Opinion and Behavior.'" Oxford Bibliographies, September 20, 2019. https://www.oxfordbibliographies.com/ view/document/obo-9780199756223/obo-9780199756223-0270.xml.

Dahl, Robert A. *Modern Political Analysis*. Englewood Cliffs, NJ: Prentice-Hall, 1963.

Dean, John. "Altemeyer on Trump's Supporters." *Verdict*. July 7, 2017. https:// verdict.justia.com/2017/07/07/altemeyer-trumps-supporters.

Delli Carpini, Michael X., and Scott Keeter. *What Americans Know about Politics and Why It Matters*. New Haven, CT: Yale University Press, 1997.

DeParle, Jason. *A Good Provider Is One Who Leaves*. New York: Penguin, 2019.

DeVega, Chauncey. "Can Members of the Trump Cult Be Deprogrammed after the Leader Falls? Steven Hassan Says Yes." *Salon*, October 22, 2019. https://www. salon.com/2019/10/22/cam-members-of-the-trump-cult-be-deprogrammed-after-the-leader-falls-steven-hassan-says-yes/.

Dionne, E. J., Norman J. Ornstein, and Thomas E. Mann. *One Nation after Trump: A Guide for the Perplexed, the Disillusioned, the Desperate, and the Not-Yet Deported*. New York: St. Martin's Press, 2017.

Ditto, P. H., B. S. Liu, C. J. Clark, S. P. Wojcik, E. E. Chen, R. H. Grady, . . . Zinger, J. F. "At Least Bias Is Bipartisan: A Meta-analytic Comparison of Partisan Bias in Liberals and Conservatives." *Perspectives on Psychological Science* 14, no. 2 (2019): 273–91. doi:10.1177/1745691617746796.

Djupe, Paul A., and Ryan P. Burge. "The Illiberal Liberalism of Religious Trump Voters." *Religion in Politics* (2017). https://religioninpublic.blog/2018/10/09/ the-illiberal-liberalism-of-religious-trump-voters/.

Dodd, Michael D., Amanda Balzer, Carly M. Jacobs, Michael W. Gruszczynski, Kevin B. Smith, and John R. Hibbing. "The Political Left Rolls with the Good and the Political Right Confronts the Bad: Connecting Physiology and Cognition to Preferences." *Philosophical Transactions of the Royal Society B: Biological Sciences* 367, no. 1589 (2012): 640–49. https://doi.org/10.1098/rstb.2011.0268.

Douthat, Ross. "Libertarians in the Age of Trump." *New York Times*, July 21, 2018. https://www.nytimes.com/2018/07/21/opinion/sunday/libertarians-in-the-age-of-trump.html.

Du Bois, W. E. B. *Black Reconstruction: An Essay toward a History of the Part Which Black Folk Played in the Attempt to Reconstruct Democracy in America, 1860–1880*. New York: Harcourt, Brace, 1935.

Duckitt, John, Boris Bizumic, Stephen W. Krauss, and Edna Heled. "A Tripartite Approach to Right-Wing Authoritarianism." *Political Psychology* 31, no. 5 (2010): 685–715. https://doi.org/10.1111/j.1467-9221.2010.00781.x.

Duckitt, John, and Chris G. Sibley. "A Dual-Process Motivational Model of Ideology, Politics, and Prejudice." *Psychological Inquiry* 20, no. 2–3 (2009): 98–109. https://doi.org/10.1080/10478400903028540.

Duckitt, John, Claire Wagner, Ilouize Du Plessis, and Ingrid Birum. "The Psychological Bases of Ideology and Prejudice: Testing a Dual Process Model." *Journal of Personality and Social Psychology* 83, no. 1 (2002): 75–93. https://doi.org/10.1037/0022-3514.83.1.75.

Duckitt, John, and Kirstin Fisher. "The Impact of Social Threat on Worldview and Ideological Attitudes." *Political Psychology* 24, no. 1 (2003): 199–222. https://doi.org/10.1111/0162-895x.00322.

Dugatkin, Lee A., and Lyudmila N. Trut. *How to Tame a Fox (and Build a Dog): Visionary Scientists and a Siberian Tale of Jump-Started Evolution*. Chicago: University of Chicago Press, 2017.

Duina, Francesco G. *Broke and Patriotic: Why Poor Americans Love Their Country*. Stanford, CA: Stanford University Press, 2018.

Dunwoody, Philip T., and Friedrich Funke. "The Aggression-Submission-Conventionalism Scale: Testing a New Three Factor Measure of Authoritarianism." *Journal of Social and Political Psychology* 4, no. 2 (2016): 571–600. https://doi.org/10.5964/jspp.v4i2.168.

Dunwoody, Philip T., and Sam G. McFarland. "Support for Anti-Muslim Policies: The Role of Political Traits and Threat Perception." *Political Psychology* 39, no. 1 (2018): 89–106. https://doi:10.1111/pops.124505.

Easton, David. "A Re-Assessment of the Concept of Political Support." *British Journal of Political Science* 5, no. 4 (1975): 435–57. https://doi.org/10.1017/s0007123400008309.

Edsall, Thomas B. "The 2016 Exit Polls Led Us to Misinterpret the 2016 Election." *New York Times*, March 29, 2018. https://www.nytimes.com/2018/03/29/opinion/2016-exit-polls-election.html.

Edsall, Thomas B. "Trump Needs His Base to Burn with Anger." *New York Times*, July 3, 2019a. https://www.nytimes.com/2019/07/03/opinion/trump-republican-base.html.

Edsall, Thomas B. "Will Trump Ever Leave the White House?" *New York Times*, October 2, 2019b. https://www.nytimes.com/2019/10/02/opinion/trump-leave-white-house.html.

Ekins, Emily. "Religious Trump Voters." Democracy Fund Voter Study Group, September 2018. https://www.voterstudygroup.org/publication/religious-trump-voters.

Elliott, Larry. "Globalisation Backlash Enters New Phase with Trump Win." *The Guardian*, November 9, 2016. https://www.theguardian.com/business/2016/nov/09/globalisation-backlash-us-economy.

Engelhardt, Andrew M. "Trumped by Race: Explanations for Race's Influence on Whites' Votes in 2016." *Quarterly Journal of Political Science* 14, no. 3 (2019): 313–28. https://doi.org/10.1561/100.00018068.

Eysenck, Hans J. *The Psychology of Politics*. London: Routledge, 1954.

Eysenck, Hans J., and Thelma T. Coulter. "The Personality and Attitudes of Working-Class British Communists and Fascists." *Journal of Social Psychology* 87, no. 1 (1972): 59–73. https://doi.org/10.1080/00224545.1972.9918648.

Federico, Christopher M., and Ariel Malka. "The Contingent, Contextual Nature of the Relationship between Needs for Security and Certainty and Political Preferences." *Advances in Political Psychology* 39, no. S1 (2018): 3–48. https://doi.org/10.1111/pops.12477.

Feldman, Stanley. "Values, Ideology, and the Structure of Political Attitudes." In *Oxford Handbook of Political Psychology*, edited by David O. Sears, Leonie Huddy, and Robert Jervis, 477–508. New York: Oxford University Press, 2003a.

Feldman, Stanley. "Enforcing Social Conformity: A Theory of Authoritarianism." *Political Psychology* 24, no. 1 (2003b): 41–74. https://doi.org/10.1111/0162-895X.00316.

Feldman, Stanley, and Karen Stenner. "Perceived Threat and Authoritarianism." *Political Psychology* 18, no. 4 (1997): 741–70. https://doi.org/10.1111/0162-895x.00077.

Feuer, Alan. "The Preppers Next Door." *New York Times*, January 26, 2013. https://www.nytimes.com/2013/01/27/nyregion/the-doomsday-preppers-of-new-york.html.

Forscher, Patrick S., William T. L. Cox, Nicholas Graetz, and Patricia G. Devine. "The Motivation to Express Prejudice." *Journal of Personality and Social Psychology* 109, no. 5 (2015): 791–812. https://doi.org/10.1037/pspi0000030.

Fortunato, David, Matthew V. Hibbing, and Jeffery J. Mondak. "The Trump Draw: Voter Personality and Support for Donald Trump in the 2016 Republican Nomination Campaign." *American Politics Research* 46, no. 5 (2018): 785–810. https://doi.org/10.1177/1532673x18765190.

Frank, Thomas. *What's the Matter with Kansas? How Conservatives Won the Heart of America*. New York: Picador, 2004.

French, David. "Why People Carry Guns: A Response to David Frum." *National Review*, February 17, 2014. https://www.nationalreview.com/corner/why-people-carry-guns-response-david-frum-david-french/.

Fromm, Erich. *Escape from Freedom*. New York: Holt, 1941.

Frum, David. *Trumpocracy: The Corruption of the American Republic*. New York: Harper, 2018.

Fukuyama, Francis. *The End of History and the Last Man*. New York: Free Press, 1992.

Gelfand, Michele. *Rule Makers; Rule Breakers*. New York: Blackstone, 2018.

Gerber, Alan S., Gregory A. Huber, David Doherty, Conor M. Dowling, and Shang E. Ha. "Personality and Political Attitudes: Relationships across Issue Domains and Political Contexts." *American Political Science Review* 104, no. 1 (2010): 111–33. https://doi.org/10.1017/s0003055410000031.

Gibson, James L. "Political Intolerance in the Context of Democratic Theory." *The Oxford Handbook of Political Science*, Robert Goodin, ed. Oxford University Press: 2011.

Gilson, Tom. "No, Liberals, You're Wrong: Conservatism Isn't about Fear." *The Stream*, March 22, 2018. https://stream.org/no-liberals-youre-wrong-conservatism-isnt-about-fear/.

Goldman, Jason G. "Man's New Best Friend? A Forgotten Russian Experiment in Fox Domestication." *Scientific American*, September 6, 2010. https://blogs.scientificamerican.com/guest-blog/mans-new-best-friend-a-forgotten-russian-experiment-in-fox-domestication/.

Goodhart, David. *The Road to Somewhere: The Populist Revolt and the Future of Politics*. London: Hurst, 2017.

Goodwin, Matthew, and Caitlin Milazzo. "Taking Back Control? Investigating the Role of Immigration in the 2016 Vote for Brexit." *British Journal of Politics and International Relations* 19, no. 3 (2017): 450–64. https://doi.org/10.1177/1369148117710799.

Gordon, Peter E. *Adorno and Existence*. Cambridge, MA: Harvard University Press, 2016a.

Gordon, Peter E. "The Authoritarian Personality Revisited: Reading Adorno in the Age of Trump." *b2o*, June 15, 2016b. https://www.boundary2.org/2016/06/peter-gordon-the-authoritarian-personality-revisited-reading-adorno-in-the-age-of-trump/.

Graham, Jesse, Jonathan Haidt, and Brian A. Nosek. "Liberals and Conservatives Rely on Different Sets of Moral Foundations." *Journal of Personality and Social Psychology* 96, no. 5 (2009): 1029–46. https://doi.org/10.1037/a0015141.

Graham, Matthew, and Milan W. Svolik. "Democracy in America? Partisanship, Polarization, and the Robustness of Support for Democracy in the U.S." Yale University Working Paper. https://www.bu.edu/polisci/files/2019/09/Graham-and-Svolik-Democracy-in-America-web-1ngqg71.pdf.

Gray, Peter. "Childrearing Beliefs Were Best Predictor of Trump Support." *Psychology Today*, February 1, 2017. https://www.psychologytoday.com/us/blog/freedom-learn/201702/childrearing-beliefs-were-best-predictor-trump-support.

Greeley, Andrew M., and Paul B. Sheatsley. "Attitudes toward Racial Integration." *Scientific American* (December 1971). https://www.scientificamerican.com/article/attitudes-toward-racial-integration-1971-12/.

Green, Emma. "It Was Cultural Anxiety That Drove White, Working-Class Voters to Trump." *The Atlantic*, May 9, 2017.

Green, Jon, and Sean McElwee. "The Differential Effects of Economic Conditions and Racial Attitudes in the Election of Donald Trump." *Perspectives on Politics* 17, no. 2 (2019): 358–79. https://doi.org/10.1017/S1537592718003365.

Grier, Peter. "Why Are Trump Voters So Angry about Immigration?" *Christian Science Monitor*, June 10, 2016. https://www.csmonitor.com/USA/Politics/Decoder/2016/0610/Why-are-Trump-voters-so-angry-about-immigration.

Griffith, R. Marie. *Moral Combat: How Sex Divided American Christians and Fractured American Politics*. New York: Basic Books, 2017.

Grossmann, Matthew, and David A. Hopkins. *Asymmetric Politics: Ideological Republicans and Group Interest Democrats*. New York: Oxford University Press, 2016.

Haidt, Jonathan. The Disgust Scale Home Page, October 16, 2012a. http://people.stern.nyu.edu/jhaidt/disgustscale.html.

Haidt, Jonathan. *The Righteous Mind: Why Good People Are Divided by Politics and Religion*. New York: Random House, 2012b.

Haidt, Jonathan. "When and Why Nationalism Beats Globalism." *American Interest*, July 10, 2016. https://www.the-american-interest.com/2016/07/10/when-and-why-nationalism-beats-globalism/.

Hammer, Espen. *Adorno and the Political*. New York: Routledge, 2006.

Harari, Yuval Noah. *Sapiens: A Brief History of Humankind*. New York: Harper, 2015.

Hart, Roderick P. *Trump and Us*. Cambridge: Cambridge University Press, 2020.

Hassan, Steven. *The Cult of Trump*. New York: Free Press, 2019.

Hatemi, Peter K., Sarah E. Medland, Katherine I. Morley, Andrew C. Heath, and Nicholas G. Martin. "The Genetics of Voting: An Australian Twin Study." *Behavior Genetics* 37, no. 3 (2007): 435–48. https://doi.org/10.1007/s10519-006-9138-8.

Henry, P. J. "The Role of Stigma in Understanding Ethnicity Differences in Authoritarianism." *Political Psychology* 32, no. 3 (2011): 419–38. https://doi.org/10.1111/j.1467-9221.2010.00816.x.

Hetherington, Marc J., and Elizabeth Suhay. "Authoritarianism, Threat, and Americans' Support for the War on Terror." *American Journal of Political Science* 55, no. 3 (2011): 546–60. https://doi.org/10.1111/j.1540-5907.2011.00514.x.

Hetherington, Marc J., and Jonathan D. Weiler. *Authoritarianism and Polarization in American Politics*. Cambridge: Cambridge University Press, 2009.

Hetherington, Marc J., and Jonathan D. Weiler. *Prius or Pickup? How the Answers to Four Simple Questions Explain America's Great Divide*. Boston: Houghton Mifflin Harcourt, 2018.

Hetherington, Marc J., and Thomas Rudolph. *Why Washington Won't Work: Polarization, Political Trust, and the Governing Crisis*. Chicago: University of Chicago Press, 2015.

Hibbing, John R., and Elizabeth Theiss-Morse. *Stealth Democracy: Americans' Beliefs about How Government Should Work*. New York: Cambridge University Press, 2002.

Hibbing, John R., Elizabeth Theiss-Morse, Matthew V. Hibbing, and David Fortunato. "Who Do People Want to Govern and How? The Style of Democracy Preferred by Americans." Paper presented at the American Political Science Associate Meetings, Boston, MA, August–September, 2018.

Hibbing, John R., Kevin B. Smith, and John R. Alford. *Predisposed: Liberals, Conservatives, and the Biology of Political Differences*. New York: Routledge, 2014.

Hill, K. R., R. S. Walker, M. Bozicevic, J. Eder, T. Headland, B. Hewlett, A. M. Hurtado, F. Marlowe, P. Wiessner, and B. Wood. "Co-Residence Patterns in Hunter-Gatherer Societies Show Unique Human Social Structure." *Science* 331, no. 6022 (2011): 1286–89. https://doi.org/10.1126/science.1199071.

Hirsh, Jacob B., Colin G. Deyoung, Xiaowen Xu, and Jordan B. Peterson. "Compassionate Liberals and Polite Conservatives: Associations of Agreeableness with Political Ideology and Moral Values." *Personality and Social Psychology Bulletin* 36, no. 5 (2010): 655–64. https://doi.org/10.1177/0146167210366854.

Hobbes, Thomas. *Leviathan: or, The Matter, Forme and Power of a Commonwealth Ecclesiasticall and Civill*. Edited by Ian Shapiro. New Haven, CT: Yale University Press, 2010.

Hochschild, Arlie R. *Strangers in Their Own Land: Anger and Mourning on the American Right*. New York: The New Press, 2018.

Hofstadter, Richard. "The Paranoid Style in American Politics." *Harper's Magazine*, November 1964.

Hopkins, Daniel J., John Sides, and Jack Citrin. "The Muted Consequences of Correct Information about Immigration." *Journal of Politics* 81, no. 1 (2018): 315–20. https://dx.doi.org/10.1086/699914.

Huddy, Leonie, and Nadia Khatib. "American Patriotism, National Identity, and Political Involvement." *American Journal of Political Science* 51, no. 1 (2007): 63–77. https://doi.org/10.1111/j.1540-5907.2007.00237.x.

Huddy, Leonie, Stanley Feldman, Charles Taber, and Gallya Lahav. "Threat, Anxiety, and Support of Antiterrorism Policies." *American Journal of Political Science* 49, no. 3 (2005): 593. https://doi.org/10.2307/3647734.

Hyman, Herbert H., and Paul B. Sheatsley. "The Authoritarian Personality: A Methodological Critique." In *Studies in the Scope and Method of "The Authoritarian Personality,"* edited by Richard Christie and Marie Jahoda, 50–122. Glencoe, IL: Free Press, 1954.

Illing, Sean. "If You Want to Understand the Age of Trump, Read the Frankfurt School." *Vox*, December 27, 2016. https://www.vox.com/conversations/2016/12/27/14038406/donald-trump-frankfurt-school-brexit-critical-theory.

Inbar, Yoel, David A. Pizarro, and Paul Bloom. "Conservatives Are More Easily Disgusted than Liberals." *Cognition & Emotion* 23, no. 4 (2009): 714–25. https://doi.org/10.1080/02699930802110007.

Inglehart, Ronald. *Silent Revolution. Changing Values and Political Styles among Western Publics.* Princeton, NJ: Princeton University Press, 2016.

Inglehart, Ronald. *Cultural Evolution: People's Motivations Are Changing and Reshaping the World.* Cambridge: Cambridge University Press, 2018.

Iyengar, Shanto, and Sean J. Westwood. "Fear and Loathing across Party Lines: New Evidence on Group Polarization." *American Journal of Political Science* 59, no. 3 (2014): 690–707. https://doi.org/10.1111/ajps.12152.

Iyer, Ravi, Spassena Koleva, Jesse Graham, Peter Ditto, and Jonathan Haidt. "Understanding Libertarian Morality: The Psychological Dispositions of Self-Identified Libertarians." *PLoS ONE* 7, no. 8 (2012). https://doi.org/10.1371/journal.pone.0042366.

Jacobs, Tom. "How Fear of a Physical Threat Can Foster Social Conservatism." *Pacific Standard*, November 1, 2017. https://psmag.com/news/how-fear-of-a-physical-threat-can-foster-social-conservatism.

Jacobs, Tom. "Trump and the Playbook of Fascist Politics." *Pacific Standard*, September 17, 2018. https://psmag.com/news/trump-and-the-playbook-of-fascist-politics.

Jardina, Ashley. *White Identity Politics.* New York: Cambridge University Press, 2019.

Jensen, Carsten, and Michael B. Petersen. "The Deservingness Heuristic and the Politics of Health Care." *American Journal of Political Science* 61, no. 1 (2016): 68–83. https://doi.org/10.1111/ajps.12251.

Jetten, Jolanda, S. Alexander Haslam, and Fiona K. Barlow. "Bringing Back the System." *Social Psychological and Personality Science* 4, no. 1 (2012): 6–13. https://doi.org/10.1177/1948550612439721.

Johnston, Christopher D., Howard G. Lavine, and Christopher M. Federico. *Open versus Closed: Personality, Identity, and the Politics of Redistribution.* Cambridge: Cambridge University Press, 2017.

Jost, John T. "The End of the End of Ideology." *American Psychologist* 61, no. 7 (2006): 651–70. https://doi.org/10.1037/0003-066x.61.7.651.

Jost, John T. *A Theory of System Justification.* Cambridge, MA: Harvard University Press, 2020.

Jost, John T., Jack Glaser, Arie W. Kruglanski, and Frank J. Sulloway. "Political Conservatism as Motivated Social Cognition." *Psychological Bulletin* 129, no. 3 (2003): 339–75. https://doi.org/10.1037/0033-2909.129.3.339.

Jost, John T., Mahzarin R. Banaji, and Brian A. Nosek. "A Decade of System Justification Theory: Accumulated Evidence of Conscious and Unconscious Bolstering of the Status Quo." *Political Psychology* 25, no. 6 (2004): 881–919. https://doi.org/10.1111/j.1467-9221.2004.00402.x.

Jost, John, and Orsolya Hunyady. "The Psychology of System Justification and the Palliative Function of Ideology." *European Review of Social Psychology* 13, no. 1 (2003): 111–53. https://doi.org/10.1080/10463280240000046.

Jung, Carl G. *The Undiscovered Self: The Dilemma of the Individual in Modern Society*. New York: Signet, 2006.

Kahan, Dan M. "Ideology, Motivated Reasoning, and Cognitive Reflection." *Judgement and Decision Making* 8, no. 4 (2013): 407–24. http://journal.sjdm.org/13/13313/jdm13313.pdf.

Katz, Daniel. "The Functional Approach to the Study of Attitudes." *Public Opinion Quarterly* 24, no. 2, Special Issue: Attitude Change (1960): 163–204. https://doi.org/10.1086/266945.

Kaufmann, Eric P. *Whiteshift: Populism, Immigration, and the Future of White Majorities*. New York: Abrams Press, 2019.

Keim, Brandon. "Conservatives Scare More Easily Than Liberals, Say Scientists." *Wired*, September 18, 2008.

Kendi, Ibram X. *How to Be an Antiracist*. New York: One World, 2019.

Kessler, Thomas, and Julia Elad-Strenger. "Essentially National: The Psychology of Right-Wing Populism." Paper presented at the annual meetings of the International Society for Political Psychology, Lisbon, Portugal, July 2019.

Kimmel, Michael. *Angry White Men: American Masculinity at the End of an Era*. New York: Bold Type Books, 2018.

Kinder, Donald R., and Cindy D. Kam. *Us against Them: Ethnocentric Foundations of American Opinion*. Chicago: University of Chicago Press, 2010.

Kinder, Donald R., and Nathan P. Kalmoe. *Neither Liberal nor Conservative: Ideological Innocence in the American Public*. Chicago: University of Chicago Press, 2017.

Kirby, Jen. "Trump Goes to the United Nations to Argue against Everything It Stands For—Again." *Vox*, September 24, 2019. https://www.vox.com/2019/9/24/20881781/unga-trump-speech-2019-nationalism-sovereignty-again.

Klaas, Brian P. *The Despots' Apprentice: Donald Trump's Attack on Democracy*. New York: Hot Books, 2017.

Klein, Ezra. *Why We're Polarized*. New York: Avid Reader, 2020.

Knoll, Benjamin R., Tyler J. O'Daniel, and Brian Cusato. "Physiological Responses and Political Behavior: Three Reproductions Using a Novel Dataset." *Research & Politics* 2, no. 4 (2015). https://doi.org/10.1177/2053168015621328.

Kosterman, Rick, and Seymour Feshbach. "Toward a Measure of Patriotic and Nationalistic Attitudes." *Political Psychology* 10, no. 2 (1989): 257–74. https://doi.org/10.2307/3791647.

Kosur, James. "Trump Supporters Are Easily Manipulated by Fear, Brain Scan Studies Claim." *HillReporter.com*, December 5, 2018. https://hillreporter.com/brain-scan-studies-trump-supporters-easily-manipulated-by-fear-16707.

Krugman, Paul. "Trump's Big Libertarian Experiment." *New York Times*, January 10, 2019. https://www.nytimes.com/2019/01/10/opinion/trump-shutdown.html.

Kurzban, Robert, John Tooby, and Leda Cosmides. "Can Race Be Erased? Coalitional Computation and Social Categorization." *Proceedings of the National Academy of Sciences* 98, no. 26 (2001): 15387–92. https://doi.org/10.1073/pnas.251541498.

Kymlicka, Will. "Liberalism and Communitarianism." *Canadian Journal of Philosophy* 18, no. 2 (1988): 181–203. https://doi.org/10.1080/00455091.1988.10717173.

Lakoff, George. *Moral Politics: How Liberals and Conservatives Think*. Chicago: University of Chicago Press, 1996.

Lamont, Michèle, Bo Yun Park, and Elena Ayala-Hurtado. "Trump's Electoral Speeches and His Appeal to the American White Working Class." *British Journal of Sociology* 68, no. S1 (2017): S153–80. https://doi.org/10.1111/1468-4446.12315.

Lampo, David. *A Fundamental Freedom: Why Republicans, Conservatives, and Libertarians Should Support Gay Rights*. Lanham, MD: Rowman & Littlefield, 2012.

Lavine, Howard, Milton Lodge, James Polichak, and Charles Taber. "Explicating the Black Box through Experimentation: Studies of Authoritarianism and Threat." *Political Analysis* 10, no. 4 (2002): 343–61. https://doi.org/10.1093/pan/10.4.343.

Lazarsfeld, Paul F., Bernard Berelson, and Hazel Gaudet. *The People's Choice: How the Voter Makes Up His Mind in a Presidential Campaign*. New York: Columbia University Press, 1948.

Lee, Richard B. "Reflections on Primitive Communism." In *Hunters and Gatherers*, vol I: *History, Evolution and Social Change*, edited by Tim Ingold, David Riches, and James Woodburn, 200–16. London: Berg, 1988.

Levendusky, Matthew. *The Partisan Sort: How Liberals Became Democrats and Conservatives Became Republicans*. Chicago: University of Chicago Press, 2009.

Levitsky, Steven, and Daniel Ziblatt. *How Democracies Die*. New York: Viking Books, 2018.

Lewis-Beck, Michael S., William G. Jacoby, Helmut Norpoth, and Herbert F. Weisberg. *The American Voter Revisited*. Ann Arbor: University of Michigan Press, 2008.

Libertarian Party. "Trump Is the Opposite of a Libertarian." Libertarian Party, March 28, 2018. https://www.lp.org/trump-opposite-libertarian/.

Lilienfeld, Scott O., and Robert D. Latzman. "Threat Bias, Not Negativity Bias, Underpins Differences in Political Ideology." *Behavioral and Brain Sciences* 37, no. 3 (2014): 318–19. https://doi.org/10.1017/s0140525x1300263x.

Lind, Michael. "Donald Trump, the Perfect Populist." *Politico Magazine*, March 9, 2016. https://www.politico.com/magazine/story/2016/03/donald-trump-the-perfect-populist-213697.

Linden, Magnus. "Trump's America and the Rise of the Authoritarian Personality." *The Conversation*, February 16, 2017. https://theconversation.com/trumps-america-and-the-rise-of-the-authoritarian-personality-72770.

Liuzza, Marco T., Torun Lindholm, Caitlin B. Hawley, Marie G. Sendén, Ingrid Ekström, Mats J. Olsson, and Jonas K. Olofsson. "Body Odour Disgust Sensitivity Predicts Authoritarian Attitudes." *Royal Society Open Science* 5, no. 2 (2018). https://doi.org/10.1098/rsos.171091.

Long, Heather, and Scott Clement. "Trump Voters Hit Hard by Tariffs Are Standing by Him—for Now." *Washington Post*, July 12, 2018. https://www.washingtonpost.com/business/2018/07/12/trump-voters-hit-hard-by-tariffs-are-standing-by-him-now/.

Lopez, German. "The Past Year of Research Has Made It Very Clear: Trump Won Because of Racial Resentment." *Vox*, December 15, 2017. https://www.vox.com/identities/2017/12/15/16781222/trump-racism-economic-anxiety-study.

Ludeke, Steven G., Camilla N. Klitgaard, and Joseph Vitriol. "Comprehensively-Measured Authoritarianism Does Predict Vote Choice: The Importance of Authoritarianism's Facets, Ideological Sorting, and the Particular Candidate." *Personality and Individual Differences* 123 (2018): 209–16. https://doi.org/10.1016/j.paid.2017.11.019.

Lupia, Arthur. *Uninformed: Why People Seem to Know so Little about Politics and What We Can Do about It.* New York: Oxford University Press, 2015.

Luttig, Matthew D., Christopher M. Federico, and Howard Lavine. "Supporters and Opponents of Donald Trump Respond Differently to Racial Cues: An Experimental Analysis." *Research & Politics* 4, no. 4 (2017). https://doi.org/10.1177/2053168017737411.

MacWilliams, Matthew C. "The Best Predictor of Trump Support Isn't Income, Education, or Age. It's Authoritarianism." *Vox*, February 23, 2016a. https://www.vox.com/2016/2/23/11099644/trump-support-authoritarianism.

MacWilliams, Matthew C. *The Rise of Trump: America's Authoritarian Spring.* Amherst, MA: Amherst College Press, 2016b.

Madison, James. "Federalist No. 10." In *The Federalist Papers*, by Hamilton, Alexander, James Madison, and John Jay, edited by Clinton Rossiter. New York: New American Library, 1961.

Malkin, Michelle. "Speech at the Conservative Political Action Conference." *Conservative Political Action Conference*. March 1, 2019. https://www.c-span.org/video/?458347-42/cpac-michelle-malkin.

Manza, Jeff, and Ned Crowley. "Working Class Hero? Interrogating the Social Bases of the Rise of Donald Trump." *The Forum* 15, no. 1 (2017). https://doi.org/10.1515/for-2017-0002.

Marcus, George E., Michael MacKuen, and W. Russell Neuman. *Affective Intelligence and Political Judgment*. Chicago: University of Chicago Press, 2000.

Marques, José, Dominic Abrams, and Rui G. Serôdio. "Being Better by Being Right: Subjective Group Dynamics and Derogation of in-Group Deviants When Generic Norms Are Undermined." *Journal of Personality and Social Psychology* 81, no. 3 (2001): 436–47. https://doi.org/10.1037/0022-3514.81.3.436.

Martin, James G. *The Tolerant Personality*. Detroit: Wayne State University Press, 1964.

Martin, John L. "The Authoritarian Personality Fifty Years Later." *Political Psychology* 22, no. 1 (2001): 1–26. https://doi.org/10.1111/0162-895X.00223.

Martin, N. G., L. J. Eaves, A. C. Heath, Rosemary Jardine, Lynn M. Feingold, and H. J. Eysenck. "Transmission of Social Attitudes." *Proceedings of the National Academy of Sciences* 83, no. 12 (1986): 4364–68. https://doi.org/10.1073/pnas.83.12.4364.

Mason, Lilliana. "The Rise of Uncivil Agreement: Issue versus Behavioral Polarization in the American Electorate." *American Behavioral Scientist* 57, no. 1 (2012): 140–59. https://doi.org/10.1177/0002764212463363.

Mason, Lilliana, John V. Kane, and Julie Wronski. "Trump Support Is Not Normal Partisanship." *Vox* (June 21, 2019). https://www.vox.com/polyarchy/2019/6/21/18679314/trump-support-is-not-normal-partisanship.

Masuoka, Natalie, and Jane Junn. *The Politics of Belonging*. Chicago: University of Chicago Press, 2013.

Maxwell, Rahsaan. "Cosmopolitan Immigration Attitudes in Large European Cities: Contextual of Compositional Effects." *American Political Science Review* 113, no. 2 (2019): 456–74. https://doi.org/10.1017/S0003055418000898.

McCarty, Nolan. *Polarization: What Everyone Needs to Know*. New York: Oxford University Press, 2019.

McCrae, Robert R., and Paul T. Costa. "Validation of the Five-Factor Model of Personality across Instruments and Observers." *Journal of Personality and Social Psychology* 52, no. 1 (1987): 81–90. https://doi.org/10.1037/0022-3514.52.1.81.

McCrae, Robert R., and Paul T. Costa. *Personality in Adulthood: A Five-Factor Theory Perspective*. 2nd ed. New York: Guilford Press, 2003.

Medved, Michael. "Why the Right Hates Mitt Romney and His 2012 Presidential Bid." *Daily Beast*, November 10, 2011. https://www.thedailybeast.com/why-the-right-hates-mitt-romney-and-his-2012-presidential-bid.

Mendelberg, Tali. *The Race Card: Campaign Strategy, Implicit Messages, and the Norm of Equality*. Princeton, NJ: Princeton University Press, 2001.

Metzl, Jonathan M. *Dying of Whiteness: How the Politics of Racial Resentment Is Killing America's Heartland*. New York: Basic Books, 2019.

Milligan, Susan. "Another Year of the Angry Voter." *U.S. News & World Report*, February 23, 2018. https://www.usnews.com/news/the-report/articles/2018-02-23/angry-voters-got-trump-elected-now-anger-may-help-democrats.

Mills, Mark, Frank J. Gonzalez, Karl Giuseffi, Benjamin Sievert, Kevin B. Smith, John R. Hibbing, and Michael D. Dodd. "Political Conservatism Predicts Asymmetries in Emotional Scene Memory." *Behavioural Brain Research* 306 (2016): 84–90. https://doi.org/10.1016/j.bbr.2016.03.025.

Mills, Mark, Kevin B. Smith, John R. Hibbing, and Michael D. Dodd. "The Politics of the Face-in-the-Crowd." *Journal of Experimental Psychology: General* 143, no. 3 (2014): 1199–1213. https://doi.org/10.1037/a0035177.

Mondak, Jeffery J. *Personality and the Foundations of Political Behavior.* Cambridge: Cambridge University Press, 2010.

Mondak, Jeffery J., Matthew V. Hibbing, Damarys Canache, Mitchell A. Seligson, and Mary R. Anderson. "Personality and Civic Engagement: An Integrative Framework for the Study of Trait Effects on Political Behavior." *American Political Science Review* 104, no. 1 (2010): 85–110. https://doi.org/10.1017/s0003055409990359.

Mooney, Chris. *The Republican War on Science.* New York: Basic Books, 2005.

Mounk, Yascha. *The People vs Democracy. Why Our Freedom Is in Danger and How to Save It.* Cambridge, MA: Harvard University Press, 2018.

Mudde, Cas. *Populist Radical Right Parties in Europe.* Cambridge: Cambridge University Press, 2007.

Mudde, Cas, and Cristobal Rovira Kaltwasser. *Populism: A Very Short Introduction.* New York: Oxford University Press, 2017.

Mueller, John, and Mark G. Stewart. "Public Opinion and Counterterrorism Policy." White Paper. Cato Institute, February 20, 2018. https://www.cato.org/publications/white-paper/public-opinion-counterterrorism-policy

Müller-Doohm, Stefan. *Adorno: A Biography.* Cambridge: Polity Press, 2005.

Mutz, Diana C. "Status Threat, Not Economic Hardship, Explains the 2016 Presidential Vote." *Proceedings of the National Academy of Sciences* 115, no. 19 (2018): E4330–9. https://doi.org/10.1073/pnas.1718155115.

Napier, Jaime L., and John T. Jost. "Why Are Conservatives Happier Than Liberals?" *Psychological Science* 19, no. 6 (2008): 565–72. https://doi.org/10.1111/j.1467-9280.2008.02124.x.

Newport, Frank. "Blacks as Conservative as Republicans on Some Moral Issues." Gallup, December 3, 2008. https://news.gallup.com/poll/112807/blacks-conservative-republicans-some-moral-issues.aspx.

Norris, Pippa, and Ronald F. Inglehart. *Cultural Backlash: Trump, Brexit, and Authoritarian Populism.* Cambridge: Cambridge University Press, 2019.

Oh, Inae. "Top Trump Official Edits Statue of Liberty Poem to Justify Rule Punishing Poor Immigrants." *Mother Jones*, August 13, 2019. https://www.motherjones.com/politics/2019/08/ken-cuccinelli-statue-of-liberty-public-charge/.

Oliver, J. Eric, and Wendy M. Rahn. "Rise of the Trumpenvolk: Populism in the 2016 Election." *Annals of the American Academy of Political and Social Science* 667, no. 1 (2016): 189–206. https://doi.org/10.1177%2F0002716216662639

Oliver, J. Eric, and Thomas J. Wood. *Enchanted America: How Intuition and Reason Divide Our Politics*. Chicago: University of Chicago Press, 2018.

Onraet, Emma, Jasper Van Assche, Arne Roets, Tessa Haesevoets, and Alain Van Hiel. "The Happiness Gap between Conservatives and Liberals Depends on Country-Level Threat." *Social Psychological and Personality Science* 8, no. 1 (2016): 11–9. https://doi.org/10.1177/1948550616662125.

O'Reilly, Bill, and Martin Dugard. *Killing Jesus: A History*. Waterville, ME: Thorndike Press, 2013.

Osborne, Danny, Petar Milojev, and Chris G. Sibley. "Authoritarianism and National Identity: Examining the Longitudinal Effects of SDO and RWA on Nationalism and Patriotism." *Personality and Social Psychology Bulletin* 43, no. 8 (2017): 1086–99. https://doi.org/10.1177/0146167217704196.

Osmundsen, Mathias, David Hendry, Lasse Laustsen, Kevin Smith, and Michael B. Petersen. "The Psychophysiology of Political Ideology: Replications, Reanalysis and Recommendations," 2019. https://doi.org/10.31234/osf.io/49hfg.

Ostrom, Elinor. *Governing the Commons: The Evolutions of Institutions for Collective Action*. Cambridge: Cambridge University Press, 1990.

Oxley, Douglas R., Kevin B. Smith, John R. Alford, Matthew V. Hibbing, Jennifer L. Miller, Mario Scalora, Peter K. Hatemi, and John R. Hibbing. "Political Attitudes Vary with Physiological Traits." *Science* 321, no. 5896 (2008): 1667–70. https://doi.org/10.1126/science.1157627.

Parker, Kim, Juliana Menasce Horowitz, Anna Brown, Richard Fry, D'Vera Cohn, and Ruth Igielnik. "How Urban, Suburban and Rural Residents View Social and Political Issues." Pew Research Center, May 22, 2018. https://www.pewsocialtrends.org/2018/05/22/urban-suburban-and-rural-residents-views-on-key-social-and-political-issues/.

Parvizi, Josef, Corentin Jacques, Brett L. Foster, Nathan Withoft, Vinitha Rangarajan, Kevin S. Weiner, and Kalanit Grill-Spector. "Electrical Stimulation of Human Fusiform Face-Selective Regions Distorts Face Perception." *Journal of Neuroscience* 32, no. 43 (2012): 14915–20. https://doi.org/10.1523/jneurosci.2609-12.2012.

Pehrson, Samuel, Vivian L. Vignoles, and Rupert Brown. "National Identification and Anti-Immigrant Prejudice: Individual and Contextual Effects of National Definitions." *Social Psychology Quarterly* 72, no. 1 (2009): 24–38. https://doi.org/10.1177/019027250907200104.

Peters, Jeremy W., Michael M. Grynbaum, Keith Collins, and Rich Harris. "How the El Paso Gunman Echoed the Words of Right-Wing Pundits." *New York Times*, August 12, 2019. https://www.nytimes.com/interactive/2019/08/11/business/media/el-paso-killer-conservative-media.html.

Petersen, Michael B., Rune Slothuus, Rune Stubager, and Lise Togeby. "Deservingness versus Values in Public Opinion on Welfare: The Automaticity of the Deservingness Heuristic." *European Journal of Political Research* 50, no. 1 (2010): 24–52. https://doi.org/10.1111/j.1475-6765.2010.01923.x.

Peterson, Johnathan C., Carly Jacobs, John Hibbing, and Kevin Smith. "In Your Face." *Politics and the Life Sciences* 37, no. 1 (2018): 53–67. https://doi.org/10.1017/pls.2017.13.

Peterson, Johnathan C., Kevin B. Smith, and John R. Hibbing. "Do People Really Become More Conservatives as They Age?" *Journal of Politics*, forthcoming. https://doi.org/10.1086/706889

Pettigrew, Thomas. "Social Psychological Perspectives on Trump Supporters." *Journal of Social and Political Psychology* 5, no. 1 (2017): 107–16. https://jspp.psychopen.eu/article/view/750/html.

Philpot, Tasha S. *Conservative but Not Republican: The Paradox of Party Identification and Ideology among African Americans.* New York: Cambridge University Press, 2017.

Pickett, Cynthia L., and Marilynn B. Brewer. "The Role of Exclusion in Maintaining In-Group Inclusion." In *The Social Psychology of Inclusion and Exclusion*, edited by Dominic Abrams, Michael A. Hogg, and José M. Marques, 89–112. New York: Psychology Press, 2005.

Pinker, Steven. *The Blank Slate and the Modern Denial of Human Nature.* New York: Viking, 2002.

Pinker, Steven. *The Better Angels of Our Nature: Why Violence Has Declined.* New York: Penguin, 2011.

Pitts, Leonard. "Do We Really Need to Understand Trump Supporters?" *Chicago Tribune*, May 8, 2018. https://www.chicagotribune.com/opinion/commentary/ct-perspec-pitts-trump-supporters-understanding-0508-20180506-story.html.

Plott, Elaina. "'We're All Tired of Being Called Racists.'" *The Atlantic*, August 2, 2019. https://www.theatlantic.com/politics/archive/2019/08/trump-supporters-called-racists/595333/.

Rapoport, Ronald B., Alan I. Abramowitz, and Walter J. Stone. "Why Trump Was Inevitable." *New York Review of Books*, June 23, 2016. https://www.nybooks.com/articles/2016/06/23/why-trump-was-inevitable/.

Rauch, Jonathan. "Rethinking Polarization." *National Affairs* 41 (2019). https://www.nationalaffairs.com/publications/detail/rethinking-polarization.

Ray, John J. "Reviving the Problem of Acquiescent Response Set." *Journal of Social Psychology* 121, no. 1 (1983): 81–96. https://doi.org/10.1080/00224545.1983.9924470.

Ray, John J. "Defective Validity in the Altemeyer Authoritarianism Scale." *Journal of Social Psychology* 125, no. 2 (1985): 271–72. https://doi.org/10.1080/00224545.1985.9922883.

Reich, Robert. "Economy Causing Strife; Trump a Mere Symptom." *Lincoln Journal-Star*, May 5, 2018. https://journalstar.com/opinion/columnists/robert-b-reich-economy-causing-strife-trump-a-mere-symptom/article_b0327c79-1a4f-5c80-adc2-fc61498a8827.html.

Robison, Joshua, and Rachel L. Moskowitz. "The Group Basis of Partisan Affective Polarization." *Journal of Politics* 81, no. 3 (2019): 1075–79. https://doi.org/10.1086/703069.

Rokeach, Milton. *The Open and Closed Mind: Investigations into the Nature of Belief Systems and Personality Systems.* New York: Basic Books, 1960.

Rokeach, Milton. *The Nature of Human Values.* New York: Free Press, 1973.

Ross, Alex. "The Naysayers: Walter Benjamin, Theodor Adorno, and the Critique of Pop Culture." *The New Yorker*, September 15, 2014. https://www.newyorker.com/magazine/2014/09/15/naysayers.

Ross, Alex. "The Frankfurt School Knew Trump Was Coming." *New Yorker*, December 5, 2016. https://www.newyorker.com/culture/cultural-comment/the-frankfurt-school-knew-trump-was-coming.

Rothwell, Jonathan T., and Pablo Diego-Rosell. "Explaining Nationalist Political Views: The Case of Donald Trump." *SSRN Electronic Journal*, 2016. https://doi.org/10.2139/ssrn.2822059.

Rupar, Aaron. "Trump Still Refuses to Admit He Was Wrong about the Central Park 5." *Vox*, June 18, 2019. https://www.vox.com/policy-and-politics/2019/6/18/18684217/trump-central-park-5-netflix.

Sanford, Nevitt. "A Personal Account of the Study of Authoritarianism: Comment on Samelson." *Journal of Social Issues* 42, no. 1 (1986): 209–14. https://doi.org/10.1111/j.1540-4560.1986.tb00217.x.

Sarlin, Benjy. "United States of Trump." *NBC News*, June 20, 2016. https://www.nbcnews.com/specials/donald-trump-republican-party.

Schildkraut, Deborah J. *Americanism in the Twenty-First Century.* Cambridge: Cambridge University Press, 2011.

Schreiber, Darren, Greg Fonzo, Alan N. Simmons, Christopher T. Dawes, Taru Flagan, James H. Fowler, and Martin P. Paulus. "Red Brain, Blue Brain: Evaluative Processes Differ in Democrats and Republicans." *PLoS ONE* 8, no. 2 (2013). https://doi.org/10.1371/journal.pone.0052970.

Schreindl, Jessica. "People Who Are 'Fearful' Tend to Be Politically Conservative, Study Says." *Mic*, February 19, 2013. https://www.mic.com/articles/26911/people-who-are-fearful-tend-to-be-politically-conservative-study-says.

Schwartz, Shalom H. "Universals in the Content and Structure of Values: Theoretical Advances and Empirical Tests in 20 Countries." *Advances in Experimental Social Psychology Advances in Experimental Social Psychology*, vol. 15, 1992, 1–65. https://doi.org/10.1016/s0065-2601(08)60281-6.

Schwartz, Shalom H., Gian V. Caprara, and Michele Vecchione. "Basic Personal Values, Core Political Values, and Voting: A Longitudinal Analysis." *Political Psychology* 31, no. 3 (2010): 421–52. https://doi.org/10.1111/j.1467-9221.2010.00764.x.

Sears, David O., and Carolyn L. Funk. "Evidence of the Long-Term Persistence of Adults' Political Predispositions." *Journal of Politics* 61, no. 1 (1999): 1–28. https://doi.org/10.2307/2647773.

Serwer, Adam. "The Cruelty Is the Point." *The Atlantic*, October 3, 2018. https://www.theatlantic.com/ideas/archive/2018/10/the-cruelty-is-the-point/572104/

Settle, Jaime E., Christopher T. Dawes, Nicholas A. Christakis, and James H. Fowler. "Friendships Moderate an Association between a Dopamine Gene Variant and Political Ideology." *Journal of Politics* 72, no. 4 (2010): 1189–98. https://doi.org/10.1017/s0022381610000617.

Setzler, Mark, and Alixandra B. Yanus. "Why Did Women Vote for Donald Trump?" *PS: Political Science & Politics* 51, no. 03 (2018): 523–27. https://doi.org/10.1017/s1049096518000355.

Shils, Edward A. "Authoritarianism: Right and Left." In *Studies in the Scope and Method of "The Authoritarian Personality,"* edited by Richard Christie and Marie Jahoda, 24–49. Glencoe, IL: Free Press, 1954.

Shook, Natalie J., and Russell H. Fazio. "Political Ideology, Exploration of Novel Stimuli, and Attitude Formation." *Journal of Experimental Social Psychology* 45, no. 4 (2009): 995–98. https://doi.org/10.1016/j.jesp.2009.04.003.

Sibley, Chris G., and John Duckitt. "The Dual Process Model of Ideology and Prejudice: A Longitudinal Test during a Global Recession." *Journal of Social Psychology* 153, no. 4 (2013): 448–66. https://doi.org/10.1080/00224545.2012.757544.

Sidanius, James, and Felicia Pratto. *Social Dominance: An Intergroup Theory of Social Hierarchy and Oppression.* Cambridge: Cambridge University Press, 1999.

Sides, John. "Race, Religion, and Immigration in 2016." Democracy Fund Voter Study Group, June 2017. https://www.voterstudygroup.org/publication/race-religion-immigration-2016.

Sides, John, Michael Tesler, and Lynn Vavreck. *Identity Crisis: The 2016 Presidential Campaign and the Battle for the Meaning of America.* Princeton, NJ: Princeton University Press, 2018.

Simon, Scott, and Emma Bowman. "African-American Gun Rights Group Grows in the Age of Trump." National Public Radio, March 31, 2018. https://www.npr.org/2018/03/31/598503554/african-americans-guns-and-trump.

Skitka, Linda J. "The Psychological Foundations of Moral Conviction." In J. Wright and H. Sarkissian (eds.), *Advances in Moral Psychology.* New York: Bloomsbury Academic Press, 2014.

Skocpol, Theda, and Vanessa Williamson. *The Tea Party and the Remaking of Republican Conservatism.* Oxford: Oxford University Press, 2012.

Smith, David N., and Eric Hanley. "The Anger Games: Who Voted for Donald Trump in the 2016 Election, and Why?" *Critical Sociology* 44, no. 2 (2018): 195–212. https://doi.org/10.1177/0896920517740615.

Smith, Kevin B., John R. Alford, John R. Hibbing, Nicholas G. Martin, and Peter K. Hatemi. "Intuitive Ethics and Political Orientations: Testing Moral Foundations as a Theory of Political Ideology." *American Journal of Political Science* 61 (2017): 424–36. https://doi.org/10.1111/ajps.12255.

Smith, Kevin B., Douglas Oxley, Matthew V. Hibbing, John R. Alford, and John R. Hibbing. "Disgust Sensitivity and the Neurophysiology of Left-Right

Political Orientations." *PLoS ONE* 6, no. 10 (2011). https://doi.org/10.1371/journal.pone.0025552.

Smith, Kevin B., Matthew V. Hibbing, and John R. Hibbing. "Friends, Relatives, Sanity, and Health: The Costs of Politics." *PloS One* 14, no. 9 (2019). https://doi.org/10.1371/journal.pone.0221870.

Somin, Ilya. "No, Libertarians Have Not Thrown in with Trump." Cato Institute, January 30, 2018. https://www.cato.org/publications/commentary/no-libertarians-have-not-thrown-trump.

Somit, Albert, and Steven A. Peterson. *Darwinism, Dominance, and Democracy: The Biological Bases of Authoritarianism*. Westport, CT: Praeger, 1997.

Spinner-Halev, Jeff, and Elizabeth Theiss-Morse. "Liberal Citizenship and the Challenge of Respect." Paper presented at the Southern Political Science Association Annual Meeting, San Juan, Puerto Rico, January 2020.

Stanley, Jason. *How Fascism Works: The Politics of Us and Them*. New York: Random House, 2018.

Stenner, Karen. *The Authoritarian Dynamic*. Cambridge: Cambridge University Press, 2005.

Svolik, Milan W. "Polarization versus Democracy." *Journal of Democracy* 30, no. 3 (2019): 20–32. https://www.journalofdemocracy.org/articles/polarization-versus-democracy/.

Talk of the Nation. "McCain Too Moderate, Some GOP Conservatives Say." National Public Radio broadcast, February 4, 2008. https://www.npr.org/templates/story/story.php?storyId=18664285.

Tate, Katherine. *What's Going On?: Political Incorporation and the Transformation of Black Public Opinion*. Washington, DC: Georgetown University Press, 2010.

Taub, Amanda. "The Rise of American Authoritarianism." *Vox*, March 1, 2016. https://www.vox.com/2016/3/1/11127424/trump-authoritarianism.

Taub, Amanda. "Why Americans Vote 'against Their Interests': Partisanship." *New York Times*, April 12, 2017. https://www.nytimes.com/2017/04/12/upshot/why-americans-vote-against-their-interest-partisanship.html.

Taylor, Charles. "Blunt Talk about Trump and His Supporters." *Boston Globe*, June 14, 2018. https://www.bostonglobe.com/opinion/2018/06/14/blunt-talk-about-trump-and-his-supporters/eOoUZ8UHmmLSHEpHuShcYI/story.html.

Taylor, Paul, Cary Funk, and Peyton Craighill. "Are We Happy Yet?" Pew Research Center, February 13, 2006. https://www.pewresearch.org/wp-content/uploads/sites/3/2010/10/AreWeHappyYet.pdf.

Tetlock, Philip E. "Thinking the Unthinkable: Sacred Values and Taboo Cognitions." *Trends in Cognitive Sciences* 7, no. 7 (2003): 320–24. https://doi.org/10.1016/s1364-6613(03)00135-9.

Theiss-Morse, Elizabeth. *Who Counts as an American? The Boundaries of National Identity*. Cambridge: Cambridge University Press, 2009.

Theriault, Sean M. *Party Polarization in Congress*. Cambridge: Cambridge University Press, 2008.

Valentino, Nicholas A., Antoine J. Banks, Vincent L. Hutchings, and Anne K. Davis. "Selective Exposure in the Internet Age: The Interaction between Anxiety and Information Utility." *Political Psychology* 30, no. 4 (2009): 591–613. https://doi.org/10.1111/j.1467-9221.2009.00716.x.

Valentino, Nicholas A., Vincent L. Hutchings, Antoine J. Banks, and Anne K. Davis. "Is a Worried Citizen a Good Citizen? Emotions, Political Information Seeking, and Learning via the Internet." *Political Psychology* 29, no. 2 (2008): 247–73. https://doi.org/10.1111/j.1467-9221.2008.00625.x.

Van Hiel, Alain, Bart Duriez, and Malgorzata Kossowska. "The Presence of Left-Wing Authoritarianism in Western Europe and Its Relationship with Conservative Ideology." *Political Psychology* 27, no. 5 (2006): 769–93. https://doi.org/10.1111/j.1467-9221.2006.00532.x.

Vance, J. D. *Hillbilly Elegy: A Memoir of a Family and Culture in Crisis*. New York: Harper, 2016.

Verhulst, Brad, Lindon J. Eaves, and Peter K. Hatemi. "Correlation Not Causation: The Relationship between Personality Traits and Political Ideologies." *American Journal of Political Science* 56, no. 1 (2012): 34–51. https://doi.org/10.1111/j.1540-5907.2011.00568.x.

Wade, Nicholas. "Nice Rats, Nasty Rats; Maybe It's All in the Genes." *New York Times*, July 25, 2006. https://www.nytimes.com/2006/07/25/health/25rats.html.

Walsh, Joe. Twitter Post. January 8, 2019. https://twitter.com/WalshFreedom/status/1082655898387001344?s=20.

Weber, Jesse N., Brant K. Peterson, and Hopi E. Hoekstra. "Discrete Genetic Modules Are Responsible for Complex Burrow Evolution in Peromyscus Mice." *Nature* 493, no. 7432 (2013): 402–5. https://doi.org/10.1038/nature11816.

Welch, Susan, and Lorn Foster. "Class and Conservatism in the Black Community." *American Politics Research* 15, no. 4 (1987). https://doi.org/10.1177%2F1532673X8701500402.

Wiggershaus, Rolf. *The Frankfurt School: Its History, Theories and Political Significance*. Cambridge, MA: MIT Press, 1995.

Will, George. "Conservative Psychosis." *Townhall*, August 10, 2003. https://townhall.com/columnists/georgewill/2003/08/10/conservative-psychosis-n952623.

Wojcik, Sean P., Arpine Hovasapian, Jesse Graham, Matt Motyl, and Peter H. Ditto. "Conservatives Report, but Liberals Display Greater Happiness." *Science* 347, no. 6227 (2015): 1243–46. https://doi.org/10.1126/science.1260817.

Womick, Jake, Tobias Rothmund, Flavio Azevedo, Laura A. King, and John T. Jost. "Group-Based Dominance and Authoritarian Aggression Predict Support for Donald Trump in the 2016 U.S. Presidential Election." *Social Psychological*

and Personality Science 10, no. 5 (2018): 643–52. https://doi.org/10.1177/
1948550618778290.

Woodburn, James. "Egalitarian Societies." *Man* 17, no. 3 (1982): 431–51. https://
doi.org/10.2307/2801707.

Wuthnow, Robert. *The Left behind: Decline and Rage in Rural America*. Princeton,
NJ: Princeton University Press, 2018.

Young, Damon. "Experiment Proves That Conservatives Are Little Baby
Snowflakes Who Act the Way They Do Because Everything Terrifies
Them." *The Root*, March 8, 2018. https://verysmartbrothas.theroot.com/
experiment-proves-that-conservatives-are-in-fact-litt-1823619179.

Zeitz, Joshua. "Does the White Working Class Really Vote against Its Own
Interests?" *Politico Magazine*, December 31, 2017. https://www.politico.com/
magazine/story/2017/12/31/trump-white-working-class-history-216200.

Zito, Salena, and Brad Todd. *The Great Revolt: Inside the Populist Coalition Reshaping
American Politics*. New York: Crown Forum, 2018.

INDEX

abortion
  African American views regarding,
    199t, 201
  securitarianism and, 85
  "social warriors" and, 179–180
  state laws regulating, 180
  Trump venerators and, 15, 29, 138t,
    141, 161, 162t
Adams, John, 208–209
Adorno, Theodor
  American Jewish Committee
    and, 49
  The Authoritarian Personality, 47,
    49–59, 63–64, 82
  Frankfurt School and, 48, 50
  on the Holocaust, 49, 106
  Marxism of, 50
  Princeton Radio Project and, 48
  racial prejudice research of, 116
  repatriation to Germany (1950)
    by, 49–50
African Americans
  Democratic Party and, 198, 199t,
    200–201
  GLBTQ rights and, 199t, 201

  gun rights and, 199t, 201
  liberals' attitudes regarding, 117,
    118–19t, 120f
  moderates' attitudes regarding, 117,
    118–19t, 120f
  non-Trump venerating conservatives'
    attitudes toward, 117,
    118–19t, 120f
  securitarian views among, 198–202
  Trump support levels among, 30
  Trump venerators' attitudes
    regarding, 116–117, 118–19t,
    120f, 122, 170t, 171–172, 182
  views on social policies among,
    199t, 201
Akesson, Jimmie, 10
Albert, Frank, 67
Alien and Sedition Acts (1798),
  208–209
Allen, Danielle, 208
Altemeyer, Bob, 58–60, 63, 128–129
American Jewish Committee
  (AJC), 49–50
American Revolution, 11
Asian Americans, 30, 90, 201

liberals' attitudes toward, 109,
110t, 122
moderates' attitudes toward, 110t
non-Trump venerating conservatives'
attitudes toward, 109, 110t
trade policy and, 15–16
Trump's rhetoric regarding, 15
Trump venerators' attitudes toward,
16, 109, 110t, 170t, 182, 186t,
196t, 198
climate change, 169, 210
Clinton, Hillary
"basketful of deplorables" comment
by, 75–76
demography of supporters
of, 26–30
Trump supporters' hatred of, 3, 62
Cohen, Michael, 8
Congressional elections of 2018, 1–4,
40, 43, 204
conservatives. *See also* non-Trump
venerating conservatives
agreeableness among, 33, 121
anger levels among, 32, 43, 45
anxiety levels among, 43
authoritarianism and, 58
belief in dangerousness of world
among, 32
bitterness among, 44
child-rearing preferences among,
130, 132
conformity among, 32, 36, 45
conscientiousness among, 33, 45, 99,
121, 168
diminished self-esteem among, 32
disgust sensitivity among, 32–33,
35–36, 72–73
dogmatism among, 32, 34, 121
ego defensiveness among, 32
emotional stability among, 33
enhanced fear of death among, 32
enhanced mortality salience
among, 32, 34

extraversion levels among, 33–34,
121, 168
fear levels among, 32, 39–42, 45, 73
government power feared by, 41–42
gun rights and, 41–42
happiness levels among, 75
intolerance of ambiguity
among, 32, 45
low concern with inequality among, 32
low integrative complexity
among, 32
low openness to new experiences
among, 32–34, 45, 121, 168
low sensation-seeking among, 32, 34
low value placed on exciting lives
among, 32, 34
low value placed on imaganitiveness
among, 32, 34
neuroticism levels among, 32,
121, 168
outsiders viewed as threat among, 75
preference for closure among, 32,
34–35, 121
preference for order and structure
among, 32–35
preference for purity among,
32, 35–36
preference for simplicity among, 32
reluctance to accept new technology
among, 32
resentfulness among, 32
suspicion of innovation at the
workplace among, 32, 34
sympathetic nervous system
responses among, 73
threat sensitivity among, 32–34, 45,
72–73, 107, 110–11t, 112
Trump supporters among, 25, 33, 65
Trump support levels among, 91,
92t, 94
willingness to engage in disruptive or
illegal action for political reasons
among, 175

political involvement and political
knowledge levels among, 166t,
167, 184t
pornography and, 188t
racial attitudes among, 170t,
181, 186t
racial demographics of, 165, 184t
religiosity levels among, 184t
resentfulness levels among, 166t,
168, 180
Right-Wing Authoritarianism
and, 190t
in rural America, 184t
securitarian worldview and,
177t, 191t
social fulfillment levels among, 166t,
168, 180
submissiveness levels among,
177t, 190t
threat sensitivity among, 170t, 186t
tobacco use among, 188t
traffic citation rates among, 188t
willingness to engage in aggressive
or illegal actions for political ends
among, 173t, 188–89t
egalitarianism, 17–18
Erdogan, Recep, 10
European Union, 13, 16, 157–158
Evangelical Christianity, 28, 44, 96–97,
166–167, 179, 184t

Falwell, Jerry, 21
Farage, Nigel, 10, 194
fascism, 50–51, 82, 85–86, 212
Federalist Party, 208
Federico, Christopher, 76–77
Feldman, Stanley, 156
Ford, Doug, 10
Fortunato, David, 34, 101
Franco, Francisco, 10
Frankfurt School, 48, 50, 56, 59
Franklin, Ben, 11

French, David, 83
Frenkel-Brunswik, Else. *See The*
Authoritarian Personality
Fromm, Erich, 56
Fukuyama, Francis, 2, 238n1

genetics, 65–70
George III (king of England), 11
GLBTQ rights
African Americans' views regarding,
199t, 201
increasing levels of support in society
for, 194
marriage rights and, 199t, 201
Republican Party and, 201
securitarians' views regarding,
80–81, 85
Trump venerators' views regarding,
15, 138t, 141, 162t
unitarians' views regarding, 90
Goodhart, David, 76, 194–195, 201
Gordon, Peter E., 63
Gorsuch, Neil, 204
Graham, Matthew, 149
Grossman, Matt, 88–90
gun rights
African Americans' views regarding,
199t, 201
conservatives' support for, 41–42
non-Trump venerating conservatives'
support for, 139t, 140
securitarianism and, 20, 83–84, 86,
182, 206
"stand your ground" laws and, 70
Trump venerators' support for, 39,
44, 136t, 137, 139t, 140, 161,
162t, 182

Haidt, Jonathan, 5, 216n22
Hanley, Eric, 31
Hanson, Pauline, 10
Hawley, Josh, 1–2

liberals
    abortion and, 138t
    aggression levels among, 126t, 129,
        143, 144t
    agreeableness among, 33, 100t, 121
    alcohol consumption levels among,
        108t, 122, 174
    anger levels among, 43–44,
        103t, 104
    attitudes regarding eavesdropping on
        criminal suspects among, 139t
    attitudes regarding healthcare
        among, 110t, 112, 113f, 122,
        135, 136t, 138t
    attitudes regarding sex education and
        birth control among, 138t
    attitudes toward China and other
        foreign powers among, 109,
        110t, 122
    attitudes toward conservatives
        among, 110t, 112, 206–207
    attitudes toward criminals among,
        110t, 122
    attitudes toward the federal
        government among, 110t, 138t
    attitudes toward immigrants among,
        90, 109, 110t, 113f, 114–115,
        122, 139t
    attitudes toward income inequality
        among, 110t, 112, 122, 135,
        136t, 152t
    attitudes toward outsiders among,
        106, 135
    attitudes toward women and
        women's rights among, 118–19t,
        120f, 135, 136t
    belief in a dangerous world among,
        111t, 112
    bitterness among, 102, 103t,
        104, 105f
    business regulation and, 138t
    capital punishment and, 139t

    chaos as a source of fear for,
        110–11t, 112
    child-rearing preferences among,
        130, 131t, 132
    college tuition policies and, 138t
    conventionalism levels among, 126t,
        143, 144t
    defense spending and, 139t, 152t
    defining qualities of, 16–17
    disgust sensitivity among, 103t
    dogmatism among, 100t, 121
    economic status of, 96t, 97–98, 98f
    education levels among, 96t, 97, 98f
    emotional stability among, 33
    English as official language policies
        and, 139t
    Evangelical faith and, 96t, 97
    extraversion levels among, 33–34,
        100t, 102f, 121
    fear levels among, 41–42, 73
    fears of natural disasters among,
        110t, 112, 113f, 122
    fears of terrorism among, 109,
        110t, 122
    gambling by, 108t, 122
    gambling policies and, 138t
    gender breakdown among,
        96t, 97–98
    GLBTQ rights and, 138t
    gun ownership rates among, 107,
        108t, 122
    gun policies and, 139t
    happiness levels among, 75, 106
    high value placed on exciting lives
        among, 32
    hunting and fishing by, 108t
    levels of support for democratic
        norms among, 150f
    lottery participation by, 107, 108t
    low conscientiousness among, 33,
        100t, 121
    marijuana legalization and, 138t

liberals (*cont.*)
  median age among, 96t, 97
  national anthem protests and, 139t
  neuroticism levels among, 100t,
    102f, 121
  off-color jokes told by, 107, 108t, 122
  openness to new experiences among,
    33, 99, 100t, 101, 102f, 121
  overseas travel by, 108t
  pornography and, 107, 108t
  preference for closure among,
    100t, 121
  preference for consensus among,
    100t, 121
  racial attitudes among, 110t, 112,
    117, 118–19t, 120f, 122, 135,
    136t, 171
  racial demographics of, 95, 96t, 97
  religiosity levels among, 96t, 97,
    98f, 99
  resentfulness among, 103t, 104, 105f
  in rural America, 96t, 97, 98f
  school prayer and, 138t
  securitarianism and, 133, 134t, 136f,
    151, 152t
  social fulfillment levels among, 103t,
    104, 105f, 106, 168
  social welfare policies and, 138t
  submissiveness levels among, 125,
    126t, 127f, 136f, 142, 144t, 176
  tax policy and, 138t
  threat sensitivity among, 107, 110–
    11t, 112–114
  tobacco use among, 108t, 122
  traffic citation rates among,
    107, 108t
  Trump support levels among, 92*t*
  Trump venerators' attitudes toward,
    38–39, 109, 110t, 122, 186t,
    206–207
  willingness to engage in aggressive
    or illegal actions for political ends
    among, 146–47t, 148–149, 175

libertarianism, 16, 81–83, 85
Lindbergh, Charles, 11
Log Cabin Republicans, 201
Ludeke, Steven, 62, 143
Luttig, Matthew, 76–77
Lysenko, Trofim, 65–66

Macri, Mauricio, 10
Madison, James, 61, 86, 208
Malkin, Michelle, 77, 84, 86
Mann, Thomas, 47
Marcuse, Herbert, 47
Martin, John Levi, 63
McCain, John, 21–22, 27, 30, 86
McCarthyism, 209
McCaskill, Claire, 1–2
Meacham, Jon, 5
Medved, Michael, 22
Mexico, 3, 10, 87
Mexico border wall proposal, 8,
    22, 36, 59
moderates
  abortion and, 138t
  aggression levels among, 126t, 144t
  agreeableness among, 100t
  alcohol consumption levels among,
    108t, 122
  anger levels among, 103t
  attitudes regarding eavesdropping on
    criminal suspects among, 139t
  attitudes regarding healthcare
    coverage among, 110t, 113f, 135,
    136t, 138t
  attitudes regarding sex education and
    birth control among, 138t
  attitudes toward China and other
    foreign powers among, 110t
  attitudes toward conservatives
    among, 110t
  attitudes toward criminals
    among, 110t
  attitudes toward economic health
    among, 135, 136t